Young Children and Picture Books

Second Edition

Mary Renck Jalongo

National Association for the Education of Young Children
Washington, DC

It's *Whether,* Not *Which,* That Matters

In this second edition of *Young Children and Picture Books,* more than 400 different picture books for young children are mentioned, excerpted, and suggested for various purposes. Many children's titles are available in multiple editions and formats by multiple publishers. To simplify things throughout this volume, only title and author or illustrator's last name—not full bibliographical data—is given for each children's book cited, as sufficient to locate a copy at your local library, bookstore, or online.

Cover design and cut-paper artwork: Sandi Collins
Book design: Malini Dominey

National Association for the Education of Young Children
1509 16th St., NW
Washington, DC 20036-1426
202-232-8777 or 800-424-2460
www.naeyc.org

Through its publications program the National Association for the Education of Young Children (NAEYC) provides a forum for discussion of major issues and ideas in the early childhood field, with the hope of provoking thought and promoting professional growth. The views expressed or implied are not necessarily those of the Association.

NAEYC wishes to thank the author, who donated much time and effort to develop this book as a contribution to our profession.

Library of Congress Control Number: 2004100521
ISBN: 1-928896-15-4
NAEYC Item #160

Mary Renck Jalongo is a teacher, writer, and editor. As a classroom teacher she taught preschool, first grade, and second grade. She worked in a parent cooperative nursery school for the children of migrant farmworkers, and taught preschoolers in the laboratory school at the University of Toledo. Currently, she is a professor at Indiana University of Pennsylvania.

As a writer she has coauthored and edited more than 20 books, many of them textbooks in the field of early childhood education, including *Early Childhood Language Arts* (3d ed., Allyn & Bacon), *Creative Expression and Play in Early Childhood* (4th ed., Merrill/Prentice Hall), and *Major Trends and Issues in Early Childhood Education: Challenges, Controversies, and Insights* (2d ed., Teachers College Press).

Mary Renck Jalongo also is the editor in chief of the international publication *Early Childhood Education Journal*, published by Kluwer Academic Publishers.

Dedication

For Miss Klingensmith, my compassionate and wise kindergarten teacher. When I played school as a child, she was my shining example, and years later, as I continue in the field of early childhood education, she continues to exemplify the behaviors I seek to develop in future teachers. The picture books she shared will remain in my heart always, stories such as *Ferdinand*, the little bull who would rather smell flowers than fight; and *Make Way for Ducklings*, the tale of a city that relaxed its traffic rules a bit to allow a mother duck and her babies to flourish. Although I reached adulthood without remembering the titles or authors of these and the other picture books that Miss K. chose to share, those images and words remained with me always and were reactivated by viewing the illustrations during my college days. Today I have the privilege of seeing "the lights go on" for new groups of early childhood practitioners as they, too, recall those first teachers who read aloud and made books come alive.

It all began with Miss K.

—M.R.J.

Contents

List of Boxes

Acknowledgments

Special recognition goes to Melissa Ann Renck, children's services librarian at Toledo Lucas County Library, who supplied several of the figures, appendixes, and recommended picture books based on her daily storytime experiences with toddlers, preschoolers, and school-age children.

The early childhood education majors at Indiana University of Pennsylvania also merit recognition for assisting with the interviews of young children. Six teachers were particularly helpful in gathering samples of children's work: Anne Drolett Creany, Frankie DeGeorge, Jamie Hodan, Sandy Malcolm, Sandy Monsilovich, and Denise Dragich. I thank them for their contributions to this project. Finally, I would like to thank Marjorie L. Stanek for proofreading the manuscript and attending to details, and Frank S. Jalongo for his thoughtful responses to the chapters as they neared completion.

Engagement with Picture Books

The picture book contributes much more than something to do during a hurried storytime. Engagement with picture books while we are young forms the basis for becoming a literate adult, one who not only decodes words accurately but also enjoys reading and takes the time to read. Teachers who share quality picture books with young children are promoting literacy in the fullest sense of the word. For this reason, exemplary early childhood educators have always made high-quality children's picture books a central part of their curriculum.

Ideally, children learn to love literature through joyful encounters with picture books shared with them by enthusiastic adults. Consider, by analogy, how we introduce a toddler to a pull toy for the first time. We do not simply throw toy and child together and then wait to see what happens. Rather, we demonstrate the toy's use to the child, all the while guided by thoughts of the enjoyment it will bring. We approach the task with high expectations for the child's success, coupled with an acceptance that success will come naturally after a certain amount of trial and error by the child. We neither insist that the child master a set of discrete skills before exploring the toy nor expect the child to sit quietly and watch until we have explained thoroughly all aspects of the toy. Rather, we follow the child's lead, fully anticipating that, with practice, the child soon will be racing around with the toy in tow. The child learns to play by playing.

How much better the world of early literacy would be if similar assumptions and practices were in place! An introduction to a new toy is based in appreciation for the child's developmental characteristics, a belief in the child's abilities, a focus on enjoyment, an emphasis on learning by doing, and the recognition that mistakes are an inevitable part of learning. A child's introduction to literature and literacy should be based in no less.

Despite the importance of early experiences with literature, many young children arrive at schools and centers lacking experience with picture books. Perhaps their parents, daunted by the persistent debates about the "best" way to teach reading and fearful that their child will fail the system, have decided to leave the mystifying task of supporting their child's literacy growth to the trained professionals. In some instances, families' own struggles with learning English or with learning to read present major obstacles, and once again they turn over the language learning of their children to us. In other cases, families may not think of literacy in quite the same way as a teacher does, and instead may value the rich storytelling traditions of their tribal culture or may assume, based on their own experiences in school, that copying and memorizing are the only sure routes to success. As early childhood educators, we have an obligation to show every family and all of the children in our care that picture books exist for and about them. They need to know that readily available to them are high-quality picture books for listeners and not-yet-readers; books online that can be translated into different languages; stories from every land that are accompanied by beautiful illustrations; "Big Books," "predictable" books, and "easy readers" to support emergent readers; and "chapter books" to invite budding readers to tackle a full-length work.

Above all, we must not be dismissive with hurtful comments such as "She has no books at home" or "His parents are barely literate" or, most destructive, "They obviously don't care about their child's education." When a family's ability to support literacy learning is inadequate and a young child's literacy needs are great, rather than point to deficiencies as a way of absolving ourselves of responsibility, we teachers must reaffirm a deep commitment to caring. Very young children and their families are counting on us.

To realize the full potential of children's literature, adults must accept two complementary guiding principles: that the purpose of picture books is to engage children with literature, and that the picture book is a major resource in children's acquisition of literacy.

Children's experiences with literature need to begin with enjoyment. The word *enjoy* literally means "to take pleasure in"; it describes active participation coupled with intense interest. Contrary to popular opinion, *enjoyment* is a synonym for *engagement*, not for *frivolity*. Engagement is essential in the learning process. Once engaged, the child can be empowered to persist at solving problems, to gain control over skills, and to increase achievement (Mosenthal 1999). Although their terminology may have differed a bit, educators for centuries have maintained that engagement is essential for effective literacy learning (Guthrie & Wigfield 1997). Contemporary experts in the field of literacy have substantiated the contention that interest, motivation, and emotions—in a word, *enjoyment*—influence learning much more than previously thought (Cambourne 2001; Turner 1997). When promoting literature, as picture book author and illustrator Erik Haugaard contends, engagement, in the original sense of the word, is a desirable result: "Those books that I have learned most from have been those which have entertained me. No one as yet, that I have heard of, has been bored into wisdom" (quoted in Burns & Flowers 1999, 577).

Although children certainly do achieve important learning goals through picture books, the process must begin with enjoyment, rather than with a dreary, adult-directed lesson. Pleasure persuades the child first to look, then to discuss and listen, next to remember and recite from memory, and finally to read a favorite story. Enjoyment is the force that sustains a young child's involvement with picture books when television and computers beckon. The enjoyment of picture books is a precursor to not only learning to read but also wanting to read. As Jonathan Kozol, the award-winning author of numerous books about race, poverty, and education, asserted in his address to the National Council of Teachers of English,

> I wish that teachers would insist that every little child in our country—rich or poor; black, brown, or white; whatever origin or background—would have the chance to read books not for any other reason than the fact that books bring joy into our lives, not because they'll be useful for a state examination, not because they'll improve SAT scores, but solely because of the intense pleasure that we get from books. If [adults are] not willing to defend the right of every child to enjoy the treasures of the earth, who will? (Kozol 1998)

Too often, picture books that do not include an obvious lesson or heavy-handed moral are viewed less favorably by adults. Teachers and families may wonder aloud, "Isn't this book telling children it's okay to try to do some of the ridiculous things in this story?" or "What are they really learning from this book?" Or maybe they worry "Won't children be confused by a story about things that couldn't happen in real life?" Fascinating that adults would impose limitations on picture books for children that they would not put on their own reading choices. The same adults who stop reading a book after a few seconds because they "can't get into it" too often believe that children's books should be like a vitamin supplement—a daily dosage of medicine with a sweet, colorful outer shell. The same adults who send jokes and humor-ous stories to family and friends often cannot appreciate that children like humor in their books as much as adults like wit in their e-mail messages.

All readers want to be engaged by what they read; all have a right to expect enjoyment. As literacy expert Margaret Meek (1991) points out, "Picture books are not simply privileged reading for or with children. They make reading for all a distinctive kind of imaginative looking" (116). One feature of the "imaginative looking" to which Meek refers calls on the child to use many different areas of the brain (Sorgen 1999). Involved in the reading process are the motor skills of holding the book, turning the pages, touching and pointing to the pictures, clutching a beloved book close to one's chest. Also involved are the visual skills of looking at the illustrations, interpreting their meaning, searching for details mentioned in the text, lingering over favorite images. Additionally, a host of language skills is brought into play as things are named, new vocabulary is used in context, wonderings are spoken aloud, and children begin their long apprenticeship of learning to read and write, inspired by what adults have written for and read to them.

Despite the value to young children of experiences with picture books, the pressure is escalating on teachers to "emphasize skills," to "stick to the three

Rs," to "teach to the test." Those pressures can push teachers and families into a no-nonsense, grim, determined approach to early literacy. But *enjoyment* is not the opposite of *thinking*. One finds pleasure when thinking through a solution to a problem, contributing a good idea during a discussion, experiencing a flash of insight, reading fluently and writing effectively. Quality picture books involve children in all of these types of thinking by inviting them into the world of literacy (Routman 1994).

What, exactly, are the pleasures of literature? Experts in the field of children's literature have identified many, including the following (adapted from Nodelman & Reimer 2003):

• Delighting in the words themselves
• Comprehending the text and pictures
• Expanding one's repertoire as a reader and writer
• Visualizing new images and exploring new ideas
• Identifying with characters
• Experiencing the lives and thoughts of others vicariously
• Enjoying a well-crafted story and sharing it with others
• Understanding a work of art in terms of its form, structure, and patterns
• Revisiting the comfortably familiar favorites
• Connecting with the book and resonating to its message
• Gaining awareness of how the parts of the picture book combine into a meaningful whole
• Appreciating history and expanding cultural awareness
• Recognizing the unique styles of authors and illustrators
• Sharing experiences of literature with others
• Learning ways of talking about responses to books
• Reflecting on connections between one's life and the story

Paradoxically, one of the great attractions of literature at any age is that it not only affirms the familiar but also shakes up our thinking with ideas that are surprising and original and that serve to enrich and enlarge perspectives beyond what we already know. In a rapidly changing society, attributes such as perceptivity, imagination, spontaneity, flexibility, and insight require every bit as much cultivation as knowledge and skills do (Jalongo 2003b). Picture books are a primary source of stimulation for young children's creative thinking processes as they become tellers of stories, writers of words, and readers of increasingly complex print and nonprint media.

The best way to become convinced of the positive role that the picture book can play in the acquisition of literacy is to bring quality picture books and young children together in ways that are developmentally effective (see Bredekamp & Copple 1997). After this dynamic interaction happens, most early childhood teachers become committed to infusing literature into the curriculum.

> My toddlers love the library storytime. I was amazed at how many activities the librarian includes in a single session.

Mary Renck Jalongo

I invited my 3-year-olds to join in the story by saying "Run, run as fast as you can, you can't catch me, I'm the gingerbread man" and now they keep begging me to read it again!

My first-graders really look forward to reading and discussing these big, poster-size books together. They are gaining confidence and learning to read.

In every case, reflective practitioners are able to see the child's emerging literacy skills being activated by the pleasures of picture books.

About this book

You may not have had an opportunity to share picture books with children, or perhaps you have extensive experience. Whatever your background, use this, the second edition of *Young Children and Picture Books*, to reflect on and to amass even richer experiences with children's literature. This volume is intended for those who are committed to the care and education of young children, including early childhood practitioners, professionals in related fields, and families.

Young Children and Picture Books, 2d ed. has purposes that align with its seven chapters: (1) to persuade adults of the importance of children's literature; (2) to enhance professional judgment about literature; (3) to suggest effective ways of linking literature with young learners; (4) to further understanding of young children's responses to literature; (5) to describe the ways that picture books promote literacy; (6) to explore the role of parents, other family members, and communities in providing picture book experiences for the very young child; and (7) to clarify the crucial role that teachers play in integrating picture books into the early childhood curriculum.

My hope as an author is that readers will gain a fuller appreciation for the many contributions made by children's literature to teaching and learning in the early childhood field. And ideally, that their reactions upon arriving at this book's final pages would be comparable to those experienced by a young child as the last page of a favorite picture book is turned—a sense of time well spent, an intention to revisit it later, and an interest in reading on to new books. Above all, I hope that any teacher, parent, or other adult who reads this book will emerge with an even firmer resolve to make children's literature an integral part of every young child's learning and life.

Importance of Picture Books

> *The name "picture books" evokes images of brightly colored, beautifully illustrated books that beg to be read. No matter what our age, most of us still enjoy reading them because of their vibrant pictures, rich and evocative language, and poignant and meaning-ful themes. Picture books speak to us in the same way photographs do. They touch our emotions, delight our senses, appeal to our whimsy, and bring back memories of our childhood. Picture books invite us to curl up and read them.*
>
> —Diana Mitchell, *Children's Literature* (2003, 71)

In the fairy tale "Sleeping Beauty," the invited guests and god-mothers bestow gifts on the infant, bequests intended to ensure the child's well-being. Teachers also have a clear idea of how to optimize a child's developmental journey from infancy through maturity. Our ideas flesh out a prototype for the adult we hope each young child will become—someone who loves and is loved, someone with insight and vision, someone who is confident and competent. These worthy objectives are difficult to challenge, but the best ways to achieve them are perpetually controversial.

For centuries, diverse groups of people have believed that children's literature can and should play an integral part in the child's developmental journey (Bader 1998; Bettelheim 1976; Cullinan & Galda 1994). In some ways, according to children's literature expert Barbara Kiefer (1995), the illuminated manuscripts of the Middle Ages were the predecessor of the picture book, because these laboriously decorated manuscripts combined print and pictures well before the printing press was invented. Graeme Harper (2001) also traces the historical origins of the modern picture book to illustrated texts across the ages, including Japanese scrolls from the 12th and 13th centuries, Caxton's 1484 edition of *Aesop's Fables*, Comenius's *Orbis Sensualium Pictus [Visible World]* from 1659 (which included a picture alphabet), Newbury's *Pretty Book of Pictures for Little Masters and Misses* in 1752, Bertuch's German *Bilderbuch fur Kinder [Picture Book for Children]* in 1796, and Harris's *The Comic Adventures of Old Mother Hubbard and Her Dog* in 1805. Clearly, the antecedents of the modern picture book are found in many times and places. (For more on the history of children's books, see Silvey 2002.)

Through experiences with picture books the young child can develop socially, personally, intellectually, culturally, and aesthetically. Books enable the newly socialized child to explore interpersonal relationships and human motives. Picture books communicate self-acceptance, and they model coping strategies for children who are just learning to deal with powerful emotions. Literature also supplies information and raises questions, thus contributing to intellectual growth. Through picture books, children meet families, settings, and cultures that are in some ways similar and in some ways different from their own. As a result, picture books contribute to the child's cultural identity and multicultural awareness. Furthermore, because the picture book is both illustrated and written, it simultaneously supports aesthetic development and growth in literacy. For all of these reasons, children's literature has an important role to play in children's learning and lives.

Nikki is a 5-year-old who is retelling a fairy tale from the Brothers Grimm. Notice how her aesthetic, cultural, social-emotional, intellectual, and imaginative abilities all have been affected by her favorite book:

> Rumpelstiltskin. One day there was a queen . . . that . . . and she was very pretty. One day, the miller's daughter came and they knew somebody, her daughter, that can do straw. So he took her to a room and she sat down and cried. And one time, the door sprang open and a little man walked in and he said, "Hi. What are you crying about?" "I have to spin all this into gold." And so, he said, "What will you give me if I do this into gold?" "My necklace." And he spun a-a-l-l-l the hay into gold.
>
> So one day she [was] put in a larger room. And so, the door sprang open *again* and the little man walked in. And he said, "What will you give me if you . . . if I spin it all *this* time?" "I'll give you the ring on my finger." So he took the ring on her finger and spinned all the hay into gold. That morning if she did another big larger room, they [the miller's daughter and the king] would marry. So they took her to a larger room. So he sprang open *again* and if he . . . and he said, "What will you give me if I do it *now-ow*?" "I have nothing to give you." "Then you promise that I'll give you . . . that *you'll* give *me* the first baby that you have. When you marry."
>
> So, one day they got married . . . and then she forgot about the little man. And he stepped in and he said, "All right. Give me your *chi-uld*." And she was frightened 'cause she forgot about him. And so he said, "All right. I'll give you three days and if you remember my name, if you say my name, then you may keep your daughter . . . your son." So she's been thinkin' about all these names after day to day. And then one day she named *all* the names on the list. He said "no" to *all* of them that people gave her on her list. So one day she spied on him and he kept saying, "Rumpelstiltskin is my name," riding on a spoon. So she went back and then she said, "Is your name Johnny? Jody? . . . In fact, your name is RUMPELSTILTSKIN!" And so *he* cri—he was *mad* on his *spoon*stick. So he flied away and she got to keep her baby. The end.

Paul O. Zelinsky's exquisite, jewel-toned oil paintings are what first attracted Nikki's attention to his *Rumpelstiltskin*. She likes the book because "it's pretty." Her favorite scene is the double-page painting of the wedding ceremony, a scene she also has illustrated herself. Clearly her aesthetic awareness

Mary Renck Jalongo

Nikki's drawing of the wedding scene from *Rumpelstiltskin*

has been affected by experiences with the book. That the story takes place in a time and culture vastly different from her own enhances her cultural awareness.

Consider, too, all the words she uses to describe emotions and motives. She has gained a perspective on the possible consequences of a bargain struck in desperation and the universality of human emotions, something that contributes to her knowledge of self and others. She tells the story expressively, changing the tone of her voice to represent the different characters. Sometimes her voice sounds crafty (when Rumpelstiltskin is making his offer), sometimes distressed (when the miller's daughter has nothing left to give), and ultimately triumphant (when the queen correctly guesses Rumpelstiltskin's name). In addition, Nikki's intellect is enriched by this encounter with a picture book; she uses vocabulary and sentence structures that are far more complex than those required in routine conversations, and she has mastered the basic story sequence.

The book also stimulates Nikki's imagination. She can envision dynamic actions such as the little man flying about, the straw being spun, or the door springing open, actions that cannot be fully represented in the freeze frame of a picture book illustration.

In this way, one book has been responsible for affecting imaginative, intellectual, cultural, social-emotional, and aesthetic development. Nikki also relates this book to her life and to her experiences with other media. As it turns out, Nikki is going to be a flower girl in a wedding, and her favorite illustration depicts a young child holding the train of the soon-to-be-queen's gown. The bride in the book also has "Princess Leia hair," something that reminds Nikki of the movie *Star Wars*.

Author Jane Yolen (1977) is a particularly eloquent spokesperson for the contributions of literature to a child's development:

> Just as the child is born with a literal hole in its head, where the bones slowly close underneath the fragile shield of skin and hair, just so the child is born with a figurative hole in his heart. Slowly it too is filled up. . . . What slips in before it anneals creates the man or woman that child grows into. Literature, folklore, mythology—they surely must rank as one of the most important intrusions into the human heart. (645)

Despite the importance of literature in children's lives, it can be ignored, neglected, or trivialized. Environments that do not support literature are characterized by teachers who are unfamiliar with books that have been published since their own last course in children's literature. Parents and families give up the struggle to find time to read to their children, and soon even an occasional bedtime story is abandoned. Education majors feel foolish carrying around copies of picture books, and defend their egos with complaints about "kiddie lit." Higher education faculty overemphasize the importance of details related to children's literature rather than teach teachers how to fully infuse picture books into the early childhood curriculum. Such environments are failing to explore the potential of the picture book.

The satisfactions of literature should not be the province of a privileged few. Children are universally entitled to meaningful experiences with memorable books. As educators we have an obligation not only to familiarize children with many different picture books but also to convince adult skeptics of the benefits of children's experiences with literature. To meet this challenge successfully,

Mary Renck Jalongo

early childhood professionals need to formulate clear, persuasive answers to three questions:

- What is literature?
- What can children learn from literature?
- How does literature meet the developmental needs of the young child?

Literature and picture books defined

Observing young children and their books makes clear the need for a broad definition of the picture book. Toddlers with a board book, preschoolers who sing along with a picture book version of a folk song, and first-graders who pore over a nonfiction book about a science topic all must be accommodated in that definition. In general, *literature* may be defined as "the imaginative shaping of life and thought into the forms and structures of language" (Huck et al. 2000, 4). *Picture books,* a special category or genre of children's literature, are publications in which the pictures stand alone, the pictures dominate the text, or the words and illustrations are equally important (Shulevitz 1989).

A useful distinction can be made between an *illustrated book* and a picture book. As children's literature textbook author Donna Norton points out, "most children's books are illustrated, but not all illustrated children's books are picture books," because to be a picture book, the work must provide "a balance between the pictures and text so that neither of them is completely effective without the other" (1999, 214). In illustrated books—e.g., many of the books that children in the middle grades read—simple drawings are placed periodically in the text, often as chapter openers. A child could read and understand the entire story without these illustrations, however. Conversely, in the vast majority of picture books for young children, both the words and the pictures are "read," and the pictures extend, clarify, complement, or take the place of words (Shulevitz 1989). Picture books for young children possess the following five features (Sutherland 1997):

- Present the story line in a brief and straightforward manner
- Contain a limited number of concepts
- Include concepts that children can comprehend
- Provide text that is written in a direct, simple style
- Provide illustrations that complement the text

Usually, the term *picture book* refers to picture *storybooks*, books that have simple plots and contain, on average, about 200 words. For example, three very popular picture books have the following word counts:

- Eric Carle's *The Very Hungry Caterpillar*—225 words
- Ezra Jack Keats's *The Snowy Day*—319 words
- Laura Joffe Numeroff's *If You Give a Mouse a Cookie*—291 words

A picture storybook usually is 32 pages long. In fact, publishers often advise aspiring picture book authors or illustrators to work with a replica of the typical picture book. To make one of your own, gather then fold in half eight pieces of paper, stapling at the fold to simulate the book's binding. The first three pages must be reserved for the inside front cover, title page, and copyright page, leaving 29 available for the story. Shaping the material to this configuration and thinking about the brief pauses of turning the pages, as well as the drama of double-page illustration, is the best preparation for designing a picture book (Mayr 1999).

Picture books embody at least three stories: "the one told by the words, the one implied by the pictures, and the one that results from the combination of the other two" (Nodelman & Reimer 2003, 295). As a result of the interdependence of the words and pictures, both children and the adults who share books with them tend to view picture books differently from other types of printed material, as they flip back and forth among the pages and search in the illustrations to confirm details mentioned in the text:

> In some picture books, it's clear that little thought has been given to these matters. Stopping to examine the pictures makes the text seem choppy. But in more carefully constructed books, this back-and-forth movement becomes a strength rather than a liability. The text is divided in such a way that the pauses in the story caused by the presence of illustrations add to the suspense. Readers want to turn the page and find out what happens next, but they also want to stop where they are and pay close attention to a picture. The characteristic rhythm of picture books consists of a pattern of such delays counterpointing and contributing to the suspense of the plot. (Nodelman & Reimer 2003, 296)

Why Read Nonfiction and Information Books to Very Young Children?

• To provide accurate, authoritative, and interesting information

• To capitalize on children's natural curiosity and encourage them to pursue answers to questions

• To demonstrate good models of expository prose, text organization, and principles of design

• To stimulate children's desire to seek additional information about topics of interest

• To encourage children to use reference materials appropriately

• To expand children's vocabularies and knowledge of the real world

• To correct children's commonly held misconceptions

• To make children aware of the contributions of individuals and groups to society

• To introduce children to different careers and occupations

Adapted, with permission, from Lea McGee & Donald Richgels, *Designing Early Literacy Programs: Strategies for At-Risk Preschool and Kindergarten Children* (New York: The Guilford Press). Copyright © 2003 by The Guilford Press.

Mary Renck Jalongo

Also available are nonfiction picture books that depend equally on words and illustrations to communicate information. They are referred to as *information books* (Duke & Kays 1998). Typically, information books for children provide factual information about people, mathematics, science topics, historical events, and how things are made or done. High quality information books "are examples of literary art and not just dreary compilations of facts" (Burns & Flowers 1999, 575). Examples of information books for the youngest child include *concept books*, which are somewhat like commercials for ideas (Roberts 1984) such as colors, shapes, counting, the alphabet, and the like. The number of these nonfiction titles in picture book format has increased significantly in recent years (Giblin 1996). Authors who are noted for high-quality information books include Tana Hoban, Ruth Heller, and Gail Gibbons.

Large-scale survey research indicates that children's responses to picture books differ according to gender, with boys tending to prefer nonfiction/ information books over picture storybooks (Hall & Coles 1999; Millard 1997). But some evidence suggests that teachers do not often choose information books for reading aloud. In a study of the reading-aloud practices of 1,882 elementary teachers over 10 days, only one-half to three-quarters of the teachers read aloud to students at all, and those who did read aloud selected information books to read just 3 of the 10 days on average (Jacobs, Morrison, & Swinyard 2000). To better satisfy the diverse interests and individual tastes of groups of young children, it is particularly important that teachers read aloud not only picture storybooks but also information books (Vardell & Copeland 1992).

The box **Why Read Nonfiction and Information Books to Very Young Children?** highlights the importance of information books in the early childhood curriculum. Reading just a portion of the text is an option if, for example, the book is rather detailed and only a portion of the material is relevant to the lesson or to a child's question. Another is to give a *book talk*—a brief "sneak preview" of the book, typically to build interest and prepare children for a full reading of the book, at one sitting or spread out over more than one reading. A useful reference book about information picture books is Cianciolo's (2000) *Informational Picture Books for Children.*

A common adult misconception is that children's literature consists of cute little books unworthy of serious consideration; because the reading level and content are simple, one book seems just as good as another. The truth, of course, is that even the simplest concepts can be presented in ways that are superb, mediocre, or inferior. Picture books are more than a useful teaching tool, as Eileen Tway (1982) notes; they also exist as an art form that transcends the functions of informing, entertaining, and providing emotional release. With good reason, children's literature is the subject of theory and research, of literary and artistic criticism, and of social controversy.

Attributes of literature

The distinction between a picture book and other printed and illustrated material can be made using a concrete example. Suppose that several books are laid out on a table. One is an ordinary coloring book on bicycle safety. The rest are children's books that have been well received by both adults and children. The contrasting dramatic differences in these two types of publications make the characteristics of literature apparent. Literature differs from other written and illustrated material in terms of its use of language; its artistic quality; its ways of depicting experience; and its content, form, and structure (Purves & Monson 1984).

Use of language. In our coloring book example, language is used in an obvious, literal way. It holds no surprises, and it does not have a cadence or rhythm. The potential of language is not fully explored, and the writing is not literary in any sense. Even literature in its simplest form does more with words than simply label the pictures. For example, Mary Murphy's book for toddlers *I Like It When . . .* includes the following lines:

> I like it when you hug me tight.
> I like it when we splash about.
> I like it when we kiss good night.
> Sleep tight. Good night.
> I love you. I love you, too.

Here, the language is lilting. It activates thought and creates images rather than simply labels what is already apparent in the pictures. Few words are used, but each one is chosen carefully. We can easily imagine some of the book's words and phrases becoming part of a toddler's good-night ritual.

Artistic quality. Just as the melody and lyrics of a beautiful song must be complementary, the illustrations and text of quality picture books work together to produce a work of art. Faith Ringgold's *Tar Beach* illustrates this cohesiveness. This picture storybook was inspired by a story quilt the author had made, and each page is illustrated with a colorful quilt border. In both creative works, the author-artist raises and answers this question: Suppose you lived in an apartment on a hot summer night and had no way to take a vacation; what would you do? The families in this story use their imaginations to turn the asphalt roof of their apartment building into a vacation spot where they can enjoy the breeze, good company, and good food. As the young African American girl who narrates the story participates, she also imagines that she and her little brother could join hands and fly over the city while gazing down on the lights and sights. Ringgold's story and illustrations in this lovely mood piece invite child listeners to take similar flights of fancy and drift off into dreams of their own.

As Wayne Harris (1997) explains, effective illustrations in picture books

> [do not] only describe what the words have already conjured up. . . . The picture should add nuance and atmosphere, it should expand the story outwards and inwards. It should provide us with a taste of subtext and the unexpected . . . and it should give the author all the adjectives that they were denied. (quoted in Morrow 1999, 141)

Thus, picture book art does not simply give a literal interpretation; it extends and complements the mood of the language. Together, images and text evoke an emotional response from reader-listeners and reward them with meaning. Quality in picture book art requires illustrations "that are understandable, evoke emotional identification and intense emotional response, that allow room for the exercise of the reader's own imagination, that provide the reader

I have told him it's very easy, anyone can fly. All you need is somewhere to go that you can't get to any other way. The next thing you know, you're flying among the stars.

with a new, wholesome (and vital) way of looking at the world and at life" (Cianciolo 1984, 847). Contrast this description with the illustrations from coloring books, whose pictures do none of those things—a case of "what you see is what you get." Rather than real art, the black outlines that define coloring book pictures are predictable boundaries waiting to corral the waxy pigment of crayons.

Ways of depicting experience. All literature has a voice, a way of speaking to the reader and a way of describing experience. Sometimes that voice speaks to the reader-listener through the dialogue of characters. At other times the voice is a sympathetic narrator who tells the story. In a coloring book, the sparse text has no voice, no feeling that these words really are spoken by someone; they are just labels or captions.

Contrast that coloring book with a book such as *Bailey Goes Camping* (Henkes). When his older siblings, Bruce and Betty, get ready to go off to camp, Bailey is told that he is "too little to go" and then reassured with, "But in a few years you can!" That feeling of being excluded cannot be dismissed so lightly, however. Bruce and Betty have described a very inviting experience, one that involves swimming, sleeping in a tent, telling ghost stories, and roasting marshmallows. Young children share in Bailey's delight when, with the help of his parents, he manages to do all of these things right at home. This example highlights another important attribute of literature: It is evocative. Literature pulls us in, involves us. Preschoolers who hear *Bailey Goes Camping* often respond with surprised laughter at the incongruity of Bailey wearing his sunglasses in the bathtub during his simulated swim. When the story is finished, they often say, "Read it again!" Responses such as these are a testimonial to a book's evocativeness and its ability to depict experience.

The difference between literature and other printed material in book form is like the difference between singing a song and singing the alphabet. True, "The ABC Song" has some of the characteristics of music—a melody and a semblance of lyrics. But it does not qualify as music in the fullest sense of the word. Similarly, if a picture book does not use language imaginatively, use art expressively, or depict experience authentically, it lacks some essential elements of literature.

Content, form, and structure. Picture books forge connections among the topics, the characters, the plot, the setting, the point of view, and the illustrations. The topics in high-quality picture books can be serious while also being lighthearted. Consider, for example, a book such as *The Patchwork Quilt* (Flournoy). The characters are family members and the setting is their home. Realistic illustrations are well suited to the story's plot, which centers on the elderly grandmother's illness. She despairs of ever completing the quilt that she started, but her granddaughter urges the entire family to participate in the project, and in the process rekindles her grandmother's will to survive. The content, form, and structure in this story combine to express a message of intergenerational understanding.

If they are read to and talked to about stories, by the time most children are 5 years old they already know key elements of story form (Applebee 1978). They know that a story has a beginning, a middle, and an end; they use words such as "Once there was" or "The End" to reflect this knowledge. Young children also recognize structural elements of picture books such as repetition or rhyme. Thus, even those children who are relatively new to literature perceive the literary attributes of content, form, and structure.

Controversies in children's literature

Opinions are not unanimous about what constitutes an appropriate picture book for a young child. In fact, the issue of what is suitable for children is sometimes the focus of considerable debate and controversy. One indication that children's literature matters to adults is that, at various times throughout history, children's picture books have been criticized, challenged, censored, and even banned. One example is Helen Bannerman's book *The Story of Little Black Sambo.* Originally published in 1899, it tells the tale of a child walking through the forest who is pursued by hungry tigers. The child gives away each of his articles of new clothing to pacify the tigers, but they get into an argument, run around him, and literally have a meltdown. As a result, the child not only recovers all of his finery but also brings home butter and shares a feast with his family. Because the word *sambo* was used as a racial slur in the American South, the book was virtually banned, even though the character in the original story was a native of India and not of African descent.

More recently, however, an African American author/illustrator team, Julius Lester and Jerry Pinkney, reissued the story as *Sam and the Tigers*: *A New Telling of Little Black Sambo.* Another illustrator, Fred Marcellino, put Bannerman's story back in India as *The Story of Little Babaji.* Together, they introduced new generations of children to the story that delighted adults so many years ago. They also helped to counteract the story's undeserved reputation for promoting prejudice.

Ways of depicting characters in picture books can also be challenged. In 1972 Charlotte Zolotow's *William's Doll* created a sensation because it depicted a boy who owned and played with a baby doll at a time when this toy generally was considered to be for girls only. Likewise, when William Steig's *Sylvester and the Magic Pebble* was first published in 1970, it was banned in several cities because the police were portrayed as pigs during an era of protest. As times change, attitudes toward picture books often change along with them.

Usually, when adults object to a book for children, they do so out of the following concerns:

• The subject or theme is considered to be inappropriate for young children (e.g., a book about childbirth or gender issues).

• The illustrations are too disturbing or graphic (e.g., a book with frightening monsters or images of war or famine).

• The book depicts behaviors a child should not imitate (e.g., a book about a child's cruelty to another child).

• The book conflicts with religious beliefs or other convictions (e.g., a book about dinosaurs that attributes their demise to climate changes rather than to an act of God).

Illustration copyright © Fred Marcellino. Used by permission of HarperCollins Publishers.

Any responsible adult is constantly making choices from among the many picture books available. One of the differences between *censorship* and book *selection* is that the person who selects certain books over others does not insist that everyone else be denied access to those others. The censor, however, wants the other books removed from the school or library so no one can read them.

Which books become targets of heated controversy is sometimes surprising. Usually, the list of the most frequently challenged books in any given year contains many of the most familiar children's literature favorites. For example, Trina Schart Hyman's version of *Little Red Riding Hood* was challenged because the pictures show a bottle of wine in Little Red's basket for her grandmother. Tomie de Paola's Italian folktale *Strega Nona [Grandma Witch]* was pulled from the shelves in some school districts because a small but vocal minority objected to the "witchcraft" of Strega Nona's magic pasta pot. Likewise, Frank Asch's gentle story *The Last Puppy* was challenged at a public library because the first cartoon-style illustration shows the puppy being born, and the parent was worried that it would lead to questions she was not prepared to answer. Thus, adults propose a wide range of reasons for pulling a picture book from the shelves, and those reasons can be as diverse as the families and communities themselves.

Mary Renck Jalongo

Proactive strategies

Before sharing any book with young children, early childhood educators should as a precaution solicit the opinions of professional colleagues and make certain they are thoroughly familiar with the book's material. If the book seems likely to stir controversy, they need to ask themselves whether they are willing to fight for it or not. A host of difficulties can be averted by educators taking proactive steps, including the following:

Keeping current in the field of children's literature. *Early Childhood Education Journal* (Kluwer) regularly reviews picture books for the young child. Two NAEYC pamphlets—*Books to Grow On: Latino Literature for Young Children* (Schon 2002) and *Books to Grow On: African American Literature for Young Children* (Brown & Oates 2001)—also suggest picture books of high quality, as does this volume.

Consulting selection criteria from national professional organizations. If a picture book includes an image or words that might offend, should teachers avoid it? On what grounds? Professional groups such as the American Library Association, the National Council of Teachers of English, and the International Reading Association all have selection criteria for children's literature and information about ways to respond to censorship.

Communicating with families and children. Often challenges to books can be avoided simply by letting families know which books are being shared and inviting parents and other family members to participate in discussion groups about the books. Once they have read a book, understand its value, know why it was included in the reading library, and see its appeal for children, they are less likely to become censors. Children also are capable of rating their own literature. In kindergarten or primary grades small groups of three to five children can be provided with a collection of about 15 picture books and asked to identify their first, second, and third choices. Results can then be tallied, and the selected books can be shared in rank order.

Preparing a center or school policy statement and complaint procedure. Having policy statements and procedures ready enables a more consistent response to the sometimes surprising objections to particular picture books. A parent who is a vegan might object to a book in which the illustrations show people eating meat, or a parent who expects obedience from a child might object to a book that shows a character who is naughty. Rather than waiting until after a problem surfaces, educators should articulate their criteria for selection. For example, in *Picture Books to Enhance the Curriculum*, authors Jeanne McLain Harms and Lucille Lettow (1996) describe what criteria they used: (1) literary and artistic quality, (2) application to the elementary curriculum, (3) child appeal, and (4) availability (e.g., book is still in print). When someone does speak out against a book, the person can be asked to fill out a form that will show he or she actually has read the book and can explain the basis for complaint. The National Council of Teachers of English has a form called "The Citizen's Request for Reconsideration of a Work" available for this purpose. After a complaint is received, a committee consisting of community members and teachers can review the complaint and make a recommendation. For more on dealing with censorship in children's literature, see Creany (1999).

Even experts can differ

Of course, the controversies surrounding picture books do not always come from families and community members. Sometimes objections are raised by educators and other professionals in the field of children's literature (Fox & Short 2003). One such issue is whether an author or illustrator who is not a member of a particular cultural, racial, ethnic, or religious group is qualified to represent that group in words or pictures. For example, is it acceptable for a person who is not a Native American to retell a Navaho legend, or who is not an African American to illustrate a book about slavery? Should a person of English descent create a picture book about the struggles of Irish immigrants, or someone not of the Jewish faith write a story about Yom Kippur? Why or why not?

Rudine Sims Bishop (1992) defines *multicultural literature* as books "by and about members of groups outside the sociopolitical mainstream of the United States" (32). This definition implies that members of a cultural group are better suited than nonmembers are to write and illustrate picture books about that group. McGuire-Raskin (1996) concurs, arguing that "outsider" perspectives can be more susceptible to "stereotyped or generic cultural motifs, adopt a tourist's view of characters and events, and are more careless with the ways culture is portrayed" (26). Of course, it can also be argued that some authors have such a rare capacity for identification, imagination, and empathy that restricting them to writing only about their own gender, culture, race, and firsthand experiences may be going too far.

Another controversy to consider is whether sufficient justification exists for including in the curriculum a picture book that is not particularly well written or illustrated because it deals with an underrepresented group. For example, if a picture book portrays a child with special needs or depicts a gay or lesbian family, should it be included based on that criterion alone, or should it be evaluated on the basis of its literary merit? As one team of authors argues, "books should not be chosen simply because they are about a certain cultural, social, or ethnic group" (Bainbridge, Pantaleo, & Ellis 1999, 185). Yet there may be sufficient justification for including a book of slightly lower quality if necessary to give the underrepresented a voice and presence in picture books.

Underlying the debate is this question: Are the pages of picture books the place to try to change society? During the Vietnam war era, for example, many of the fairy tales and folktales were rewritten to be less violent in hopes that this approach would create a less violent next generation (Bettelheim 1976). In 1992, Eve Bunting's *The Wall* was controversial because it depicted the emotional effect on a young boy of searching for his grandfather's name on the Vietnam Veterans Memorial. In 1993, her book *Fly Away Home* told the story of a homeless father and child who live in an airport. Some felt such topics were too sad and serious for a picture book, whereas others felt that books of this kind were long overdue, groundbreaking works.

This small sampling represents only some of the controversies that picture books can spark. In general, the best approach is to be well acquainted with four

Mary Renck Jalongo

factors: the child or children, the professional judgment of colleagues, the values and attitudes of families and communities, and the picture book itself.

Learning through literature

Katz (1988) has identified four kinds of learning fundamental in a young child's education and development: knowledge, skills, dispositions, and feelings. These categories of learning are directly applicable to a child's experiences with literature. *Knowledge* is typically acquired through the senses, personal experience, and direct instruction. *Skills* are learned through practice, beginning with guided practice and eventually developing into independent practice. *Dispositions*, says Katz, are "habits of mind." Some of the habits of mind that are immediately associated with very young children are flexibility, curiosity, and enthusiasm. Dispositions become lifelong traits after children observe and emulate role models. The young child's curiosity, for example, can mature into a tendency to seek out authoritative information when he or she has a question. The fourth essential component, *feelings,* has to do with the emotional lessons learned during an experience.

How do these four types of learning relate to literacy? Even a single book can promote all four. Learning to decode and understand words requires knowledge and skill. Wanting to read is a disposition linked with the feeling tone of experiences with books (whether pressured or relaxed, competitive or cooperative, frustrating or enjoyable). The realization that the text of a book heard so many times originates not from the mind of the person reading aloud but from those marks on the page is a breakthrough for the young child. Children want to be able to perform this magical feat of reading all by themselves. One of the best ways for them to acquire the disposition to want to read is to see enthusiastic, literate adults in action, not only at home and in the community but also in a wide array of educational settings.

Positive feelings about literacy are built when the young child associates warmth, closeness, and pleasure with picture books (Zeece 2000). As any early childhood teacher knows, children's early experiences exert an influence on their later experiences. If initial experiences with books impress on a child that learning to read is a difficult and perplexing task that will lead only to a heavier workload, then the child may, unsurprisingly, balk at reading, express dislike for literacy activities, or avoid any reading assignments that are not required and graded.

Thus, literacy seems to operate on the "iceberg principle"—that is, that knowledge and skills are only its visible tip. Dispositions and feelings make up the substantial portion that lies beneath the surface. Emphasizing knowledge and skills to the exclusion of dispositions and feelings results in an *aliterate* population. In other words, it produces learners who know how to read but refuse to. The educational implications of research on reading and neuroscience bear out the importance of dispositions and feelings in learning to read. That research supports the following conclusions:

Holding attention. Concrete, vivid images are the most powerful in capturing the child's interest and maintaining attention (Rushton & Larkin

2001); therefore, picture books with high-quality illustrations are particularly well suited for inviting children into the world of literacy.

Accommodating difference. The brain's development and timing is "as individual as DNA" (Sorgen 1999); therefore, lockstep literacy programs are counterproductive in meeting the literacy needs of diverse groups of children.

Giving pleasure. Because the brain functions best when it is in a state of "relaxed alertness" (Caine & Caine 1997), fear can interfere with intelligence (Ayers 1995); therefore, it is particularly important that the child's initiation into literacy be pleasurable yet intellectually stimulating.

Challenging the brain. The brain can operate on several levels simultaneously (Jensen 1998). Within seconds our thoughts can touch on dozens of ideas and we take in myriad pieces of information; the brain is oriented toward seeking patterns out of all this chaotic complexity. Picture books offer intellectual stimulation on two levels simultaneously—text and illustrations.

Provoking conversation. Both listening and reading are categorized as *receptive* language arts because the message has to be taken in, processed, and interpreted. For children without hearing impairments, a high positive correlation exists between listening comprehension and reading comprehension (Collins & Shaeffer 1997). Listening to and talking about picture books is an effective way to transition into reading, because each requires the child to make meaning of a message and to understand vocabulary. When the vocabularies of struggling and successful young readers are compared, the differences are enormous; successful young readers know as many as 2,000 more words (Baker, Simmons, & Kameenui 1998). Researchers attribute much of that vocabulary advantage to the children having had opportunities to hear stories read aloud and to discuss books with interested adults during their early childhood (Allor & McCathren 2003; Nagy & Scott 2000).

Connecting experiences. Even though children today have extensive experience with visual materials, prior life experience plays a key role in making sense of illustrations; therefore, picture books that are created specifically for children according to their developmental levels, interests, and activity settings offer the best opportunity for linking visual literacy, listening comprehension, and reading comprehension. A team of experts on reading comprehension concludes, "Comprehension processes emerge early in life as children learn to talk about their experiences, listen to stories, and experience the world. These early experiences provide the foundation for comprehension instruction" (Reutzel, Camperell, & Smith 2002).

How are the feelings, dispositions, skills, and knowledge associated with literacy affected by a child's early experiences with picture books? A discussion between 5-year-old Leah and her librarian about *The Nutcracker* (Hoffman) offers some insight. Leah not only has learned about stories but also has made them her own, made them part of her daily life. In the process, she has become quite a storyteller herself:

> *Leah:* The little girl was named Clara . . . she, she was sick and she wore a blue party dress and her doctor gave her a nutcracker for Christmas. And her brother stamped on it. Well, her *godfather* gave her the nutcracker.

Mary Renck Jalongo

What Can Children Learn from Picture Books?

Through meaningful experiences with picture books, children—

• Develop the skills of visual literacy
• Appreciate excellence in art and language
• Understand people, relationships, feelings, and motives
• Think more expansively about the real world and about imaginary ones
• Apply skills in all areas of the language arts—listening, speaking, reading, and writing—as well as in the arts in general
• Reflect on how real storytellers, writers, and artists work, and become inspired by them
• Interpret and evaluate literature in its many different forms (Roser & Martinez 1985)
• Communicate more effectively by incorporating the content, vocabulary, and linguistic complexity found in literature (Solsken 1985)
• Broaden their perspectives to view different cultures and individuals in less stereotypic ways (Sims 1982)
• Learn to select books that are suited to their reading levels and interests (Hepler & Hickman 1982)

And her brother stamped on it and kicked it and his godfather picked him up on the hair and pulled him out—*ordered* him out. Because, he didn't like that. And she had a dream that it danced around and her nutcracker grew and grew and grew until it was a person. There was a beautiful ballet dancer named the Sugar Plum Fairy and she was all purple and there was a Castle of Sleeps and there was a jewelry box lady and the flowers were dancing and the bees and butterflies and see, the doctor had put some dolls out, some wind-up dolls and they *danced.* And you know what else? You know what I got for Christmas? . . . My Aunt June got me a ballet suit.

Librarian: A ballet suit?

Leah: Yeah! It came with a tutu and it came with the tights and the shirt and it came with ballet shoes.

Librarian: So, are you going to be a ballet dancer?

Leah: Well, yes, I *want* to . . . I got that book because Stacy gave it to me—our next door neighbor. And you know what? You haven't heard at all—I have a boyfriend . . . Derek. He was at school and he moved (*lowers voice*) to Lima, Ohio.

Librarian: Oh, no.

Leah: And you know what? Every ti—when he was at school, every time he saw I went, he always kissed my hand. And I WAS GETTING SICK OF IT! I *was.* And I thought . . . and one day when he was about to kiss my hand, I put my gloves on so he wouldn't. (*laughs*) He said, "How about kissing your cheek?" and I said, "*No way.*" I thought, "Oh, no—I should have my scarf on!" (*giggles*) But I took my mittens off after that because he wanted to kiss my cheek. I don't like that at all, I really don't. He *always* did that. I keep *dreaming* of him every night. I miss him. And before he went—And you know what? I gave him a going-away present. I gave him a COMIC BOOK! . . . And I miss him now a lot, a whole lot. . . . Do you know the tape of Peter Wolf? I keep *dreaming* of that, and I kept *reading* about big bad wolfs. So every time when I dreamed of it, I snuggled up close because I was afraid that it would come and eat me so I snuggled up close to my Mama so it wouldn't. I thought that big bad wolf was *real* . . . sheesh!

Librarian: Do you think that now?

Leah: No, but one morning I dreamed about the story that you lent out one time about the little girl and the Gunniwolf.

Chronology of Language Development and Literacy Needs

Age	Language development	Literacy needs
Birth–6 mos.	Comforted by soft sounds; cries, gurgles, and coos	To hear rhythmic language, rhymes, chants, songs
6–9 mos.	Produces one-syllable sounds; sounds develop intonation patterns; may attempt to imitate "Ma" and "Da"	All of the above—plus, to participate in using repetitious books, point-and-say books, books that pose simple questions, books that have clear pictures of familiar objects, simple stories with predictable plots
9 mos.–18 mos.	Responds to some words; begins using holophrases (one-word utterances) such as "doggie," "juice," "ball"; may produce unusual pronunciation that may make the child's words difficult to understand	
18 mos.–2 yrs.	Points to objects; has developed a vocabulary of 20 to 200 words; understands simple questions; uses telegraphic speech such as "Daddy bye-bye"	
2 yrs.–2½ yrs.	Has developed a vocabulary of 50 to 400 words; continues using two- and three-word phrases; begins using pronouns and prepositions, but may get them confused (e.g., saying "inside" when meaning "outside")	All of the above—plus, to respond to simple stories that can be dramatized and to stories that include families, important changes, interesting characters, predictable outcomes

Mary Renck Jalongo

Librarian: Oh, the puppet show that we did here. Did that scare you?

Leah: Oh, not that much. Know what? Now they're showing it on television . . . but the Gunniwolf, it looked real funny—it looked like a *spider*! (*laughs*) The little girl . . . got some yellowish and white flowers and yellow flowers and she dropped all of them and she got some orange flowers and she dropped all of them and she got home and her mother told her stay out of the woods and she got home and she *cried*. And her mother went away at the end of the book. She went in there because she saw some flowers. She thought they were nice for her Mama and she just *almost* got eaten. But she didn't. (*laughs*) Yeah, that's the whole story! (provided by Melissa Ann Renck, children's services librarian, Toledo Lucas County Library)

Age	Language development	Literacy needs
2½ yrs.–3 yrs.	Uses three- and four-word utterances; uses correct word order more often; applies some grammatical rules; comprehends better; is more intelligible to others; asks questions such as "What's that?"	All of the above—plus, to enjoy simple counting rhymes and songs, answering questions, repetition of captivating phrases
3–4 yrs.	Has developed a 1,000-word vocabulary; demonstrates better articulation of certain sounds (*s, th, z, r, l*); generates more complex sentences and questions; is beginning conversation	All of the above—plus, to retell or memorize stories; to use characters and situations from literature in sociodramatic play
4–5 yrs.	Can use 1,500–1,800 words; correctly names many objects, actions, colors, etc.; may be able to identify some letters or read simple words; can converse with other children and adults	All of the above—plus, to memorize favorite stories and "read" them; to sustain interest in stories with more plot and character development; to enjoy stories that explore basic concepts, human emotions, and relationships; to distinguish between real and make-believe or between good and bad behavior

Based on Lamme et al. (1980) and Papalia & Olds (1998).

Where knowledge and skills are concerned, Leah clearly has been influenced by literature. She has acquired new vocabulary (e.g., *stamped* and *ordered*), and she can construct a narrative about her experiences. Her favorite stories have had an effect also on her dispositions. She has been motivated to borrow books from the library, listen to tapes, attend a puppet performance, and even critique a film version of *The Gunniwolf* (Harper), an earlier version of the Little Red Riding Hood story. Additionally, Leah has used literature as a safe way of confronting one of the most prevalent fears of preschoolers, a fear of animals. It is apparent that this 5-year-old's experiences with literature have deeply affected all aspects of her life.

Armed with an understanding of the structure of stories, an expanded vocabulary, ways of discussing books, and ways of representing the ideas in books, Leah will arrive at school able to present herself to others as a competent and well-informed kindergartner. Additionally, literature has captured her imagination and made her eager to learn to read so that she can further explore and enjoy the pleasures of picture books.

Conclusion: The contributions of picture books

A considerable investment goes into developing a high-quality picture book that will be developmentally effective with children at various points in their lives. The box **Chronology of Language Development and Literacy Needs** summarizes the ways that picture books can satisfy those needs. For more information on meeting children's needs through quality picture books, see Zeece (2001a/b).

What is best where literature is concerned? Choices in picture books have long-term significance in children's lives. Ideally, picture books would have the effect described here:

> Books do for children the same things they do for adults: they inform, they stimulate, delight, amuse, and transport us all into other worlds of thought and experience. Most importantly, they make us think and feel and respond, and they put us in intimate touch with the best that has been known and thought. ("A Note to Grownups" 1985, n.p.)

Mary Renck Jalongo

CHAPTER 2

Quality in Picture Books

*Only the rarest and best kind of anything can be good enough for
the young.*

—Walter de la Mare, *Bells and Grass* (1942)

Arriving at a definition for *quality* is exceedingly difficult. Why is
any one thing more valued or worthwhile than something else?
As a cultural artifact, the picture book is deemed valuable when

• it is judged to have made an exceptional contribution that advances the field
of children's literature;

• it compares favorably with other books of its type or genre;

• it is recognized as art by the intended audience or culture;

• it retains its value over time; and

• it is produced by someone who is considered to be an artist.

Of course, the success of a book is affected by additional variables, including the process through which the literature evolved, readability, marketing, and audience appeal (Temple et al. 1998).

Books considered children's literature "classics" have managed to endure as favorites. How does this continued appeal happen? Picture books that become classics appeal to both children and adults; they are written in a captivating and original style. The classics also introduce us to unforgettable characters who change and grow; their stories remain fresh rather than becoming outdated as years go by. Great picture books live in our memories, rather than being quickly forgotten, and as a result, they become part of our childhood (Jalongo 2002). Appendix A highlights authors and illustrators who consistently emerge as leaders in the field of literature for young children.

Nevertheless, the task of defining quality in picture books remains a challenge:

> The question of what is good is a dangerous one. The appellation of "good" is a fragile raft of opinion resting precariously on the shifting quicksand of taste.

Quality in Picture Books

> What is acclaimed today may be ignored or criticized only a few years hence. Obviously one answer to the problem is to wait until a book has stood the test of time before declaring it good. (Stewig 1980, 10)

As social mores change, our concepts of what is suitable for children and what represents quality also change. Books that have been roundly criticized can be resurrected by a retelling or new illustrations and books that were once popular sometimes fall into disfavor because they clash with prevailing attitudes (Kohl 1995). Consider, for example, recent criticisms of two longstanding favorite stories among young children, *Curious George* (Rey), first published in 1941, and *The Story of Babar, the Little Elephant* (DeBrunhoff) from 1931. Recent critics of these books have argued that they are metaphors for imperialism and white domination of other races (MacCann 1998). Some educators point to the child appeal of *Curious George* as justification for continuing to include it in the curriculum, whereas others disagree. The controversy raises this question:

> If texts like *Curious George* and *The Story of Babar* do have the racist and colonialist implications that they seem to have, should we continue to hold them up as cultural icons worth keeping? . . . If we do not pay careful attention to the artifacts of childhood culture, we risk blithely passing on damaging, static traditions that inhibit social growth. (Coats 2001, 406, 409)

Whatever the decision, the passage of time, cultural and political influences, and individual preferences clearly affect prevailing concepts of quality in children's literature. The number of works, the formats of those works, and the uses of children's literature are constantly growing, changing, and developing.

Formulating professional judgments about picture books

Young children depend on adults to lead them to literacy. Families and teachers must decide which of the many books on library or bookstore shelves are written and illustrated better than others (see Horning 1997). According to the American Booksellers Association (2003), there were 460.3 million children's books purchased at a cost of $1.9 billion in 2002 alone (www.bookweb.org/aba).

Identifying quality in picture books poses some of the same challenges as deciding on the basis of an interview who among several candidates will be an esteemed co-teacher and colleague. In many ways, to say what is not acceptable is almost easier than to define what is. In *The Way to Write for Children*, Aiken (1982) describes what a high-quality picture book is not:

> [It] is not something that can be dashed off to schedule, turned off a production belt like a piece of factory goods. It should not be anything with an axe to grind, propaganda for something, a hidden sales message. It should not be perfunctory, meaningless, flat, coy, or second rate. (15)

According to *Publishers Weekly*, 376 children's titles have met its criteria for all-time best-selling children's books by having sold at least 750,000 hardcover copies or 1 million paperback copies since first publication (http://publishersweekly.reviews.news.com). What makes a picture book a "keeper" from among the thousands in print or recently published? In an article for *The Horn Book Magazine*, Burns and Flowers (1999) contend that high-quality

Picture Book Trends

Increase in the number of picture books published. Only 2,640 children's books were published in the year 1970; by 1995 that number had more than doubled (Lynch-Brown & Tomlinson 1999). Currently more than 120,000 different children's books are in print in the United States. In the United Kingdom, 8,000 children's books were published in 1997 alone (Astbury 1998).

Use of children's literature for reading instruction. A trend has developed toward the use of literature for reading instruction. For emergent readers, oversize or Big Books that typically are about 18 by 22 inches are used to introduce young children to reading. Picture books are also found in reading series referred to as *basal readers*. Increasingly, picture books are being published with older readers in mind, which makes careful selection even more important so books appropriately match the interests and abilities of younger listeners and readers.

Consolidation in the publishing industry. For the last three decades, companies have been engaged in mergers and acquisitions; a few huge corporations rather than many small presses now dominate the publication of picture books. To illustrate, 87 different publishers had produced the books reviewed in *The Horn Book Magazine* during 1967; three decades later, just 5 publishing companies had produced 60 percent of the books reviewed during 1997 (Hade 2001). Additionally, concerns are growing that as a result of these changes, originality in children's literature will suffer and first-time and minority authors will not be supported.

Increased commercialization of children's literature. Commercialization is a concern to many experts, who fear that profits alone, rather than quality, will dictate decision making. For example, objections have been raised (Raugust 2000) about picture books being used to advertise and sell food items—such as Cheerios, Pepperidge Farm Goldfish crackers, or M&M's.

Promotion of items other than books in bookstores. Increasingly the big publishing companies are selling licenses to companies authorizing those companies to make products based on one of the publisher's story characters. Mehren (1999) reports that bookstores now devote nearly a third of their space to the display of nonbook items. In 1998, 13 of the 16 top-selling hardcover children's books were licensed properties (Raugust 1999). A child who likes Norman Bridwell's big red dog can own not only a wide range of picture books about Clifford but also an array of items with a Clifford theme, including stuffed toys, board games, computer software and videos, articles of clothing, a backpack, and a lunch box.

Basing books on the mass media, and converting books into media. Books that promote toys, movies, and television programs can attain quick popularity; because these characters already are familiar to children and families, they may be chosen first. Some see media violence and the toys linked to it as particularly problematic, due to the multiple effects on children's play (see Levine 1998; Levine 2003). Of course, children's books can also yield mass media, particularly movies and television programs (Maughan 1999). For example, *Stuart Little*, E.B. White's 1945 tale of

continued . . .

Picture Book Trends, continued

a little white mouse with a spunky personality charmed another generation when computer-generated imagery made it possible to create a film that brought the imaginary character to life in convincing, photo-realistic detail (Jobson 2001). Another work of high fantasy, Chris Van Allsburg's *Jumanji*, a picture book about a board game gone wild, also inspired a feature-length film. In addition, after the Marc Brown story character Arthur became a television program, more than 20 million copies of the various books about Arthur were sold (Raugust 1999).

Interactive websites linked with picture books. Just beginning to emerge are appealing, high-quality, interactive websites that focus on picture books and that are intended specifically for children (e.g., www.peterrabbit.com). For older children, websites that focus on favorite authors, such as Eric Carle (www.eric-carle.com), offer interesting information and activities. Thus far, websites for toy and broadcasting companies such as the Public Broadcasting Service (www.pbs.org/kids) have been leading the way in interactive website development related to children's literature. Meanwhile, sites for huge conglomerates such as The Walt Disney Corporation might report 20 million hits per month (Jobson 2001). One advantage of high-quality interactive websites is that many of them offer children the opportunity to select the language they want to use to view the material, thus providing additional support for bilingual instruction.

New formats and technologies for picture books. Most early picture books relied on black ink sketches for their illustrations. Today, advances in high-speed color printing have made it possible and financially feasible to produce illustrated books that delight the eyes of young viewers. Some contemporary books are illustrated with color photographs of three-dimensional artworks such as collages, clay, and various textile arts (Dickman 1998; O'Malley 1998). Additionally, books such as lift-the-flap or pop-up books, which have moving parts, have become increasingly elaborate paper-engineering marvels. Not only the production methods but also the books themselves have become increasingly high tech as picture books are equipped with computer chips that make animal sounds, play music, or enable children to follow along with words that are read aloud by a computer voice.

A range of services provided for teachers. Teacher book clubs such as those sponsored by Scholastic Corporation offer inexpensive paperback books. They also

picture books are memorable; that is, while some books are "merely popular or timely," good picture books "have the power to endure" (575). Much of a book's success, in their opinion, is attributable to

> unforgettable characters . . . the consummate nanny Mary Poppins; Charlotte, the wisest of spiders; the iconoclastic Cat in the Hat; and Max, forever in search of Wild Things. These and similar figures have endured in our traditions and in our memories, giving rise to new metaphors, to new ways of seeing. (575)

Mary Renck Jalongo

provide a wide range of classroom book collections, reading programs, Big Books, classroom magazines, and school supplies. Additionally, teachers who promote the book clubs among children can earn points to obtain free teaching resources such as videos about popular author-illustrators. Teachers can also access free online lesson plans indexed to each state's academic standards (Hade 2001). Increasingly, publishers of picture books are marketing their wares to teachers.

Research on children's visual and textual literacy. Picture books are big business, and publishers conduct research into children's visual and textual literacy to increase the chances that their investments will pay off. Factors such as "eye bites" (the length of a line of text a child can read without difficulty), the legibility of different fonts, as well as the connection between textual and visual understanding, are investigated but may not be freely shared, a strategy that enables companies to beat the competition (Jobson 2001). Publishers are also becoming increasingly sophisticated at inventing accompanying activities. They know, for example, that simple point-and-click websites are preferred by toddlers. They also know that when children seek information about a book, they tend to search by character, not by author or title.

Interventions that provide access to high-quality books. When Krashen's (1997) research indicated that middle-class children had better personal libraries at home than many low-income children had at school, the findings reinforced what many educators and activists promoting literacy had known all along—that book ownership matters. Interventions, reflecting a growing recognition of the need to give children opportunities to read and own books, are increasing—both internationally, as evidenced by the literacy projects supported by the International Reading Association, and at the national level, in projects such as Reading Is Fundamental (www.RIF.org) and In2Books (www.in2books.org/national). When Britain declared 1999 the "Year of Reading," some 23 million children's books were put into schools to increase access to literature (British Broadcasting Corporation 1999). After the Pennsylvania Department of Education reported that less than one U.S. dollar per week per child was spent on supplies in government-subsidized child care (Neuman & Celano 2001b), a two-year program in Philadelphia called "Books Aloud" not only supplied picture books to urban child care centers and to families but also trained child care providers in how to use the books more effectively. As a result, classroom libraries increased to an average of seven books per child, and children made impressive gains in reading (Neuman 1999).

The best picture books

> offer new ways of thinking, fresh ways of re-examining the past and the present, an invigorating vocabulary, and unusual characters and settings. They are not predictable, nor are they trite. In fact, they are sometimes disturbing, even as they entertain. (578)

In thinking about the books that last, that are memorable, and that stimulate thinking, it is helpful to recognize that many different people exert an influence on the process of producing picture books. Clearly, children, families, and community members affect publishers' decision making. Likewise, professionals who share books with children and recognized experts in the field of children's literature affect assessments of picture books' quality.

How difficult is writing a quality children's book?

Talk to aspiring writers and they will often say that they want to begin by writing a children's book. Why? Because they assume that writing a short book must be easier than writing a long one. Before agreeing with this idea, consider the following information:

• A good picture book must appeal not only to the child but also to the adults who purchase and read stories to children. Publishers, families, librarians, teachers, and critics are often the book's first audience; children, its second.

• The book must grab the young child's interest initially and maintain that interest through repeated readings; it can be simple, but not trivial or condescending. It has to be memorable and worthy of being revisited.

• Although the number of words might range from zero to a thousand, any words that are used must be selected carefully because the book will be read aloud like poetry.

Who Influences the Children's Book Market?

In the rapidly changing marketplace, the ability of a new picture book to remain in print even a few years is a complex interaction of variables:

The child affects adults' ideas about good books by his or her individual response to literature. If the child does not appear interested in a particular book, the adult will try a different book or, perhaps, try the same book at another time. In this way, the child's response affects both current and future book selections by adults.

Family members and communities influence children's literature by deciding which books to share with children, including which picture books to borrow, buy, recommend, or reject.

Professionals in the field of children's literature—picture book authors, illustrators, children's book editors, and reviewers—affect what is published. Authors determine which manuscripts will be submitted; editors decide which ones will be published; and those who review children's literature can choose to celebrate, overlook, or criticize a book.

Professionals who share literature with children—teachers, librarians, and teacher educators—help to determine through their use, endorsement, and purchase of picture books whether a book will be recognized and successful in finding an audience.

The popular media—Celebrities who endorse or write picture books (such as Will Smith or Jamie Lee Curtis) affect what is published; huge corporations, such as Walt Disney Studios, generate ubiquitous icons that frequently yield mass market books and other media.

Mary Renck Jalongo

• If an author writes only the text for a picture book, the publisher will assign an artist to the project. Even though picture book authors are not required also to be artists, they often are. Being the story's illustrator too is one way an author can ensure that the text and the images the author envisioned are perfectly matched.

• A typical picture book is 32 pages on a six-by-nine-inch paper size. A picture storybook or information book might contain some 100 to 400 words. Within these constraints, a picture book author needs to accomplish worthy goals such as informing, enlightening, entertaining, and stimulating the imagination of the young child.

• Year after year, the list of the great books for children remains relatively unchanged (Aiken 1982). Considering that more than 5,000 new picture books are published annually (Tomlinson & Lynch-Brown 2003), an author has only a small chance of creating the Great American Picture Book.

• The typical child reads only about 600 books of all types from early childhood through adolescence. Ideally, each book should enrich that child's life "with new ideas, insight, humor, or vocabulary" (Aiken 1982, 10). This requirement is perhaps the most intimidating of all. How many authors and illustrators can hope to contribute to children's lives in a significant way?

For more on writing children's picture books, see Clifton (1981), Lewis (1981), and Mayr (1999).

Deciding which books are good

Eventually, adults who select books for children must rely on good instincts, which result from thorough and frequent examination of the best that literature has to offer (Hearne 2000). Evaluating children's literature is like appraising the worth of anything, from breakfast cereal to the family car—before reaching a decision we study the features, do some comparison shopping, and establish evaluation criteria (see the boxes **Selecting** and **Evaluating a Picture Book**). Adults must also consider the needs and personality of the individual child and try to match that child with the best possible books.

It is unrealistic to assume that during a professional career, every early childhood educator can obtain, much less read and evaluate, the thousands of new picture books published annually. One way to identify which books children will like is by asking a children's librarian; another way is by consulting one of the many resources on the Web (see Appendix B for recommendations). Educators also can consult published reviews of picture books (see the box **Sources of Children's Book Reviews**). In addition, they can borrow picture books from the library every week, share them with children, and give children themselves the opportunity to identify their favorites. Children and adults develop a sense of quality in literature by being surrounded with the best so often that mediocre and poor picture books are no longer appealing.

Picture books and diversity

Literature has the power to influence ideas and expectations (Cartledge & Kiarie 2001; Cress & Holm 2000; DeGeorge 1998; Hodges 1995). One illustration of that influence is that throughout history, when one group wanted to control others completely, it burned or banned books that challenged its views. Because literature exerts strong influence on children's perceptions, it is important to choose books that treat women, minorities, and other cultures fairly: "Young children are the most vulnerable to stereotypes and bias in books because books play a major role in shaping children's first images of the larger society" (Chambers 1983, 91–2).

Consider these findings from research on diversity and multicultural children's literature:

• Young children are beginning to see the disparity between the way society should be and the way it is; they are gradually acquiring a sense of social justice (Wade 2000).

• "Children cannot be expected to develop a sensitivity toward others merely because they are told to do so. Attitudes are difficult to change. . . . Literature allows individuals to share in the lives of others; it can also provide an avenue for multicultural understanding" (Wham, Barnhart, & Cook 1996, 2).

• "Multicultural literature is one vehicle through which teachers can support and encourage tolerance and understanding among children. Multicultural

---

Selecting a Picture Book

Step 1—Quickly look over the book to get a feel for the tone and approach

Step 2—Read just the text, mentally blocking out the art

Step 3—Read the story carefully while focusing on the harmony of words and pictures, backtracking and pausing whenever you feel like it

Step 4—Examine critically other details such as book design, paper, typeface, endpapers, dedications, etc.

Questions to consider:

• What is the illustrator attempting to do?

• Why is a certain effect used? Is it successful?

• Are the illustrations or photographs aesthetically pleasing and of good quality?

• Are story and pictures well integrated?

• Is there flow from page to page?

• Has the artist considered the constraints of format?

• Has the child been kept in mind? What age child?

• Could a young child get a sense of the basic concepts of story sequence by looking just at the pictures?

• Are balance, harmony, mood, composition, line, and color apparent?

Based on Elleman (1986).

Evaluating a Picture Book

General evaluation questions

- Does the book compare favorably with other picture books of its type?
- Has the picture book received the endorsements of professionals?
- Are the literary elements of plot, theme, character, style, and setting used effectively?
- Do the pictures complement the story?
- Is the story free from ethnic, racial, or sex-role stereotypes?
- Is the picture book developmentally appropriate for the child?
- Do preschoolers respond enthusiastically to the book?
- Is the topic (and the book's treatment of it) suitable for the young child?
- Does the picture book also appeal to the parent or teacher?

Additional evaluation questions for illustrations

- Are the illustrations and text synchronized?
- Does the mood expressed by the artwork (humorous or serious, rollicking or quiet) complement that of the story?
- Are the illustrative details consistent with the text?
- Could a child get a sense of the basic concepts or story sequence by looking just at the pictures?
- Are the illustrations or photographs aesthetically pleasing?
- Is the printing (clarity, form, line, color) of good quality?
- Can children view and re-view the illustrations, each time getting more from them?
- Are the illustrative style and complexity suited to the age level of the intended audience?

Based on Huck et al. (2000).

literature is literature that depicts and explores the lives of individuals who belong to a wide range of different groups" (Bainbridge, Pantaleo, & Ellis 1999, 183).

- Picture books offer socially provocative content that motivates children to think critically about their social worlds and to evaluate those worlds (Koeller & Mitchell 1996).

- "Research has shown that storybook reading, accompanied by discussion, can significantly improve a child's acceptance of difference" (Bainbridge, Pantaleo, & Ellis 1999, 185).

- Several studies link students' reading about their own cultures and the cultures of others to higher self-esteem, greater academic achievement, and positive influences across subject areas (Diamond & Moore 1995).

Sources of Children's Book Reviews

Sponsor	Publications	Purpose
Organizations		
American Library Association (ALA)	*School Library Journal* *Booklinks* *Booklist*	Some regularly review picture books in a section of the publication
Association for Childhood Education International (ACEI)	*Childhood Education*	Some publish articles about children's literature, books about early
Council on Interracial Books for Children	*Interracial Books for Children Bulletin*	literacy, or both
Horn Book, Inc.	*The Horn Book Magazine*	
International Reading Association (IRA)	*The Reading Teacher*	
Kluwer Academic Publishers	*Early Childhood Education Journal*	
National Association for the Education of Young Children (NAEYC)	*Young Children*	
National Council of Teachers of English (NCTE)	*Language Arts*	
University of Chicago	*Bulletin of the Center for Children's Books*	
Newspapers		
New York Times	*New York Times Literary Supplement*	Publishes an annual supplement of children's book reviews
Indexes of reviews		
Gale Research Publishing	*Children's Book Review Index*	Synthesizes major children's book reviews published in a variety of sources
Publishing companies		
Various publishing companies such as Dial, Harper & Row, and Putnam	*Trade Publishers Annual*	Binds publishers' catalogues into large volumes; each catalogue advertises that company's award-winning books

As this summary of the research suggests, picture books have the power to counteract stereotypes. What is a stereotype? A filmstrip from the Council on Interracial Books for Children (1978) defines it as follows:

> A stereotype is an oversimplified, generalized image describing all individuals in a group as having the same characteristics, that is to say, in appearance, in behavior, in beliefs. While there may be a germ of truth in a stereotype, the image usually represents a gross distortion, or an exaggeration of that truth, and has offensive, dehumanizing implications.

Campbell and Wirtenberg (1980) offer these four questions for exposing stereotypes in children's books:

Are people of different races, cultures, ethnic groups, and religious groups accurately portrayed? In the 1960s, some publishers responded to the call for greater diversity simply by shading in the faces of characters who had obviously Caucasian features! Teachers are often shocked to find out that the first picture book portraying an African American child was *The Snowy Day,* written and illustrated by Ezra Jack Keats and first published in 1962, because it seems ridiculous that a book of this nature would have taken so long to be produced. Likewise, picture books about children with disabilities did not emerge until the 1960s. Even though we are into the next century, many groups of children remain underrepresented in picture books. How many classrooms that include young children of the Islamic faith have a picture book portraying a peer from that religious group? How many classrooms that include young children from Central America have books about its countries?

Moreover, when diversity is portrayed, is it shown in a positive light? Is it used to also highlight the similarities that connect us all, not just our differences? Teachers can make the cultural *connections* explicit through their choice of books. It is worth the effort, for example, to connect the two tales of cities that endeavored to help a family of ducks survive—Robert McCloskey's classic *Make Way for Ducklings,* which takes place in Boston, and Julia Takaya's picture book *Chibi: A True Story from Japan*, with a similar theme.

Are girls and women portrayed as active and successful? Children's books sometimes suggest that females are intellectually inferior and should be subservient to males. Studies of children's books suggest that boy characters in active roles far outnumber girls in similar roles, and that healthy, active lifestyles are seldom in evidence for women and girls in stories (Nilges & Spencer 2002). Beware of books that portray women as helpless or as needing male protection or intervention to succeed. Such books encourage dependency in girls and dominance in boys. They also communicate the message that girls are incapable of solving problems or pursuing leadership roles. Something as simple as a female principal in a story about school or a female veterinarian in a story about animal care can help girls to see those careers as possibilities for themselves.

Are families portrayed in all their structural diversity? Too many books for children express the message that a family is always defined as a mother, a father, and children. Presenting that family configuration exclusively can suggest to the child that a single-parent family, an extended family, a stepfamily, a two-mother or two-father family, or another family grouping is

From *Full, Full, Full of Love*. Text copyright © 2003 Trish Cooke. Illustrations copyright © 2003 Paul Howard. Reproduced by permission of the publisher Candlewick Press, Inc., Cambridge, MA, on behalf of Walker Books Ltd., London.

inferior. Vera Williams's *A Chair for My Mother* tells the story of a young child who lives with a mother and grandmother. The mother works very hard as a waitress, and after a tragic house fire, she saves enough money to buy a chair that is the right size for holding the child (the story's narrator) on her lap to share picture books. Picture books should affirm that care, affection, and responsibility are the things that define "family." A powerful example of this message is communicated in *Full, Full, Full of Love* (Cooke).

Mary Renck Jalongo

On Sunday, Jay Jay had dinner
at Grannie's house.
And when it was time to go,
he climbed on Grannie's lap.

He kissed her and she kissed him back.
And then they hugged
and hugged and hugged,
and full of hugs
they hugged some more.

Are other cultures and groups represented as strange or quaint? Children need to identify with people who seem different from themselves to become aware of what they have in common and what is unique to each. For example, children can relate to the importance of names (e.g., Sanders, *What's Your Name*); they can think about how climate, culture, and income affect the types of homes people live in (Morris, *Houses and Homes*); and they can appreciate what it means to feel homesick when they have to go away (Williams, *When Africa Was Home*). When groups of people are depicted stereotypically, children acquire inaccurate impressions. If the only depictions that children see of Native Americans, for example, show them in the 1800s wearing feathers and face paint, children may conclude wrongly that no one they know can be Native American because no one they know looks like that, or that Native Americans no longer exist today.

A book that allows children to glimpse another culture should highlight the universality of human emotions, motives, and experience. When differences are overemphasized and these common bonds are ignored, children tend to see other cultures as quaint or bizarre. Ask an elementary school child to draw or describe a peer from Holland and the probable result is a person in wooden clogs surrounded by tulips and windmills. When books perpetuate stereotypes, they hinder the child's ability to identify with other people.

Owens and Nowell (2001) suggest that children's books can be categorized around 10 themes that have significance for promoting an understanding of and appreciation for diversity in young children: (1) community, (2) decision making, (3) diversity, (4) economics, (5) employment, (6) environment, (7) justice or

Does This Picture Book Value Diversity?

As you examine a picture book, ask—

• Are the characters real and authentic?

• Are the characters in active roles?

• Are the characters' actions nonstereotypical?

• Do the characters grow and change in acceptable ways?

• Are different cultures portrayed in a positive fashion?

• Does the story increase understanding and acceptance?

• Does the story help members of the portrayed minority or group feel greater pride in their own background?

• Is the speech of the people in the book accurate and appropriate?

• Does the style of the illustrations complement the text and enhance the story?

• Do the illustrations reflect an authentic portrayal of physical features and other details?

• Did the author and illustrator have experiences that prepared them to produce this particular book?

• What is the copyright date of the book, and how might that have affected the accuracy and authenticity of the story?

• Have reviews of the book been issued by various minority groups representing ethnicity, age, gender, or education?

• Does the book encourage children to become more socially conscious?

From *All for the Children: Multicultural Essentials of Literature* by D. Finazzo. © 1997. Reprinted with permission of Wadsworth, a division of Thomson Learning: www.thomsonrights.com. Fax 800-730-2215.

fairness, (8) media (power, bias, influence), (9) perspective taking, and (10) relationships (interpersonal). For more on diversity, see the box **Supporting Children with Differences** in Chapter 3.

The child's perspective on quality

Every teacher has at one time or another presented an award-winning picture book to children only to have this object of rave reviews from literary critics be panned by its target audience. Like the parents who purchase an expensive toy for their child only to watch her play delightedly with the wrappings instead, professionals who evaluate, purchase, and share children's literature are occasionally disappointed by children's responses to a book they loved. Sometimes, those books selected as outstanding by adult critics are not the most popular with children (Nilsen, Peterson, & Searfoss 1980).

Kiefer (1985) suggests the best resolution to this issue: "Rather than argue about whether to give children books which are good for them or books which we think they will like, perhaps we ought to ask how it is that children come to love the books which are good for them" (706). With so many choices available,

Mary Renck Jalongo

we often can accomplish both: to find literature worthy of children's time and attention and to find picture books with undeniable child appeal.

Why might adults' and young children's preferences differ? Several logical explanations exist for discrepancies in children's and adults' choices:

Availability and familiarity. Young children may not have access to quality literature. They may learn to prefer what is advertised, just as they might learn to prefer the junk food they see on commercials over a well-balanced meal. As a result, children might select books that are actually commercials for popular toys or syndicated cartoon characters because those characters are highly advertised in the media.

Inexperience. Appearances can be deceiving, and young children must truly judge a book by its cover until an adult reads the book to them. Picture books (at least initially) require interaction between an adult and a child. Just surrounding children with books is not enough. Young children need caring adults to show them the way (Prescott 1965). *The Story of Jumping Mouse* by John Steptoe is a good example. It is a rich and complex Native American legend, one that a child would need to hear and discuss many times before grasping its message of self-sacrifice. What follows is an excerpt from 5-year-old Anna's retelling of the story. Note that Anna has internalized the story structure even though the book asks a lot from a kindergartner. Anna became intrigued by this picture book because adults took the time to read it to her and to answer her questions. The mythical aspects of the story captured her imagination and, with repeated readings, it became her favorite book. A child without similar opportunities would have a difficult time unlocking the potential of *The Story of Jumping Mouse,* just as adults without training and experience would have difficulty reading and following a book on home repair even though the instructions and pictures are right in front of them.

Text of the book	Anna's retelling
Once there was a young mouse who lived in the brush near a great river. During the day he and the other mice hunted for food. At night they gathered to hear the old ones tell stories. The young mouse liked to hear about the desert beyond the river, and he got shivers from the stories about the dangerous shadows that lived in the sky. But his favorite was the tale of the far-off land.	*(Anna reads title)* The Mice, by John Step. I'm holding it here. Sit where you guys can see. *(Anna points to the page)* Right here. *(Pointing to the mouse)* The little mice—that's a picture of the little mice.
The far-off land sounded so wonderful the young mouse began to dream about it. He knew he would never be content until he had been there. The old ones warned that the journey would be long and perilous, but the young mouse would not be swayed.	One morning the little mouse went out to see the leaves, but it was raining, not raining hard. One morning he went out running in the forest 'cause he wanted to see what he could see.

He set off one morning before the sun had risen. It was evening before he reached the edge of the brush. Before him was the river; on the other side was the desert.

He was tired of his city. He saw a pond.

The young mouse peered into the deep water. "How will I ever get across?" he said in dismay.

(Anna raises the pitch of her voice to sound like the mouse) "How will I ever get across the pond?"

"Don't you know how to swim?" called a gravelly voice. The young mouse looked around and saw a small green frog.

A frog speaked to him.

"Hello," he said. "What is swim?" "This is swimming," said the frog, and she jumped into the river. "Oh," said the young mouse. "I don't think I can do that." "Why do you need to cross the river?" asked the frog, hopping back up the bank. "I want to go to the far-off land," said the young mouse. "It sounds too beautiful to live a lifetime and not see it. . . . "

(Again, in her high-pitched tone of voice) "Hello, Mrs. Frog. I would like to get across to see the rest of the city. . . . "

Poor selections by adults. Of course, adults can be misguided in their own book choices and can consequently inflict those preferences on children. Sometimes adults approach picture books with a "take-this-it's-good-for-you" mentality. Usually these "good-for-you" books are one of three types: (1) sermons disguised as picture books, which extol particular social virtues, (2) workbooks disguised as picture books, which emphasize drill and memorization of academic skills, or (3) syrupy children's stories that reflect an adult's highly sentimentalized view of childhood. Furthermore, adults may choose a book because it was shared with them during their childhoods, rather than because it meets current high standards in children's literature.

Developmental differences. Sometimes an audience at one stage of development (adulthood) has difficulty responding as an audience at other stages of development (childhood) would. This difference in adults' and children's perspectives can account for some discrepancies in book preferences. In Greenlaw's (1983) study of nearly 10,000 children, humorous books were the first choice of children in the primary grades, yet few humorous books ever earn adult acclaim, perhaps because adult and child senses of humor differ. We know, for example, that preschoolers tend to appreciate slapstick and incongruity, but only the rare adult can appreciate the child's sense of humor and can predict what children will consider funny.

A good example of this discrepancy involves *The True Story of the Three Little Pigs* (Scieszka). Adults who know the original Three Pigs tale will find the satire

What Makes a High-Quality Book for the Primary Grades?

Characterization: High-quality books include memorable, well-portrayed characters; characters often are about the same age as the intended audience of child listener-readers.

Plot: High-quality books present a sequence of events and issues that are interesting and understandable to students at this stage of development.

Setting: High-quality books portray settings accurately (in the case of nonfiction) and imaginatively (in the case of fiction); new settings become familiar, and familiar settings are seen afresh.

Use of language: High-quality books incorporate language that is concrete and vivid, reads smoothly, evokes images of actions, and reflects the mood of the story.

Appropriateness of theme or motif: High-quality books contain a subtle, worthy, and truthful theme that will capture children's interest and be understandable to them.

Quality of art and design: High-quality books include illustrations that use the elements of media, design, and style in original and expressive ways that capture the readers' attention.

Interplay between pictures and words: High-quality books include illustrations that move the story forward, enhance the meaning and tone of the story, establish the mood, clarify information, and enrich the story.

Adapted from Cullinan & Galda (1994); Huck et al. (2000); Lynch-Brown & Tomlinson (1999); Temple et al. (1998); and Hefflin & Barksdale-Ladd (2001).

in Scieszka's version amusing, whereas preschoolers and kindergartners are more likely to protest "But that's not how it goes!" when the story violates their expectations for it. Such "fractured fairy tales" are seldom appealing to very young children, who are just getting acquainted with the original story, so reserve them for children in the primary grades. Send-ups of old stories that such older children enjoy include *The Principal's New Clothes* (Calmenson), a variant of "The Emperor's New Clothes"; *The Bootmaker and the Elves* (Lowell), a retelling of "The Elves and the Shoemaker"; *The Princess and the Pizza* (Auch), a new version of "The Princess and the Pea"; *Cinderella Bigfoot* (Thaler), a satire of "Cinderella"; and *The Wolf Who Cried Boy* (Hartman), a role reversal of the fable "The Boy Who Cried Wolf." The box **What Makes a High-Quality Book for the Primary Grades?** provides some specific selection guidelines.

Social and temporal influences. Adult critics might identify a book as a landmark in children's literature because it is timely or remarkably different. The 1976 Caldecott winner *Why Mosquitoes Buzz in People's Ears*, written by Verna Aardema and illustrated by Leo and Diane Dillon, is a good example. At the time, the African influence on the story and art of the book filled a gap existing in children's literature of the day and moved it forward. Considerations such as these often influence adults' choices. They may base decisions on comparisons with other publications or intuition about the long-term significance of a book. Children, however, are new to the world of books. They will respond in a much more direct and immediate way.

Conclusion: Books that children love

The Comic Adventures of Old Mother Hubbard and Her Dog (de Paola) is 4-year-old Leon's favorite book because "it has funny pictures." *A House Is a House for Me* (Hoberman) is 5-year-old Suzanna's current choice "because it has words in, that when you say one word, the other one rhymes with it." Teresa, a kindergartner, read *Happy Birthday, Moon* (Asch) "because my birthday's coming up. That's the reason I picked it out!" Miguel, a second-grader, is captivated by *Eight Animals on the Town* (Elya) because he "used it to teach my reading buddy some Spanish words."

Children who "connect" with a picture book are attracted to it by the same magnetism that causes a busy toddler to stop and listen to a song with complete concentration. What do adults say when a novel is too good to miss—"It was a real page-turner. I couldn't put it down!" The same holds true for a young child's favorite book, only in a much more literal sense. An adult puts a treasured book in a briefcase or on a bedside table, a child carries or drags it around everywhere; an adult re-reads and highlights the not-to-be-forgotten passages, the young child scrutinizes and touches pictured objects. Literature is a paradox in that it seems to rivet readers-listeners to each page yet propels us forward with the lure of what happens next. The same dynamic applies to beloved picture books. Children are intrigued by the individual illustrations, often seeing details that escape an adult's notice, yet they are eager to see what will occur with the turn of the page.

In ways that are sometimes grand and in ways that are sometimes small, the reader is better for having experienced a good book. Adults seldom persist at reading a book that does not engage them, even when someone they respect has liked it. We can expect no less from the young child. Quality picture books have enough substance to fascinate a child even after repeated encounters with the same story. A preschooler hears *Morris's Disappearing Bag* (Wells) for the first time and derives the meaning of words such as *invisible* and *disappear* . . . hears it a second time while examining the pictures closely to find out more about the Christmas presents each of the three siblings receives . . . hears it a third time and takes delight in the youngest child's triumph over an older brother and sister who try to exclude the baby of the family with those hurtful words "You're too little to play" . . . and after the fourth reading, our preschooler

  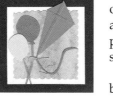

imagines what it would be like to own a disappearing bag by announcing to the family, "I'm pretending to be invisible, so don't see me, okay?"

In this way, a single story has been responsible for grabbing the attention, educating the mind, affecting the emotions, and stimulating the imagination—the effects of a quality book. It delights children and adults. It deserves to be called literature.

Mary Renck Jalongo

CHAPTER 3

Bringing Children and Books Together

Narrative is an important way of understanding human motives, particularly of understanding misunderstanding. One explanation for this is that narratives present both action and what is in the characters' minds, providing insight into what the characters are thinking, feeling, and believing.

—Jerome Bruner, *Acts of Meaning* (1990)

Spring has arrived in kindergarten, and Anna, who just turned 6, is busily drawing ants on a piece of paper. Each one consists of two circles with tiny dashes to represent its legs. At the computer, Anna types the following story about something that made an impression on her while she was at her grandmother's house over the weekend:

> My Nanni have asz in her huse. and She can't get tam out of her huse. they cep on cozing and mar and. Mar and mar cep on cazing.

> [My Nanna has ants in her house and she can't get them out of her house. They keep on coming and more and more and more keep on coming.]

Anna's personal narrative illustrates what teachers and teacher educators have believed passionately for centuries: Story plays a vital role in our lives. More specifically, a wide array of experiences with stories of all types—personal narratives, oral storytelling, and fiction as well as nonfiction books—enable us to

- grow in knowledge and understanding;
- remember information;
- construct autobiographical memory;
- learn to read and write;
- organize and interpret experiences; and
- participate in ethnic and cultural traditions (Armington 1997; Nelson, Aksu-Koc, & Johnson 2001; Sylwester 1995).

Meeting the needs of young children

Children learn the ways of the storyteller through repeated experiences with event-structured material (Jalongo 2003a). Picture storybooks are a major resource for supporting children's development. Interactions between children and picture books that are effective, first and foremost, meet the criterion of developmental appropriateness and effectiveness (see Bredekamp & Copple 1997). Furthermore, because the world of literature is so richly diverse, picture books can do the following (Baker & Greene 1987; Berman 2001; Bettelheim 1976; Neuman, Copple, & Bredekamp 2000):

• Stimulate children's imaginations by introducing them to a wide range of story-sharing experiences

• Increase children's knowledge and understanding of other eras, cultures, and places, both real and imaginary

• Connect children to their own cultural heritage and teach them to appreciate the heritage of others

• Teach children more about narrative structures such as plot sequences, story language, and character development

• Respect individual and cultural differences in discourse styles

• Expand and enrich children's voice, gesture, and vocabulary, as well as provide children with good models of oral language

• Suggest models for children's own stories, both oral and written, and help them to learn how to captivate listeners through language and gesture

• Encourage children to listen to, concentrate on, and follow event-structured material

• Challenge assumptions and introduce new ideas to children in a nonthreatening way

• Develop children's thinking skills, problem-solving strategies, and understanding of cause-effect, compare-contrast, and the like

• Nurture and encourage a sense of humor and entertain children so they associate pleasure with stories

• Increase children's appreciation of literature and various literary forms

• Contribute to children's social and ethical development by providing a warm, personal, shared experience that enables them to feel joy for another's happiness or sadness at another's misfortune

• Foster children's mental health by helping them to cope with powerful emotions and to explore their daydreams and fantasies

• Build children's self-confidence and self-esteem as they learn to interpret and share stories with others through language

The box **Meeting Children's Needs through Picture Books** highlights the main categories of picture books for children and how each addresses the developmental needs of the very young child.

Meeting Children's Needs through Picture Books

Young children need to:	Young children are:	Categories of books:
Participate actively	*Physically active*—learn through the senses and exploration of the environment	Self-help skill books, cloth and board books, novelty books
Explore, imagine, invent	*Imaginative and playful*—enjoy pretending; take pleasure in identifying ridiculous situations such as slapstick, role reversals, and incongruous situations	Humorous books, fantasy, adventure
Build self-esteem	*Unique*—need positive self-image and an appreciation of individuality	Mood books, books about dealing with powerful emotions, books about children with special needs
Form secure attachments	*Social and affiliative*—need to relate interpersonally and to develop prosocial skills	Books about relationships with significant others
Expand and enrich knowledge	*Expressive and inquisitive*—need to acquire knowledge and classify information	All picture books, particularly concept books, information books, wordless books
Establish social and cultural connections	*Culturally diverse*—need to appreciate cultural diversity and to begin to understand human motivation	Nursery rhymes, books with multicultural concepts, folktales, fairy tales
Master and enjoy oral language	*Communicative*—need to explore language, use verbal symbols, and appreciate the rhythm of words	Picture storybooks, song picture books, poetry and stories told in verse
Acquire literacy with print	*Literate*—need to acquire literacy to participate more fully in school, community, and life	Predictable books and easy readers to build confidence as a reader; chapter books to present new literacy challenges

Supporting Children with Differences

Children with physical disabilities or learning difficulties

Key statistics

• Children with special needs constitute about 14% of the total U.S. school population.

• Four categories describe 95% of children with special needs: (1) learning disabled, (2) speech and language impaired, (3) mentally disabled, and (4) emotionally disturbed (Wiles 1999).

• About 6% of all children with special needs possess superior intellects and are capable of high performance; another 6% display distinctive talent in a particular area (e.g., academics, art, music, social) (Wiles 1999).

The contributions of picture books

• Children's books can serve social and academic purposes by helping peers to become more socially conscious and understand the challenges confronted by some children (Braus & Geidel 2000).

• Children with special needs often benefit from techniques that build motivation, focus attention, and are more concrete. Teachers may find that creating 60-second "commercials" for a book, called *book talks,* can capture children's interest (Bodart 1988; Sitarz 1997; Thomas 1993) or that creating different types of diagrams, drawings, maps, and webs to represent stories and concepts from literature (Bromley 1996; Nyberg 1996) is a way to increase children's comprehension and motivation.

• Literature can serve as the impetus for more concrete ways of interpreting and representing understanding through guided dramatization (Brown, Althouse, & Anfin 1993).

Children of various ethnic and cultural backgrounds

Key statistics

• No one ethnic group exceeds 50% of the U.S. population (Bohn & Sleeter 2001).

• People who were once thought of as "language minorities" are now the majority in certain areas; for example, children whose first language is Spanish in areas of the American Southwest (Billings 1998).

The contributions of picture books

• Children who have immigrated from certain cultures may have more experience with storytelling and forms of puppetry than with picture books or reading per se. For them, teachers may find that storytelling is an avenue into the pictures and print in books (Zipes 1995).

• Many excellent storytelling books offer recommendations for more interactive forms of presentation that use props, puppets, and audience participation (Bauer 1993; Cliatt & Shaw 1988; Edmiston 1993; Marshall 1998; Van Schuyver 1993).

• Storytelling books are also a good source of literature from other lands and cultures (Pellowski 1984, 1995), as well as a good source of multicultural stories about friendship (Roberts 1997) and interdisciplinary themes (Rubright 1996).

• *Reader's theater,* in which groups of children read the text in unison, can be another way for all children to participate in literature (Barchers 2000; Bauer 1987).

• For more sources on multiethnic literature, see Harris (1997) and Steiner (2001).

Children who are learning English

Key statistics

• Of the roughly 45 million school-age children, the non–English-speaking population totals nearly 9.9 million (Waggoner 1994).

• By the year 2020, 46% of all Americans will be members of various minority groups and many of them will need to meet a variety of language challenges (Wiles 1999) such as mastering English or overcoming low literacy levels at home.

• Adoption by American families is one of the biggest routes of influx into U.S. schools of nonnative English-speaking children (Enge 1998–99).

• That some languages are spoken by hundreds of millions of people (400 million speak English as their native tongue) and other languages by only a few thousand does not make one language "superior" to another (Fox 1997).

• Students who are learning English tend to receive lower grades, are rated as less intellectually competent by their teachers, score below peers on tests of reading (Moss & Puma 1992), and are 1.5 times more likely to drop out of school than are native speakers (Cardenas, Robledo, & Waggoner 1988).

• Children who enter U.S. schools not speaking English take 7 to 10 years to reach age- and grade-level norms in language when all of their instruction is in English (Thomas & Collier 1997).

The contributions of picture books

• Particularly for newly immigrated children, books that provide information that will support their academic success are important (Duke & Kays 1998). A useful resource on information books is Bamford and Kristo's (1998) *Making Facts Come Alive: Choosing Quality Nonfiction Literature, K–8.*

• Children who are learning English can profit from practicing their conversational skills during various types of book discussions called *literature groups* or *literature circles* (Daniels 1994; Dugan 1997; Peterson & Eeds 1990; Strube 1996).

• Providing additional practice in literacy through on-screen materials (Buckleitner 1996) and digital audiobooks is another way to support English language learners (Minkel 2000).

Children from low-income backgrounds

Key statistics

• According to the Forum on Child and Family Statistics (www.childstats.gov/ac2002/pdf.econ.pdf), 9% of white, non-Hispanic children; 27% of Hispanic children; and 30% of African American children lived in poverty in 2000.

The contributions of picture books

• One way to get books in children's hands is to create small, thematic, portable lending libraries that children and families can borrow. These collections, variously referred to as *home literacy bags* (Barbour 1998–99), *book packs* or *book backpacks* (Cohen 1997), or *home kits* (Gorter-Reu & Anderson 1998), typically include three to six paperback books, a brief letter explaining the purpose of the theme, enjoyable and simple activities for the child and family to do together, and a way of reporting back on the usefulness of the collection.

To further illustrate how picture books can support children's development, the box **Song Picture Books to Support Emergent Literacy** examines one genre of literature, *song picture books,* which are illustrated lyrics of songs familiar to children and adults. Song picture books particularly support children's language and aesthetic development.

Further, today's classrooms are more culturally, socially, academically, and physically diverse than ever before (Glazer 1998; Soriano-Nagurski 1998); therefore, early childhood educators need to see possibilities beyond their own customary ways of looking at the world (Jones & Nimmo 1999). They need to have a *multicultural* perspective, which according to the National Council for Accreditation of Teacher Education is "an understanding of the social, political, economic, academic, and historical constructs of ethnicity, race, socioeconomic status, gender, exceptionalities, language, religion, sexual orientation, and the geographical area" (2002, 54).

The box **Supporting Children with Differences** describes some major categories of children with linguistic and other differences and how picture books can support their development and learning.

Which book for which child?

Heinrich, a 3-year-old, likes *Where's Spot?* (Hill) because it is a lift-the-flap book "with a monkey in the cupboard." Bruce, a first-grader, appreciates *Goodnight, Moon* (Brown) because "I never read a book where it says good night to everything." Maria, a 4-year-old, likes *The Three Little Kittens* (Galdone) because "it has a happy ending." These comments from children relate to three ways of describing books: by format, by genre, and by the five basic elements of literature.

Format. The physical configurations of a book such as size, shape, illustrations, arrangement, and spacing are all examples of *format*. In terms of size, books that are very popular such as *The Very Hungry Caterpillar* (Carle) are sometimes available in several formats—a Big Book size, a storybook size, and a board book/pocket size so they are more portable. Often the theme of the story influences its format. Not surprisingly, a book called *The Little Tiny Woman* (Zemach) is undersize. Books for children sometimes have unusual characteristics such as pages made of cardboard for toddlers, movable parts, or "pop-up" three-dimensional objects. Such books are variously referred to as *toy books, participation books*, or *novelty books*.

Two books by Ahlberg and Ahlberg emphasize the uniqueness of format. In *Peek-a-Boo!* a small circle is cut out of every other page. The pictures and the words encourage a young child to describe whatever the baby in the story sees from different vantage points, such as from his crib. In the pages of *The Jolly Postman or Other People's Letters*, these same authors use various types of correspondence—friendly letters, business letters, greeting cards, postcards, invitations, and envelopes—written by and mailed between familiar folk and fairy tale characters. Of course, to see the humor a child must be thoroughly familiar with the tales and must have some knowledge of different types of correspondence, so this book is actually better suited to children in second or third grade.

Song Picture Books to Support Emergent Literacy

There are song picture books suitable for any age.

• **Babies**—lullaby book-and-tape collections, such as *Un Regalo de Arrullos para Niños [A Child's Gift of Lullabies]* (Brown)

• **Toddlers**—board book versions of songs, such as *Hush Little Baby* (Long)

• **Preschoolers**—songs that invite participation, such as *Do Your Ears Hang Low?* (Church) and *The Bear: An American Folk Song* (Spengler)

• **Kindergartners**—song picture books that invite reading based on familiarity with a song, such as *Down by the Bay* (Raffi) or *Take Me Out to the Ballgame* (Norworth)

• **Primary grade children**—song picture books that tell a story, such as *Abiyoyo* (Seeger), or that invite children to write their own parodies, such as *I Know an Old Lady Who Swallowed a Pie* (Jackson)

Authors and illustrators who have published numerous song picture books include Aliki, Nadine Bernard Wescott, Iza Trapani, Raffi, Steven Kellogg, Paul O. Zelinsky, Mary Ann Hoberman, and Pete Seeger.

The song picture book is a fusion of literature and art. Children respond to the language and lyrics as well as to the melody and the illustrations. Because children usually have previous knowledge of the words from singing the song, song picture books support them in their efforts to read (Risher & MacDonald 2001).

The emergent literacy skills that can be built through responses to song picture books include the following:

• familiarity and enjoyment
• repetition and predictability
• vocabulary and knowledge of story structures
• critical thinking and problem solving
• creative expression and language play

Children should also have the experience of comparing and contrasting different versions of the same story. Third-graders who were presented with several song picture books—e.g., versions of the song "Six Little Ducks"—were found to be very capable of comparing and contrasting the same song in different versions (Jalongo & Ribblett 1997). Another way of providing different versions of the same songs is to visit any of the children's websites that include familiar songs. See Appendix B for some website suggestions.

When a child responds enthusiastically to a particular format, teachers can suggest additional books with unusual formats, such as *The Very Busy Spider* (Carle) in which children can touch and feel the web as it is being built.

Of course, books also can be converted into audiovisual formats. In this era of visual media, many excellent picture books for children are available as book-

and-tape sets, videocassettes, DVDs, and CD-ROMs as well as on interactive websites. Many large libraries now have extensive collections of such materials to be loaned free of charge.

Genre. Another dimension of literature, *genre,* refers to the specific type or category of book. Prose (nonfiction and fiction) and poetry are the two major genres for picture books. Poetry for young children includes nursery rhymes recited aloud, picture book versions of nursery rhymes such as *The House That Jack Built* (Taback), picture books based on songs, and stories told in verse such as *Barn Dance!* (Martin & Archambault).

Nonfiction prose includes *concept books, information books,* and *biography.* Roberts (1984) has developed some interesting analogies for children's nonfiction prose. She likens a concept book to a commercial for an idea; the book "sells" the child a basic concept such as letters, colors, shapes, numbers, or opposites. The alphabet book *Alphabatics* (MacDonald) is an example of a concept book. Roberts regards an information book as a child's version of an article in *National Geographic* or *Scientific American*; the child has questions about a topic that can be answered by factual information. Children may wonder aloud "Who made this book?" and Aliki's *How a Book Is Made* gives a clear and accurate explanation. They may want to understand a complex social issue such as adoption, and an information book such as *Being Adopted* (Rosenberg) answers their questions. How-to books also fit into this category; a book that explains how to conduct a simple science experiment or how to make popcorn is a subcategory of the information book.

Information books that tell a true story about an actual person are biographies. Generally speaking, the biography genre is more appropriate for children in the primary grades or older. One biography suitable for children in the primary grades is *The Man Who Loved Animals* (Hoff), which tells the story of Henry Bergh, the founder of the American Society for the Prevention of Cruelty to Animals (ASPCA).

Fictional prose is less dependent on fact and more dependent on the writer's imagination. Most picture storybooks for young children fall into this category. The story characters often are animals who behave like people or people with extraordinary powers. If its action is similar to real-life situations, the book is called *realistic fiction.* If it bears little resemblance to objective reality, then the book is categorized as *fantasy.* A good example of fantasy is *Click, Clack, Moo: Cows That Type* (Cronin). Fantasy for young children is found, for example, in familiar folktales such as *The Little Red Hen* (Wilburn) or modern folktales such as *One Fine Day* (Hogrogian). Fairy tales also are included in fictional prose.

Basic elements. Another way to describe and discuss picture books is by referring to the five basic elements of literature: *plot, characters, setting, style,* and *theme/motif.* Several books might share the same basic plot. *Squawk to the Moon, Little Goose* (Preston), *A Crocodile's Tale* (Aruego), *The Tale of Tricky Fox* (Aylesworth), *Chicken Little* (Rader), and an updated version of *Henny-Penny* (Wattenberg) are all stories in which a small character is captured by a hungry predator, outwits the villain, and safely returns home. Picture books might also be categorized by the main characters—books about children with imaginary companions or physical handicaps, for example. Books also might share similar

Click, clack, **moo.**
Click, clack, **moo.**
Clickety, clack, **moo.**

Bringing Children and Books Together

settings. *Crictor* (Ungerer), *Miss Nelson Is Missing!* (Allard & Marshall), and *Next Year I'll Be Special* (Giff) all have school and classrooms as their primary setting.

Style, where picture books are concerned, refers to the author's and illustrator's individual ways of relating and portraying the story. Just as two singers can produce very different versions of the same song by virtue of their unique choice of tone, rhythm, emphasis, instrumentation, and so on, authors and illustrators can produce unique versions of the same story by virtue of their unique choices of language, format, imagery, and media. Take, for example, the folk lullaby "Hush Little Baby." Although the words of the song remain similar ("Hush, little baby, don't say a word. Mama's going to buy you a mockingbird. . . ."), the song has been transformed into a picture book by Aliki in an illustrative style that harkens back to the song's origins in Victorian England, by Sylvia Long as a board book in ink and watercolors depicting a bunny mom and child, and by Shari Halpern in cut-paper collage and acrylics with bordered pages reminiscent of a quilt.

Finally, theme or motif refers to the central message of the story. Spitz (1999) categorizes the motifs of books for young children into four broad psychological themes of concern to that age group: bedtime, loss, behavior, and identity. Two books that focus on the bedtime motif are the picture storybook *David and Dog* (Hughes) and the counting book *Ten, Nine, Eight* (Bang). *David and Dog* tells a realistic family story about a child who accidentally loses his favorite toy (which he misses terribly because he always sleeps with it) and his big sister's successful effort to get it back. By way of contrast, *Ten, Nine, Eight* describes a nightly "countdown" ritual designed to gently prepare a child to settle down and go to sleep.

Any of these ways of describing literature, singly or in combination, might explain why a particular child loves a particular book. One issue that makes the teacher's role difficult is that many excellent books for young children are hard to put in a single category. A book such as *Watch the Stars Come Out* (Levinson) is a good example. It relates a young girl's experience as an immigrant to the United States. Although the story is written in prose, it is definitely poetic. Factual information—such as detail about arriving at Ellis Island—is evident, but the book also has a nostalgic quality. One could argue that the book is historical fiction (genre), a story about coming to America (plot), a metaphor for the immigrant experience (theme/motif), or a story that takes place in New York City in the late 1800s (setting).

Quality literature is so rich that it can be described in many different ways. An attempt to classify literature is like trying to describe the taste of a delicious dish by naming the ingredients in the recipe. We may be able to say with certainty that it contains paprika or serves in a casserole dish, but the blending and presentation of the components are what produces the appealing product.

Sharing books effectively with young children

Quite naturally, what makes a difference is not only which book is shared but also how it is shared with children. The following steps outline the process of sharing effectively, beginning with preparation (steps 1–4) and moving into presentation (steps 5–7).

Mary Renck Jalongo

Some Common Themes or Motifs in Picture Storybooks

Question and answer—Questions are posed and answered

> *Jesse Bear, What Will You Wear?* (Carlstrom)
> *Is Your Mama a Llama?* (Guarino)
> *Are You My Mother?* (Eastman)
> *Green Eggs and Ham* (Seuss)

Cumulative tales—Each element of the story is repeated as new characters or events are added

> *The Napping House* (Wood)
> *Today is Monday* (Carle)
> *The Wright Brothers* (Edwards)
> *Drummer Hoff* (Emberley)
> *The House That Jack Built* (Winter)

Chronological stories—Time elements such as days of the week, hours of the day, ordinal numbers, or other definite sequences are used to organize the story

> *Cookie's Week* (Ward)
> *Chicken Soup with Rice: A Book of Months* (Sendak)
> *We're Going on a Bear Hunt* (Rosen)

The quest—The main character searches for something, has an adventure, and decides to go back to the way things were

> *Hey, Al* (Yorinks)
> *El Tesoro/The Treasure* (Shulevitz)
> *The Salamander Room* (Mazer)
> *Little Nino's Pizzeria* (Barbour)

Security—The book creates a warm and comfortable mood

> *Owl Moon* (Yolen)
> *In Daddy's Arms I Am Tall: African Americans Celebrating Fathers* (Steptoe)
> *Snow Ponies* (Cotten)

Role reversals—The smallest one performs remarkable deeds that surpass even the accomplishments of adults

> *Music, Music for Everyone* (Williams)
> *The Gigantic Turnip* (Tolstoy)
> *The Carrot Seed* (Krauss)

Trickster tales—A less powerful character outwits a more powerful one

> *One Grain of Rice* (Demi)
> *Anansi and the Moss-Covered Rock* (Kimmel)
> *Borreguita and the Coyote: A Tale from Ayutla, Mexico* (Aardema)
> *Flossie and the Fox* (McKissack)

Goodness is rewarded—The character who is honest, loyal, and kind wins out over those who are not, as in the Cinderella story and its many variants

> *The Empty Pot* (Demi)
> *Andy and the Lion* (Daugherty)

The immigrant experience—Stories of families who come to the United States to build a new life

> *How Many Days to America?* (Bunting)
> *Grandfather's Journey* (Say)

1. Begin with a quality book. Identify some possibilities using one or more of the many resources available. Among these resources are the list of outstanding authors and illustrators in Appendix A; bimonthly reviews of picture books in *Early Childhood Education Journal*; "Children's Editors' Choices" published by the American Library Association annually in *Booklist*; and "Teachers' Choices" and "Children's Choices," published in *The Reading Teacher* and available online (www.reading.org/choices). Make a list of several books that sound interesting after reading their descriptions in the various annotated bibliographies. Then go to the library.

2. Review several books. Begin by locating several of your choices. Skim through each book, first looking at the pictures. This visual impression is what children will see, so it is important. If the pictures of a book appeal to you, go back through and read the text. If the text of the book also is appealing, go back through and read the text and pictures together. Imagine presenting the book to the intended audience of young children and try to anticipate what their responses are likely to be.

3. Select books the children will enjoy. Sometimes we assume that the stories we enjoyed as children are still the best selections. But many books published before 1970 include stereotypes about women and minorities (Chambers 1983). Or maybe the books you heard as a child were selected for you more on the basis of availability than on the basis of quality. Or your childhood favorites, though excellent, may not be well suited to the developmental level of the children in your group. Even though *Charlotte's Web* (White) is a children's classic, it is too sophisticated for most preschoolers and many first-graders. Introducing a book too early can sometimes ruin it for children. If they miss much of its meaning, they might decide they do not like the book and refuse to give it another chance later.

4. Select books that suit your curriculum. Look for books such as *Wolf's Favor* (Testa) that are suitable for storytelling and dramatization; seasonal books such as *The Polar Express* (Van Allsburg); books that tie in with specific content, such as *Sophie's Bucket* (Stock) for a unit on the seashore; and books that support emergent reading such as the cumulative rhyming book *The House That Jack Built* (Taback).

Make notes about when and how to share these stories with children. Discuss several of your long-term projects with the librarian and ask for recommendations. Many resources are available for teachers to quickly locate stories on a particular topic or theme (see, e.g., Gillespie 2001; Lima & Lima 2001; Appendix B in this volume).

5. Keep language and literacy development in mind as you choose picture books and read them to children. Clearly the language an author uses is part of what sets a great book apart from a mediocre one. Many of the books that engage children do delightful things with sound. So you won't find it difficult to select books rich in sounds and sound patterns such as rhyming, alliteration, and coined words that play with sound (as in Dr. Seuss's *The Lorax*: "'Once-ler!' he cried with a *cruffulous* croak. 'Once-ler! You're making such *smogulous* smoke!'"). As you read aloud books such as these, you will find countless opportunities to heighten children's phonological awareness.

You'll also want to consider vocabulary: Does the book use words that will be new to most of the children? Children enjoy learning new words and benefit in many ways from expanding their vocabulary. At the same time, if a book has so many unfamiliar words that children can't understand the story, you should choose a different book.

Of course, all the things we do as teachers to expand children's book knowledge and appreciation contribute to their becoming eager and competent readers. Examples of the sorts of questions teachers can ask (see #7 below) show other ways that we can enhance children's literacy and language development by sharing books with them.

6. Prepare your audience and yourself. Presenting picture books effectively also involves making decisions about what to emphasize as children listen to a story. The adult sets a focus for listening, which considers the background that children need before they can "get" the point of the story. For example, consider Janet Stevens's book *Tops & Bottoms*. The astute teacher notices that to appreciate the tricks that the enterprising sharecropper rabbit plays on a landowner bear, the children have to know something about how plants grow. The gist of the story is that a poor but hardworking and intelligent creature (Rabbit) outsmarts a wealthy but lazy and foolish one (Bear). Rabbit strikes several deals with Bear and always manages to get the better of him. First, Rabbit offers to plant crops and share profits. He gives Bear the choice: tops or bottoms? After Bear agrees to tops, Rabbit plants root vegetables such as carrots and beets. Next time, Bear insists upon bottoms, so Rabbit plants cabbage and lettuce. Then Bear gets furious and demands *both* tops and bottoms; Rabbit plants corn and takes the middles.

Teachers I know who love this book have gone to great lengths to help their students be in on the joke. One teacher actually planted the mentioned vegetables in a clear plastic container so children could see them growing. Another made flannel-board cutouts for each vegetable. Still another went to a farm to get the vegetables, roots and all, to show to the children. Still another used the historical notes about the story in the book with her third-graders, many of whom were the children of migrant farmworkers, and devised a theme about less powerful characters outwitting those with more power.

Even if there is no "joke" to prepare for, still consider how you will introduce each book to the children. One teacher showed her preschool class several eggs of different shapes, sizes, and colors before reading *Chickens Aren't the Only Ones* (Heller). Another teacher used a real hermit crab to introduce *Is This a House for Hermit Crab?* (McDonald).

When reading aloud to children, remember that your voice is an important tool. It can be used to differentiate among characters or to emphasize an important story element. An adult reading *Chicken Little* (Kellogg) can give Chicken Little a squeaky little voice and make Fox sound sly and gruff. Sometimes adults who read to children get overly dramatic. After a 3-year-old heard a particularly chilling rendition of "The Three Billy Goats Gruff," she handed the book to her mother and said, "Here, burn this." It is possible for adults to get carried away and "perform" a book rather than share it. A manner of presentation too flamboyant can become distracting or overshadow the book.

Bear stared at his pile. "But, Hare, all the best parts are in your half!"

"You chose the tops, Bear," Hare said.

"Now, Hare, you've tricked me. You plant this field again — and this season I want the bottoms!"

Hare agreed. "It's a done deal, Bear."

Illustration from *Tops & Bottoms,* copyright © 1995 by Janet Stevens, reprinted by permission of Harcourt, Inc.

Mary Renck Jalongo

The human voice can be used far more subtly and effectively. To appreciate how slight those changes might be, try this experiment: Read a sentence while smiling, then read the same sentence with a neutral expression on your face. Notice that you can actually hear the smile in your voice; it softens your consonants. Practice reading the book aloud so your voice communicates effectively.

7. Develop questioning skills. Although children need to understand that during book sharing time the book is the focus of the conversation, recognize that a child's "agenda" usually differs from an adult's. When the adult-child interaction about a book becomes stilted and predictable, the adult likely is being too directive. What follows is a less effective way of talking about books exemplified by this father's conversation with 2½-year-old Joshua about the book *ABC* (Szekeres). Notice that the child's question "What eated this?" is ignored.

Father: And what's this over here?

Joshua: It a bunny.

Father: And what's that?

Joshua: That gwasses.

Father: Glasses, okay, . . .

Joshua: What eated this?

Father: . . . and what is that?

Joshua: It's a bagel.

Father: It's a bagel, too. Okay.

Compare that less effective approach with the following dialogue between 33-month-old George and his dad. Here, the parent follows the child's lead more as they look at a picture book that shows animals in their homes: a kitten in a basket, a bird in a nest, and a frog in a pond:

George: *(pointing to the picture of the kitten)* Him sleeps on soft pillow. *(pointing to the picture of the bird)* Birdy.

Father: Where does the bird sleep?

George: Nest! *(imitates bird opening mouth for food)*

Father: Do you eat worms?

George: No! Yuk! Gross! *(looking at the picture of the frog)* Frog swims on water. Ribbet, ribbet.

Father: Does George like to swim in the water?

George: I kick, kick, kick. I go swim in baby pool, not big pool.

Here, the conversation is focused on the book, but the parent manages to make the book "all about George," a practice that is supported by the research on reading aloud to very young children (see Lonigan & Whitehurst 1998; Rabidoux & MacDonald 2000).

When teachers share stories with groups of children, there is a limit to the amount of discussion that can transpire before a story begins to lose momentum. Expert teachers use professional judgment to decide when the children's attention needs to be redirected to the book. As children acquire additional

A Sample Interactive Storytime with *Too Many Tamales*

1. Build interest and define key vocabulary

Teacher: I stopped at a restaurant today and bought some tamales. Let's look at them to see if we can figure out how they might have been made. After we look, I'll cut them in small pieces so you can taste them if you want to.

2. Set the children's expectations for the story

Teacher: Has anyone here eaten a tamale before? Did your tamale look like these? Does anyone here know how to make tamales? How are they made? Even if you have not made tamales before, you probably have seen bread dough, and tamales are a type of bread that is made out of corn. This book is called *Too Many Tamales*. Look at the children's faces in this picture on the cover. What might cause them to look this way?

3. Help children to construct the essential message of the story

Teacher: Have you ever tried to play with something belonging to your mom or dad or other family member and accidentally wrecked it? Did you ever make such a big mistake that you got really scared, wanted to cry, and felt your heart pounding hard and fast? There's a word for that feeling. It is *panic*. It's the way we feel when we make a mistake so bad that we want to run away or hide or pretend it did not happen. Well, that's what happens in this book to Maria. But, instead of running away, she tries to figure out a way to solve her problem with the help of her cousins.

4. Read the book

Teacher: As I read, think about Maria's problem and how she solved it.

5. Interject questions that extend children's understandings of the book
Teacher: Was it wrong to try on the mother's ring? What makes an engagement ring important? I wonder why the children were so worried about losing a ring. What might Maria's mom do if her ring is lost and cannot be found? If they are sure the ring is inside one of the tamales on that big plate, what could they do to find it? They're going to have to be careful!

6. Relate the story to children's experiences
Teacher: That big plate of tamales reminds me of when my grandmother used to make ravioli. There were so many of them and it took a long time to make them. I brought a food wrapper that shows a picture of what ravioli look like—sort of like little pillows with meat and cheese inside. Is there a food that your family makes that is stuffed or rolled up like this? What is it called? What does your family put inside? What are your favorite fillings? Is there anyone in this story who reminds you of yourself? Who? Why?

7. Revisit the story theme
Teacher: What did you think of Maria's solution to her problem? If you could talk to the children in the book, what do you think they might say about what happened? Let's have somebody pretend to be Maria and say what she would say. Now let's have someone pretend to be her cousin and tell about the problem with the ring. Did you ever get a big scare like this one and then figure out a way to solve your problem?

experience with literature, they will become more skilled at focusing discussions on the story rather than on their personal experiences unrelated to the story.

Effective questioning strategies can capitalize on the learning potential inherent in experiences with books. Fisher (1995) suggests that teachers use questions at various times to accomplish the following, plus make storytime more interactive:

• Check on children's knowledge and understanding (e.g., "What does [*insert a vocabulary word that is critical to understanding the text*] mean?")

• Link with a previous work (e.g., "How is [*insert book title*] different from yesterday's story?" "What other stories do you know where a little character outsmarts a bigger, stronger one?")

• Encourage prediction (e.g., [*when using a repetitive text*] "What do you think the next words will be?")

• Focus attention on particular features of the text (e.g., "Is the [*insert character's name*] good or bad? How do you know? What made you think so?" "How do you know the monster is not really mean?")

• Encourage children to think about how they know something or how they managed to figure it out (e.g., "Did that ending surprise you?" "What clues did you have about how the story would end? Can you go back and point out the hints the author gave?")

• Invite comparison of one text with another (e.g., "How is this story like [*insert title of another story*]?" "How were the words of this song a little different from the one that we usually sing?")

• Make links with writing, especially for wordless books (e.g., "What words would you write for this book?" "What would you have this character say?")

• Encourage evaluation of the text (e.g., "If you could change this story in any way, how would you change it?" "What did you find out [*when using an information book*] that you did not know before?")

The box **A Sample Interactive Storytime with *Too Many Tamales*** is an example of an interactive storytime that would be suitable for most children in first or second grade. *Too Many Tamales* (Soto) is the story of Maria, who tries on her mother's engagement ring while mixing the masa dough for the corn tamales. Not until after the relatives arrive and a huge plate of tamales is prepared does Maria discover that her mother's ring is gone. Maria confides in her cousins, urging them to eat the entire plate of tamales and find the ring. Notice how the introductory activity is designed not merely to grab children's attention but also to help them arrive at a deeper understanding of the story. Notice, too, how the questions are focused on fostering children's listening comprehension and encouraging them to respond to the story's central message.

Talking about picture books becomes far more pleasurable when adults ask questions that do not have obvious right-and-wrong answers, questions that challenge children's thinking. When teachers use open-ended discussion techniques, children have opportunities to talk about literature in more meaningful ways (Conrad et al. 2003; Hoffman & Knipping 1988; Paley 1981).

Getting Books in Children's Hands and Homes

Book format. Paperbacks often are one-third to one-fourth the price of a hardbound book, particularly if they are ordered through teacher book clubs such as Scholastic or Trumpet. Thus, you may want to rely primarily on inexpensive paperbacks when building a lending library. That way, if a paperback book is accidentally ruined, the loss will not be as substantial. You may want to keep certain books, such as those with moving parts or copies signed by the author, on a teacher's shelf, reserved for supervised use with young children.

Book use. Teaching and demonstrating the proper care of books, rather than expecting children to know automatically how to handle books, is important. For toddlers who are just learning about books, sturdy cardboard, plastic, or cloth pages that will withstand hard use are best. For young preschoolers, show them how to turn a page, then offer some guided practice with a book that will not cause too much upset if a page gets wrinkled. Demonstrate how to operate the pull tabs or pop-ups in a book without ripping them. Give children a chance, with gentle coaching and supervision, to operate books with moving parts. Be aware, also, that even older children may not have much book-handling experience.

Book lending. A good idea is to invest in some heavy plastic bags with zipper-type closures and have families use them for carrying books back and forth between the early childhood program and children's homes. This practice can be an effective way to keep the books clean, dry, and out of mud puddles. If you are creating *book packs*—small collections of books and accompanying activities that are centered on a particular theme—inexpensive waterproof containers such as tote bags, backpacks, or small plastic bins make good containers for carrying these collections to homes and around the classroom or center.

Book care and repair. A book whose cover is rather worn can sometimes get some additional use if a plastic book cover is placed over it. Book covers usually are easy to find in stores right before school begins in the fall. If a book page tears, use high-quality invisible tape to fix it. If stray pencil or crayon marks appear, try using an art gum eraser to remove them. If the cover is falling off, duct tape placed carefully along the edge where it won't obscure the pictures might keep it together long enough to circulate a bit longer. When books get sticky or need to be sanitized, try this method: Begin with a clean, dry cloth or sponge. Spray it with disinfectant mixed at the ratios specified on the bottle. Gently wipe the book's surfaces and allow to air dry thoroughly before closing the pages.

Book loss. If a book is never returned despite efforts to get it back, take the attitude that losing a few books is unavoidable, and hope that the book is being loved and used.

Dialogue about a book is not the same as quizzing children about the story's details. Rather, when it is skillfully done, dialogue about books can and should be a window on each child's thought process, a means of developing children's communication skills, and a way for teachers and families to glimpse children's growth in literacy.

Getting books into children's hands

In a study of 325 child care homes in Philadelphia, just 20 percent had some sort of book corner, whereas 30 percent had a television (Neuman & Celano 2001b). The goal of the project and the research that followed was to "put books in children's hands," literally and figuratively. In a literal sense, child care providers had been given new books as part of a grant; but sometimes they did not share the books with children because they feared the precious resource would be ruined. In more than one instance, the books were shelved out of children's reach. The goal of the intervention, however, was to see to it that children, including toddlers, were given books to look at during every available opportunity—during quiet times, toileting, centertime, and so forth. The tips in the box **Getting Books in Children's Hands and Homes** will make books available yet keep these materials in useable condition. Because board books have heavy cardboard pages rather than pages made of paper, they are particularly able to withstand hard use in the classroom (see Appendix C for some board book suggestions).

The project put books in children's hands in a figurative sense as well, by urging caregivers to give children more control over operating the books, asking questions, and looking at the books in their own way and time—a practice that has been supported by research (Bus 2001). Evidently many adults underestimate the contributions that books can make to toddlers' literacy growth when literature is shared in developmentally effective ways. Too often adults operate on the mistaken assumption that good practice—even for toddlers and 3-year-olds—is to make the children sit still and listen intently while the adult reads the book from cover to cover without "interruptions." Actually, most good picture book sharing sessions with the youngest children should be more like "talking about pictures" than reading the book. Using these more relaxed approaches to story sharing, Neuman and Celano (2001b) found, meant that toddlers benefited as much as preschoolers did from looking at books.

Conclusion: Connecting with picture books

The scene is a college classroom in September; the course is children's literature. A third grade teacher and graduate student is making a presentation on her students' responses to Marilee Heyer's *The Weaving of a Dream*. In this Chinese folktale about a good mother who works to support her sons by sewing, the mother sees a painting of a beautiful palace at the marketplace and becomes determined to re-create it in an elaborate tapestry, which takes her three years to complete. Yet, on the very day the final stitch is sewn, a strong wind sweeps the brocade away. The mother is so grief stricken by the loss that she becomes

gravely ill. All three of her sons vow to recover the brocade, but the two eldest sons succumb to greed and do not keep their promise. Only the youngest son remains loyal and succeeds. When he arrives home as his mother is dying, the son drapes the tapestry over her, and she and the palace scene that the elaborate tapestry depicts magically spring to life.

How did this practicing teacher's third grade students respond to *The Weaving of a Dream?* They connected with the theme of goodness being rewarded; one girl mentioned that it reminded her of Cinderella. The third-graders talked about sibling rivalries, and one child mentioned parallels between this tale and the Bible story of Joseph and his coat of many colors. The children wondered whether the older brothers who "sold out" (as one boy put it) should be allowed to rejoin the family (in the story, they are turned away by the son and mother now residing in the magical palace). Quite a discussion ensued about forgiveness. The children also reflected on how wonderful it would be if a magic cloth did exist; they talked about the people and animals they would bring back to life, using it, as one child mentioned, "sort of like ET's finger." The teacher also reported that children wanted to study the illustrations and raised many questions about China and Chinese customs.

After the teacher finished her presentation, three other graduate students, who were from China, remarked that they were familiar with a similar tale shared by storytellers called "The Chuang Brocade," but that they had never seen a picture book version. The Chinese students were obviously delighted to be in a position to help with the correct pronunciation of the characters' names and to answer their classmates' questions about ancient China. Everyone wanted *The Weaving of a Dream* to be passed around so they could linger over its richly detailed illustrations.

As the session came to a close on that crisp September evening, the students were no longer clustered by language and nationality. Rather, the American teachers were seeking out the Chinese teachers to get authoritative answers to their questions about the book, asking them to write each character's name in Chinese, or inviting them to visit their schools. And as everyone spilled out into the hallway, conversation continued as they shared their plans for how and when they would use *The Weaving of a Dream* with primary students. In this way, a single book had been responsible for fostering new respect and understanding between and among classmates.

Ultimately, one of our defining characteristics as human beings is our capacity to imagine. We think in stories, resonate with stories, and relate to one another through stories. Sharing picture books is a way of building connections and breaking barriers, not only for children but also for their teachers. That is the most compelling reason to bring young children and picture books together.

Mary Renck Jalongo

CHAPTER 4

Young Children's Responses to Picture Books

Many of us certainly remember our picture books vividly and treasure our association with them. The naturally generative quality of such pictorial representation works well with the interconnectedness of memory. Memory is never linear, never "historicist." Rather, memory is fluid and multi-layered: the sensations of sight, sound, and touch reach across time and space. . . .
—Graeme Harper, *Enfranchising the Child* (2001, 398)

Donald Hall's book *Ox-Cart Man* is a simple story that chronicles the change of seasons from the perspective of one person's work life. The central character is a somber-looking, bearded farmer. The setting is colonial America. An adult unfamiliar with the book would probably read this description and decide that young children would not like it very much, as its time, place, events, and activities are alien to their experiences. And yet, when the ox-cart man takes the ox he raised from a calf to be sold and kisses it once on the nose in farewell, many adults and children connect with the pictures and words. So many readers connect, in fact, that *Ox-Cart Man*, illustrated by Barbara Cooney, earned one of the most prestigious picture book awards, the Caldecott Medal. *Ox-Cart Man* effectively communicates to young children the abstract concept of the recurring rhythm of the seasons. On one occasion after the story was shared with preschoolers, there was a satisfied silence from the group, then a 4-year-old boy remarked softly, "Now it can start all over again" (Jalongo & Renck 1984).

How can children's responses to literature be measured? The most common way of evaluating responses is simply to tabulate; publishers report sales figures, while librarians report circulation statistics. For those of us who care about young children and their books, tabulation has its place but is definitely inadequate. Numbers alone do not capture the value of the quiet, reflective mood of that preschool boy's response to *Ox-Cart Man*, for example. The child who spontaneously comments on his own sense of wonder and feelings of pleasure would be overlooked in a purely numbers-driven assessment. Important changes are taking place, however, in identifying and interpreting children's responses to literature.

Influences on a child's response to literature

Understanding children's responses to literature has a value beyond research; just as important, understanding their literary responses enables teachers to use picture books more effectively. The box **Variables Affecting Literary Response** is an overview of the many variables that can affect how children respond to literature. Although each variable may exert an influence, responses to literature are simultaneously individual and universal, simple and complex.

In preparation for a presentation on children's literature in Tanzania, I brought along a paperback copy of Karen Williams's *Galimoto*, a picture book about a young boy who searches and barters for the wire, scrap metal, and sticks he needs to construct an original wheeled toy to race down the streets of his African village at night. To my delight, when I arrived in the capitol city of Dar es Salaam, I saw young boys playing with such homemade toys at dusk, just as had been depicted in the book. They ran alongside their inventions, tapping them deftly with sticks to keep the wheels moving. In fact, the next day, when I started to throw away my empty soda can, my hostess touched my arm

---

Variables Affecting Literary Response

Within the child

Age, gender, race, and ethnicity

Socioeconomic status

Interests and experiences

Cognitive-developmental level

Preferences in literature

Disposition toward books and reading

Prior experience with picture books

Within the book

Content

Literary style

Book format

Illustration style

Quality

Characterization

Within the environment

Availability of books

Families who enjoy reading

Teachers and other professionals who make books part of their practice

Adults who present literature effectively

Peers who recommend and discuss books

Communities that support literacy

Based on Favat (1977); Galda (1983); Monson (1985); and Norvell (1973).

Mary Renck Jalongo

and instructed me to leave it on a rock. "You'll see," she confided, "a child shall claim it almost instantly. They flatten the metal from the cans and use it to make their toys." Moments after her words were spoken, a boy who looked to be about 8 years old and flashing a brilliant smile appeared and whisked the can away. That soda can had a future in recycling far more imaginative than the waste bin.

When I spoke with East African early childhood educators at the conference, I mentioned the incident and shared *Galimoto.* Afterward, a first grade teacher with a class of 50 students stopped to study its illustrations and text. "The children would be so proud," he said as he brought his hand to rest lightly on the front cover, "to know that someone admired their work enough to write a book about it." I could see in the young man's eyes that he was imagining all the pleasure this picture book could bring to his students. I gave the book away, confident that my spare copy would do far more good in his hands than on my bookshelf. I had chosen the book because of the setting; however, I sensed that this teacher was tuned in to the developmental levels of his students, many of whom were no doubt seeking ways to prove their competence and independence.

Thus, responses to literature consist of a curious combination of the subtle and the obvious, the particular and the general, as well as the individual and the universal, with different works eliciting different responses from individual children and adults. To summarize, it is important for young children not only to encounter the familiarity of the known but also to explore the unfamiliarity of the unknown through the pages of picture books. An African child may find affirmation in *Galimoto,* whereas many other children will find other interesting surprises in the same book.

Nevertheless, young children may not be able to articulate exactly what causes them to connect with a particular book. A second-grader greeted the librarian with the following request: "I want to read a book about a kid just like me!" As adults, we may be amused at this need of the child to seek and find him- or herself in a book, but identification is one of the basic ways that readers build connections with books. In fact, enhanced opportunities for identification are often a rationale for including multicultural, multiethnic, and global literature. Not true, however, is the notion that "just like me" has to mean another 7-year-old with freckles and red hair. When children are brought together with high-quality picture books, "likeness" and "otherness" are apt to be based on emotional similarities as much as the physical or cultural. Consider, for example, *Amazing Grace* (Hoffman), a story about a young girl with a passion for drama. The child yearns to play the role of Peter Pan, but her peers tell Grace she is not suited for it (because she is female and non-white). Grace remains undaunted. When children hear this story, they see that Grace is "like" them, because they can relate to the pain of criticism from peers. The support Grace gets from her family and her resulting triumphant performance inspire and encourage all readers.

Over the years, I have read *Amazing Grace* to diverse groups of children, and the response is always the same: The children love it and are bursting to tell their own stories of times when they felt excluded. As Robin Morrow (1999)

From *Amazing Grace* by Mary Hoffman, illustrated by Caroline Binch, copyright © 1991 by Mary Hoffman, text. Copyright © 1991 by Caroline Binch, illustrations. Used by permission of Dial Books for Young Readers, A Division of Penguin Young Readers Group, A Member of Penguin Group (USA) Inc., 345 Hudson Street, New York, NY 10014. All rights reserved.

Mary Renck Jalongo

contends, "all children should be able to see something of their own lives in picture books—not mirrored, as no book can mirror life, but transformed into art" (38). Just as an adult feels reassured by the sight of friendly, familiar faces in a crowded room, children can be reassured by seeing on the pages of picture books interesting characters they consider to be like themselves in some fundamental way. Herein lies one compelling argument for populating the pages of picture books with characters as diverse as the children in our centers and classrooms.

Although a young child does not necessarily determine "likeness" by race or culture, young children should be able to see others like themselves in those ways represented on the pages of picture books. For example, in 1998 some 4,500 children's books were published in the United States; just 3 percent featured African Americans as main characters, and of them only two-thirds of the books were the work of African American authors or illustrators (Horning, Moore-Kruse, & Schliesman 1999). Without a doubt, African American children are underrepresented in picture books (Lechner 1995); and even when they are represented, they are often portrayed in subservient roles (MacCann 1998). What might be the consequences for young African American readers? Hefflin and Barksdale-Ladd (2001) suggest the following:

> To read for years and not encounter stories that closely connect with one's own cultural understandings and life experiences is problematic. . . . If teachers continually present African American children with texts in which the main characters are predominantly animals and white people, it stands to reason that these children may begin to wonder whether they, their families, and their communities fit into the world of reading. (810–811)

> Culturally sensitive stories, views, and insights can allow children to realize that literature has value for them as individuals. . . . [T]hrough repeated exposure to engaging literature in which children find themselves establishing personal connections with characters, the likelihood is great that reading will become an appealing activity. (818)

See Rand, Parker, & Foster (1998), Brown & Oates (2001), or Walters (2002) for books featuring African American characters; for Latino children's books, see Schon (2002).

As important as it is for the pages of picture books to show people of color, with disabilities, with diverse families, and so forth, representations clearly are not enough to foster in children the sense of connection we hope to evoke. In discussions about the picture book story *More Than Anything Else* (Bradby), children in the primary grades who had prior knowledge of Booker T. Washington's life and who understood that denying access to literacy was a form of oppression were better able to grasp the book's message (Conrad et al. 2003).

High-quality literature can keep children feeling connected even as it transports them to other lands. Books such as *Jacks around the World* (Lankford); *Bread, Bread, Bread* (Morris); *This Is the Way We Go to School* (Baer); *Everybody Cooks Rice* (Dooley); *Hopscotch around the World* (Lankford); *Wake Up, World! A Day in the Life of Children around the World* (Hollyer); or *Throw Your Tooth on the Roof: Tooth Traditions from around the World* (Beeler) communicate the message that one can find commonalities as well as differences in the human family.

Understanding children's responses

Literary response develops in the interface: between thinking over what has occurred and anticipating what is yet to come, between detachment from the book and involvement with it, and between unconscious drives and conscious desires (Benton 1979). Responses to picture books can be conceptualized as functioning simultaneously along several different dimensions, as depicted in the box **Encouraging Literary Responses from Children.**

For the child without serious vision impairments, the initial route of access to picture books is the illustrations and responses to the pictured characters and objects. We all have seen what Piaget (1962) referred to as "picture realism" in action—treating illustrations as if they were alive. Toddlers will sometimes stroke an illustration of a furry pet, slap a "bad" book character, kiss the other baby who beams back at them from the page, back away in fear from an illustration of a monster or wild animal, or grasp at a picture of delicious food and pretend to put it into their mouths. The response of older children to the illustrations may be less concrete and naïve, but it is no less intense. What preschooler has not pointed to or lovingly touched an engaging illustration? What child in the primary grades has not scrutinized the details of a book that reveals the inner secrets of a castle (Macaulay) or studied ships and other manufactured items from a cross-section perspective (Biesty)?

Encouraging Literary Responses from Children

Selection	Reflection	Interaction	Preparation	Access
Children who connect with a particular story are supported in finding other books of interest that can be shared and enjoyed with parents, families, teachers, and peers.	Children are encouraged to connect story characters, events, and issues with those in other stories and with their own lives.	Children have an opportunity to make comments, ask questions, and revisit both pictures and text to construct meaning from pictures and print.	Children's prior knowledge is expanded to make the story more understandable and meaningful. Adults set children's expectations and point out key words, events, and ideas.	Books are in children's hands, and children personally own several quality books. They also have access to more competent readers who will lead them to literature, and eventually they will become readers themselves.

Evidently, as children mature, their ability to reason about pictures grows with them. According to Norman Freeman's research on pictorial reasoning, children first treat art as imitative (i.e., "picking up" beauty from the world around), as just something to look at. As they gain experience with art, however, they begin to appreciate art for its power to evoke an emotional response and value it for its freshness, originality, and control over what it represents. The observant adult can recognize listeners' or readers' delight in picture books from

> their faces, their voices, their hands. . . . [T]he excitement in their voices . . . is matched by the actions of their hands pursuing meaning by pointing, tracing, flipping back to earlier pictures. The fixed nature of the book means that you can hold it in your hands, touch the words and pictures, remember where they are and return to them later. Meaning is developed through a very active form of handling the text, yet at the same time it dances in a third space beyond any form of touch. (Mackey & McClay 2000, 193)

Picture books have remarkable power to evoke a positive response from young children. In an observational study of children who were living under the most desperate of circumstances, a relatively brief intervention involving an enthusiastic adult reader and an assortment of picture books had a positive effect on children's interest in picture books and their motivation to learn more about them (Gregory & Morrison 1998). One child who was in his grandmother's custody because of his mother's drug addiction and who had virtually no prior experience with picture books became captivated by audiocassettes and by book-and-tape sets of picture books. Books that enabled him to follow along by signaling when to turn the page became not only a way of learning to read but also a source of solace.

How children learn to respond to literature

Many theorists and researchers now believe that children *construct* meaning from what they read (Rosenblatt 1978). Although this concept may not seem very surprising, it is. The previous assumption was that the text of a book had a preestablished meaning and that understanding this meaning involved simply a more or less accurate reading of the words. From this view, the young child's literary response was usually seen as inferior (i.e., less skilled, naïve) in comparison with the response of older children or adults. But that perspective has changed; now meaning is considered to be a "transaction" between the reader and the book (Rosenblatt 1978, 1982). The nature of that transaction is greatly affected by the life experiences that a listener or reader brings to the book.

Adults can easily grow weary of reading the same book over and over again. But observational research with parents and young children sharing favorite books reveals that children use imitation, questions, and comments to arrive at fuller, richer understandings of texts in revisiting them (Doake 1985; Snow 1983; Wells 1986). By holding one factor in the interaction constant (experiencing the same book repeatedly), children build a foundation and keep adding additional pieces until they have produced an intricate network of ideas and their interrelationships (Rand 1984; Rumelhart 1980). Thus, a child might repeatedly hear a book about starting school such as *My First Days of School*

(Hamilton-Merritt) and gain from those repeated readings a much more sophisticated concept of facts and feelings about initial classroom experiences.

Additionally, young children can deliberately approach text with varying purposes. Sometimes they are listening primarily to obtain information. At other times they might be looking and listening primarily to find out what happens to a character, or to enjoy the beauty of the art and language.

Picture books also can be used to develop the skills of *visual literacy,* defined as the ability to understand and produce visual images (Semali 2003). For example: A first grade teacher is sharing the Big Book version of Ed Young's *Seven Blind Mice* with her class, and this book of bright colors against a glossy

How Visual Literacy Supports Literacy with Print

Using *The Gingerbread Boy* (Cook; Galdone) as an example

Visual literacy skills	Child's comments	Implications for reading comprehension
Comprehension of the main idea—The ability to understand the intended message of the visual work	"Here's the page where he comes alive." "He gets away from all the people and the animals—except the fox."	*Literal recall*—Remembering details, the main idea, sequence, cause-effect, and character traits
Part-whole relationship—The ability to perceive details that contribute to the whole	"Look, he has raisins for his eyes." "The fox is gonna trick him."	*Inference*—Making inferences, predicting outcomes, understanding figurative language
Differentiation of fantasy and reality in illustrations—The ability to infer relationships between symbols and reality	"A gingerbread boy can't really run, but he does in the story." "I never tasted gingerbread for real."	*Evaluation*—Judgments of reality or fantasy, fact or opinion, acceptability, and worth
Recognition of artistic medium—The ability to identify unique properties of the medium used	"Somebody drew these pictures and painted them, maybe." "I like the part where he says, 'Run, run fast as you can. You can't catch me, I'm the Gingerbread Man!'"	*Appreciation*—Reader's and listener's emotional response to the author's plot, theme, characters, and use of language

Visual literacy skills adapted from Lacy (1986); implications for reading comprehension from Sutherland (1997).

Mary Renck Jalongo

black background truly is a feast for the eyes. *Seven Blind Mice* is a variant of the Indian folktale "The Blind Men and the Elephant," and its lesson is that knowing in part may make a fine tale but wisdom comes from seeing the whole. In Young's version, the basic plot is that a strange "Something" has come to the pond, and the mice set out to determine its identity, one at a time. Each day of the week, a different primary-color mouse goes to the pond. Because the first through the sixth mice are satisfied to investigate just one part of the mysterious "Something," each returns with an inaccurate report. For example, the mouse who touches only the trunk reports that the "Something" is a snake, the one who touches only the tail reports it to be a rope, and so forth. It is not until the seventh mouse goes to the pond and walks all over the mystery animal that he returns with an accurate report and correctly identifies the "Something" as an elephant.

As the first-graders examine and talk about the pictures, retell the tale using flannel-board figures, and experiment with painting pictures on black construction paper in the style of the book, they are using the three fundamental skills of visual literacy: (1) *visual thinking*, the organizing of mental images to make them meaningful; (2) *visual learning*, the ability to accurately interpret and construct meaning from nonprint messages; and (3) *visual communication*, the process involved in using a variety of media and symbols to express ideas and communicate with others (Trumbo 1999). Picture books are a tremendous resource in developing skills in visual literacy (Giorgis & Johnson 1999). Unlike television and similar media, which present images that are fleeting, picture books provide the child with images that hold still long enough to be studied. Second, the illustrations in a high-quality picture book are worth more than a quick glance; they are designed to warrant close examination and to prompt wondering aloud (Prudhoe 2003).

One teacher used a pair of funny glasses with a plastic nose attached to model for her students "special looking" in studying the illustrations in a book. First she put the glasses on herself and described aloud, in considerable detail, what she saw. Then, after some good-natured giggling, the children tried the glasses on for themselves and followed her example, describing what they saw in the pictures (Saracho 2003). A book that lends itself to such "special looking" is *Bear Wants More* (Wilson), in which the bear wakes up lean and hungry after hibernating all winter. Its illustrations invite children to practice the skills of visual literacy, while the rhythmic text and the refrain "but the bear wants more" enourage them to chime in.

Many adults assume that looking at pictures alone is not sufficiently challenging for a 5-year-old. A common misconception is that visual images are easy to understand. But images are not understood unless we have sufficient background information to make meaning from what we see. An adult can purchase a piece of electronic equipment or an appliance, look at the schematic diagram, and still have no clue about how it operates or ways to repair it. The same holds true for young children:

> That so many children *can* interpret many different kinds of pictures at an early age doesn't mean that understanding pictures is easy. . . . [B]ecause

contemporary culture provides children with the experience of so many pictures—not just in picture books, but also on television and in video games—children do often become amazingly sophisticated interpreters of the language of pictures, long before they're able to decode the visual signs that represent words. (Nodelman & Reimer 2003, 276)

Observing young children's responses to literature

It is important for adults to know whether children are responding favorably to a particular book. Observable responses may be physical, attentional, verbal, and artistic/creative. The following sections describe these responses in more detail.

Physical. Young children are action-oriented, so their enjoyment of books is often expressed in a physical way. They will position themselves in close to the book, pore over illustrations, hug the book like a treasured toy, or move closer to the reader. During a successful group story session, young children will often start out in a neat semicircle and end up clustered tightly around the reader. A group of young children who heard *The Quicksand Book* (de Paola) rushed up to the teacher afterward clamoring to be the first to borrow the book—which just happens to contain a recipe for making quicksand!

Attentional. When reading a book to a child or a group of children, we can easily identify their look of rapt attention. Children lean forward with a transfixed facial expression and will protest if the pages are turned too quickly or they cannot see the book well. They will also chime in at the appropriate moment if a book is predictable or repetitive. Sometimes the children's nonverbal responses will show that they are really listening, understanding a story, and being caught up in it even when they are not sitting still. A group of preschoolers who listened to *Hazel's Amazing Mother* (Wells) demonstrated a range of intense emotions. When little Hazel is tormented by a gang of bullies who tear apart her favorite doll, the children were outraged and audibly gasped. Later, when Hazel's mother frightens the bullies so much that they "quivered like Jello" and they "sewed like a machine" to repair Hazel's doll, the preschoolers laughed delightedly and breathed a sigh of relief. They were engrossed in the story, and their emotional involvement was reflected in their attention to the book's details—in pictures and in print.

Verbal. Young children often let adults know that they enjoy a story through their words (Zack 1983). On first hearing a book, children often ask for definitions of unfamiliar words or request clarification about something in the picture. Then, at a subsequent story session, they often seek confirmation of something that was explained earlier or bring the topic up again for further elaboration. Later still, during conversations about books, children advance to higher-level questions that evaluate what they have heard. Mem Fox's picture book *Koala Lou* tells the tale of a little koala in Australia who enters an animal "Bush Olympics" but does not succeed. Win or lose, the little koala's mom still says, "Koala Lou, I do love you!" A 4-year-old first asked, "What's Olympics?" and "Why's she sittin' like that?" At a subsequent session, he remarked, "She's

Mary Renck Jalongo

Eleanor's carriage worked without a squeak.

Eleanor was perfect except for her eyes, which Doris could not find in the grass.

The moment Doris and the boys left, Hazel's mother dropped to the ground.

Observing Young Children's Responses to Picture Books

Physical and Attentional Indicators	Verbal and Artistic/ Creative Indicators	Recommended Read-Aloud Picture Books
Infants and toddlers, 6 months–2 years		
Interested babies often stop what they are doing (e.g., stop sucking a pacifier) for a moment to focus. Excited lap babies may perform a physical action more rapidly (e.g., kicking feet or waving arms). Toddlers may grab the book, want to touch or kiss the page, or point to items of interest. Toddlers may show their appreciation for a particular book by carrying it around, holding it close, or refusing to share.	Infants may vocalize in ways that gradually begin to sound like some of the words in the book (e.g., saying, "bah, bah" in response to a picture of a baby). In a small group setting, toddlers may spontaneously dance around or clap hands together in delight. Older toddlers may provide words or sounds (e.g., the sounds that animals make).	*A Mother for Choco* (Kasza) *Big Fat Hen* (Baker) *Cock-a-Doodle-Doo* (Lavis) *Duck in the Truck* (Alborough) *Good Job, Little Bear* (Waddell) *Gossie and Gertie* (Dunrea) *Helen Oxenbury's Big Baby Book* (Oxenbury) *"Hi, Pizza Man!"* (Walter) *Joshua James Likes Trucks* (Petrie) *Maisy's Pool* (Cousins) *Mama Cat Has Three Kittens* (Fleming) *One Cow, Moo Moo!* (Bennett) *Owl Babies* (Waddell) *Please, Baby, Please* (Lee & Lee) *Ten Red Apples* (Hutchins) *Trashy Town* (Zimmerman)
Preschoolers, 3 years–5 years		
Often move closer to the reader and book, or stand up if they cannot see the pictures. If the story is familiar, they may protest if the story is changed in any way. May point out details in illustrations that sometimes escape adults' notice.	Demonstrate interest by participating in some way (e.g., joining in on a refrain, repeating the elements in a cumulative story, singing along). Usually enjoy rhythm, rhyme, and repetition. Generally appreciate incongruity and slapstick humor.	*A Birthday Basket for Tia* (Mora) *Baby Duck and the Bad Eyeglasses* (Hest) *Bear Wants More* (Wilson) *Black All Around* (Hubbell) *Circus* (Ehlert) *Countdown to Kindergarten* (McGhee) *Five Little Monkeys Wash the Car* (Christelow) *Hondo and Fabian* (McCarty) *I Love to Cuddle* (Norac) *"Let's Get a Pup!" Said Kate* (Graham)

Begin to form tastes and attitudes about picture books (e.g., "I like stories about animals"), to notice similarities between books (e.g., "This is like that other book you gave me"), and to notice differences (e.g., "That's not the way the song goes").

Max Found Two Sticks (Pinkney)
Old Black Fly (Aylesworth)
Pete's a Pizza (Steig)
Ruby's Beauty Shop (Wells)
"Slowly, Slowly, Slowly," Said the Sloth (Carle)
Snowballs (Ehlert)
Ten Flashing Fireflies (Sturges)
Ten Terrible Dinosaurs (Stickland)
That's Good! That's Bad! (Cuyler)
The Animal Boogie (Harter)
The Hat Seller and the Monkeys: A West African Folktale (Diakité)
The Mitten (Brett)
What Mommies Do Best, What Daddies Do Best (Numeroff)

Primary grades, 6 years–8 years

Children with prior book experiences are often able to sit still for a longer story, provided that it is presented effectively and does not have dense text on each page.

With numerous opportunities to share stories, children know what they need in order to enjoy books. They may ask for adjustments in presentation (e.g., "Show that picture again!"), request clarification (e.g., "Could that really happen?"), seek affirmation (e.g., "He's lost, right?"), or criticize characters' behavior (e.g., "That's not how you're supposed to ride a bike!").

If a book presented to a group of children is successful, several children may clamor to be the first to borrow it.

With extensive book experiences that have pointed out illustrators and authors, children may begin to recognize favorites (e.g., "That's a Patricia Polacco book" or "I like Lois Ehlert's pictures").

Chicken Sunday (Polacco)
Epossumondas (Salley)
Halmoni and the Picnic (Choi)
Ice Cream Larry (Pinkwater)
Saturday Night at the Dinosaur Stomp (Shields)
Shaggy, Waggy Dogs (and Others) (Calmenson)
Stellaluna (Cannon)
The Boy of the Three-Year Nap (Snyder)
The Hunterman and the Crocodiles: A West African Folktale (Diakité)
Two Bad Ants (Van Allsburg)
Who Came Down That Road? (Lyon)

crying because she lost, right?" Later, after the book was familiar, he said, "Her mommy loves her a whole bunch."

Another verbal behavior that reflects children's appreciation is the incorporation of storybook language into their vocabulary and play. After Amy heard *Gregory, the Terrible Eater* (Sharmat) several times, she used a verbal expression and a gesture from the book while she was playing house: When a boy who was pretending to be Amy's offspring misbehaved, she slammed her hand down on the table and said "That does it!" just like Gregory's father does in the story.

Artistic/creative. Children often respond to their favorite stories through drawing, painting, and other art; drama; original stories; dance/movement; and song (Gallas 1994). Thus, picture books can function as a way of stimulating children's creative thought. Opposite are some examples of young children's artistic responses to literature: Richard, a 5-year-old, drew Clifford the big red dog from *Clifford, the Small Red Puppy* (Bridwell); his original drawing was on 18-by-22-inch paper. Two first-graders illustrated their favorite part of *Sylvester and the Magic Pebble* (Steig).

The child as critic

Canaan, a 5-year-old, thinks that *Some of Us Walk, Some Fly, Some Swim* (Frith) "was very boring at the beginning . . . because it just keeps telling you the names of things, different animals." But the book "has a real happy ending. Since the fish were halfway dead, all of the birds and the other animals helped the fish, and they put them in the water."

Melissa, a first-grader, thinks that *A Children's Zoo* (Hoban) could be improved: "I would put different words in it, and I'd put in more *baby* animals, too."

Corey enjoyed *Clay Boy* (Ginsburg) "'cause he ate people." But something about the plot bothered him. In the story, the Clay Boy devours people until a billy goat offers to be Clay Boy's dinner. Once the goat is eaten, he then batters his way out, breaking the clay into bits and allowing the people to escape. Corey reasons that volunteering to be eaten is foolhardy: "Instead of saying 'I'll stand here and jump into your mouth,' I would say 'Okay, come over and try to get me' . . . and I would bust him just by runnin' into him, because it sounds dumb that he is gonna help him eatin' him."

As these comments illustrate, young children have the ability to respond evaluatively to picture books, and spontaneously do so. Perhaps young children's reactions to literature are more sophisticated than we realize, and maybe what they lack is vocabulary rather than judgment. At the very least, children have definite preferences and ways of expressing those preferences. Certainly, children who have opportunities not only to listen to stories but also to talk about them are better equipped to engage in the higher-level thought processes associated with evaluation. Several studies have documented that children's comments tend to grow more sophisticated when they revisit familiar books (Yaden 1988).

Mary Renck Jalongo

Sources of picture book appeal

Today in kindergarten, Kasey has dictated a story to accompany *Picnic*, a wordless book by Emily Arnold McCully. A *wordless book* is a picture book with little or no text; it tells the story entirely through a series of illustrations. In this picture story, a large family of mice pack a picnic lunch and pile into a pickup truck. Along the way they hit a big bump, and the littlest mouse falls out with her doll. In all of the excitement of the picnic, it takes a while before the mouse family realizes that the littlest mouse is missing, goes in search of her, and is finally happily reunited. Here is Kasey's rendition:

> Once upon a time there were 12 mouses. And they were going to go to the park to have a picnic. So they drove away, but one of the mouses fell out of the truck. And she fell down and a dolly slipped out of her hand. So they got out of the truck and they set the picnic blanket out. While they were setting up the picnic, the kids went out and played. They were having so much fun. They forgot about the girl mouse that fell out of the truck. She was lost and she found a bush of berries. They were still having fun and they still forgot. So she tried to pick berries but she was too short. But finally she got them and she started to eat them. And finally they realized that she was gone. They were so sad they were crying and yelling for her. So they packed up and went back to the truck. She was tired of where she was lost. So they drove away and started looking for her. She was trying to look for them, but the more she looked, the more she got lost. So they finally found her and they cheered "Hooray!" So when they got out of the car, they were so happy. And so she told them the story of how she got lost. So they had the picnic happily ever after. THE END.

The story that this 5-year-old invented to go along with the illustrations in *Picnic* exemplifies how picture books can evoke responses from young children. In fact, wordless books can be used to encourage children to create longer, more involved stories than the ones they might choose to tell without the support of plot-sequenced illustrations. Many curricular uses of wordless books have been developed (Jalongo et al. 2002).

Children respond more intensely to picture books that are a treat for the mind, the senses, and the emotions.

Intellectual stimulation. Young children are inquisitive. They want to understand themselves and others; they wonder about other people, places, and times. Picture books enable children to ask questions, to obtain answers, and to explore other possibilities. *Mufaro's Beautiful Daughters: An African Tale* (Steptoe) is a good example. This book instantly transports the listener to another continent that is lush, green, and magical. The characters are clothed in traditional African dress, and children immediately notice that the king, prince, and two princesses in this setting are distinctly different from most other portrayals of royalty in books. This lavishly illustrated book also stimulates children's imaginations by presenting a prince who can transform himself into a harmless garden snake or an old lady, all in the interest of learning more about the true personality of his future bride. Even the conclusion of the story stimulates children's minds; the wicked sister's prophecy that her sister will become a

Illustrations copyright © 1987 John Steptoe. Used by permission of HarperCollins Publishers.

servant in her house does not come true, rather just the reverse happens in this African variant of the Cinderella story. Young children take notice that the roles predicted at the story's beginning have been reversed at the story's conclusion. The motif that inner beauty is important can be revisited in a growing number of Cinderella tales from around the world, including Mexico (Coburn), China (Louie), North America–Algonquin tribe (Martin), and Indonesia (Sierra).

Sensory appeal. Turn the beautifully illustrated pages of *Pumpkin Pumpkin* (Titherington), and the visual and tactile stimulation is satisfying. Each page is alive with images, and the paper feels good against the reader's fingertips. Even the senses not directly affected by the book can be evoked. A listener imagines the smell of the earth as the seed is planted and the taste of salted and toasted pumpkin seeds. Additionally, when a beautifully crafted story is read aloud, the rhythm of language brings pleasure through the sense of hearing as children listen to language that is designed to be spoken.

Emotional resonance. The picture books that children love also evoke emotional responses. In Jonathan London's *Froggy Gets Dressed,* a little frog wakes up early and is determined to play outside in the snow. He goes through the arduous process of dressing for the weather, complete with a host of sound effects to go along with buttoning, zipping, and so forth. Children usually laugh out loud when Froggy is finally bundled up in winter clothes and has forgotten his underwear! Of course, not all picture books are designed to evoke hilarity. Picture books with more serious topics can be an important way to reassure children that they are not alone in experiencing intense emotions and to show how characters successfully cope with these situations (Jalongo 1986). *Timothy Goes to School* (Wells) is a fine example. Rather than present the stereotypical story about starting school—all fun and instant friendship—Wells deftly portrays the understandable anxiety about doing something for the first time, functioning as a member of a group, and contending with a know-it-all classmate.

Responses to literature involve feelings, ideas, and sensory perception. How might this knowledge about children's responses to literature be used to improve adults' use of picture books with young children?

Predicting how children will respond

When an adult goes to the library shelf to choose a picture book to share with young children, the ability to predict which books those children will prefer makes the process more efficient. Here are three strategies.

In the first strategy, the adult uses the developmental issues facing the child. For example, for a toddler, typical issues might be waiting for a parent to return and being reprimanded for making a mess. These ideas are presented in two board books by Jan Ormerod, *Dad's Back* and *Messy Baby*.

A second strategy is to base a current selection on the past preferences of the child or a small group of children. If a humorous story such as *Bea and Mr. Jones* (Schwartz), in which an advertising executive and a kindergartner trade places, was well received then another amusing role reversal such as *Swamp Monsters* (Christian) would be worth a try.

The third basic strategy in predicting children's picture book preferences is to know many excellent books very well. With this knowledge, the adult can compare an unfamiliar picture book with others of its type and make equally appropriate choices in the future. A helpful resource for locating award- and prize-winning picture books is the website of the Children's Book Council (www.cbcbooks.org/awardsandprizes). For a useful summary of picture book awards and honors, see Zeece (1999). Additionally, many teachers and librarians keep lists of favorite authors and illustrators whose books never disappoint; some suggestions appear in Appendix A. More and more, these authors and illustrators have their own websites, and some are listed in Appendix B; for example, Patricia Polacco (www.patriciapolacco.com) or Jan Brett (www.janbrett.com). Often, just typing the person's name into your browser's address field will bring you to his or her website, or try a search engine such as Google.com.

In every case, by anticipating how children might respond to the story, effective teachers can enhance the listeners' responses to a particular book. Lois Ehlert's book *Snowballs,* for example, is the perfect way to prepare for a major snowfall. The book is a marvel of stereotype-breaking ideas about creating snow figures outdoors—not just snow*men* but snowwomen, snowchildren, and snowanimals, all decorated in surprising ways with found materials such as pieces of broken toys or bottle caps and natural materials such as leaves or pieces of pine boughs. Not only does the book contain illustrations that elicit surprised laughter from children (such as Spot, the snowdog, completely decorated with buttons!), it also includes photographs of snow creatures in people's yards, a recipe for making popcorn balls, a photograph of mittens from many lands hanging on a clothesline, and sample weather reports that predict snow. The teacher who involves children in collecting and saving materials from Ehlert's "good stuff" pictorial list surely will do a better job of teaching the skills of visual literacy and inviting responses to literature with this book as support.

Conclusion: Making picture books part of daily practice

To optimize children's opportunities to respond to a book, the teachers and families who choose and share books with them need to implement practices that address the particular needs of young children for picture books. At least five compelling reasons support making picture books part of every young child's day:

Young children rely on adults for experiences with quality literature. Therefore, classrooms should be places where many different types of books are accessible to children, shared with children, and recommended to families and children.

Young children's literacy growth depends, to a considerable extent, on the opportunity to share literature on a one-to-one basis with adults.

We rolled
three snowballs
and made a
snow dad.

Therefore, children who come to school without these kinds of experiences at home must be able to obtain them in other ways. Teachers have an obligation to provide each young child, particularly toddlers, with individual storytime through community volunteers, college students in education, sessions involving cross-age tutoring, and parent education programs.

Young children can respond to literature in many ways. Therefore, teachers and other adults should model a range of responses—verbal, artistic, physical, attentional. They also should provide children with authentic opportunities for self-expression and creative thought.

Young children's previous experiences exert a great influence on their literary response. Therefore, teachers and other adults should be deliberate in connecting picture books with direct experience. After children hear a musical performance, adults should then read and display picture books about music. When children in the primary grades are curious about the trees and leaves they see around their neighborhood, adults can provide information books such as *Are Trees Alive?* (Miller) or *Tell Me, Tree: All about Trees for Kids* (Gibbons). If children become captivated by a book's format, such as books with pop-ups, pull tabs, or other moving parts, adults can then introduce more of those books such as *Colors* (Crowther) or *Big Red Fire Truck* (Wilson-Max) or *The Mouse Who Ate Bananas* (Faulkner).

Young children are in the process of forming literary preferences. Therefore, the opportunity to choose from among many high-quality books is essential to prevent those preferences from narrowing rather than expanding with time. Adults should introduce a wide variety of book types, including fiction and nonfiction, traditional and innovative.

As Betsy Hearne (2000) advises in *Choosing Books for Children: A Commonsense Guide:*

> Today's children are tomorrow's reading adults. If today's adults don't care about children's imaginations or their books, if they don't sense the strong connection, children certainly won't. Today's children will lose a golden opportunity for pleasure and tomorrow's adults may lose the passion for literature and learning. (5)

When parents, other family members, and teachers consider children's responses to literature and fulfill these roles, they create environments in which love of literature and growth in literacy can flourish.

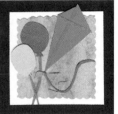

CHAPTER 5

Acquiring Literacy through Picture Books

> *Thinking about reading ability has shifted drastically in the last decade. Instead of assessing children's reading abilities, we ask questions about their prior experiences or opportunities to learn in literacy events at home, in preschool, and in kindergarten. We know that most children, although not all, who have had early experiences with reading and writing have higher reading and writing achievement scores on a variety of measures even at the time of school entry than [do] children who had relatively few literacy experiences. Instead of viewing these children's high achievement as being directly related to their high reading ability, we now recognize that these children have high achievement levels as a direct result of their extensive early literacy experiences—they have had many opportunities to learn.*
>
> —Donald McGee & Lea Richgels,
> *Designing Early Literacy Programs* (2003, 3–4)

Carl is a 3-year-old boy from Appalachia who will be traveling with his parents to visit his cousins. As he climbs into the car, he sees a map and directions that his father printed off the Internet lying on the seat. "This shows how to get to them houses," Carl comments.

Tracy, a 5-year-old from Kenya, notices a set of coasters decorated with Chinese characters lying on a coffee table. "That's Chinese writing," she says confidently, as she gently touches the raised images on each one.

Mari is an 8-year-old from Japan who recently immigrated to the United States. The second-grader watches a DVD of *The Karate Kid* at a friend's house and is disturbed to discover that Japanese internment camps existed in the United States during World War Two. She wants to try to understand why this unfairness happened, and with her school librarian's help Mari locates and reads two picture books on the topic, *Baseball Saved Us* (Mochizuki) and *The Bracelet* (Uchida).

Most people would use the word *literacy* only in reference to the child who is reading independently, yet every one of these children is demonstrating literate behaviors. Carl has acquired the concept of a symbol and realizes that a map can show the way. Tracy has observed her Mom's international student friends reading, writing, and typing in Chinese; she understands that certain symbols with particular features are readable as words and that different languages exist. In fact, Tracy has seen her own name written in three different ways—in Kiswahili, in English, and in Chinese characters. Mari, who is gifted in language, is capable of independent reading and writing both in Japanese and in English.

As the lives of these children illustrate, the acquisition of literacy is not simply accruing a set of skills; it is a progression of realizations about the forms and functions of print and nonprint messages. We live today in a time when expectations on young children for literacy behaviors are higher than ever before:

> There can be no doubt that the need for individuals to achieve high standards of literacy is increasing. And this is not only an economic imperative on a national scale but also an individual exigency at a very personal level. Literacy is one of the key tools for success in today's world and also an unparalleled means of recreation and personal discovery. (Fisher 2002, 6)

Links between literacy and literature

Every day in America, we are barraged with discouraging literacy statistics; take note of the following sobering facts, for example:

• National adult illiteracy rates range from 11 percent to 30 percent in various states. Forty (40) percent of the adults living in poverty are functioning at the lowest levels of literacy (Chandler 2000).

• According to the National Assessment of Educational Progress (2003), wide gaps exist in young children's ability to read. At the Proficient level, children need to be able to apply and reason effectively about what they read. In a large, national sample of fourth-graders, only 48% of Asian children, 43% of white children, 16% of Hispanic children, and 10% of African American children scored at the Proficient level.

But at the same time, public discussion of American literacy levels does not do justice to the complexities of learning to read. Many people, including some early childhood teachers, oversimplify learning to read as simply a set of mechanical skills, each acquired separately. In many instances what is emphasized is bearing down hard on these component skills, with little recognition of the learning experiences young children need to spark and sustain their interest and for the context for making sense of the various component skills. These portrayals of literacy acquisition are inaccurate and destructive, because they lead to ineffective teaching practices that disrespect young children's characteristic ways of learning, which are more "hands on," playful, and interactive.

In fact, the link between picture books and the acquisition of literacy is well-established (Fox 2001; Krashen 1993). Reading to children equips them to navigate a world of cultural objects, including movies, videos, television shows, and computer programs (Spitz 1999). And research supports that being read to is positively linked to a child's overall academic achievement, reading skills, and interest in reading (Routman 2002; Snow, Burns, & Griffin 1998). What is less well understood is the process by which this influence occurs. For help, let us look at another type of reading ability that is less clouded by controversy—learning to read musical notation—and examine how children acquire that ability.

• What types of activities and settings build a young child's interest in and motivation to learn music reading?

• Why is learning to read music highly valued by some individuals but not as valued by others?

• Why don't all children achieve the same level of proficiency in learning to read music?

Consider the issue of interest and motivation. Most professional musicians report becoming attracted to music through informal, pleasurable activities such as listening to music and participating in song in family and other recreational settings. Few were pressured as young children to master musical notation, the musical equivalent of the alphabet, right from the start. Sharing and enjoying music, rather than testing children's knowledge of musical symbols, was the focus. When an adult shares music with young children, typically they are not expected to remain motionless and keep quiet. Rather, they are involved with action songs, creative movement, and so forth (Isenberg & Jalongo 2000).

The same should hold true for inaugurating children's experiences with literacy. Children need to be active participants in pleasurable language activities, such as experiencing picture books. As toddlers, they need to point at and comment on the pictures. As preschoolers, they need to chime in on the refrain of a book whose content (text or images) is predictable (a *predictable book)*, dramatize the stories they love, and recite the text of books so thoroughly familiar that they have been committed to memory. And, as children begin to read, they need to apply their skills in meaningful contexts, as they read to find out what happens next in an engaging story or write to communicate with family, friends, and teachers. Just as the young child with a lifelong passion for music begins with song and movement, the child who acquires a lifelong passion for literacy with print begins with talk, story, and drama. Unfortunately, where learning to read is concerned, Americans instead tend to begin with bits of language (the letters of the alphabet, sight words, vowel sounds) and try to convince young children to stay interested until they know enough to put the pieces together. Many children simply cannot sustain their interest and motivation in the face of so much drill and practice.

Next, consider the value placed on music. Wide variations exist in the importance afforded to music in different families, communities, and social contexts. Some families place music at the center of their lives, whereas others experience music peripherally, as little more than background sounds. The value placed on singing, learning to read music, and acquiring performance skills varies tremendously, depending on whether or not musical ability is thought to enrich life in significant ways.

This same variation holds true for literacy with print. Mainstream American society greatly values literacy, and regards it as providing the key to success in life and work. This conviction, however, is not equally embraced by all, particularly not by members of cultures that consider oral language to be sufficient—even preferred—as the way to communicate and conduct business, as is the case with many tribal and indigenous groups. Neither is the conviction embraced by those in America who can look around and see neighbors who *did* acquire literacy (and *did* complete school) yet are still locked out of "the American dream" (Ogbu 1988). Those families want something better for their children, yet daily experiences disconfirm the assertion that all good things will come if only the children learn to read and write.

Such circumstances require teachers to argue literacy's contributions to families in ways that make sense in particular contexts. Vague pronouncements about the value of literature or enthusiasm for picture books will not suffice; families will rightfully insist on evidence that literature leads not merely to success in school but to voice and choice in work and life for their children (Vasquez 2003). Moreover, children need to be initiated into literature to see what reading can do for them and to be convinced that reading is an ability developed over time rather than an act of magic that some can perform and others cannot (Gallas 1997).

Finally, consider the issues surrounding level of proficiency. Members of our society vary widely in their musical abilities, with little upset. A person can be tone deaf and totally lacking in musical literacy without being considered a scourge on society or a potential criminal (Smith 1989). Not so with knowing how to read. Those who fail at literacy with print are subjected to public scorn. Clearly, the acquisition of literacy with print arouses strong societal reactions in a way that mastering musical notation does not. The question of "who's to blame" for low levels of literacy in America is constantly in the media and hotly debated.

Those who work with young children might reassure themselves that because they are responsible for a child's *earliest* experiences, they thus can distance themselves from any disappointing outcomes later in the child's life and adulthood. But we early childhood educators play a crucial role in setting that child on an appropriate path where literacy is concerned. The seemingly small or ordinary things that we do to support early literacy—for example, making a commitment to sharing picture books with young children—exert a powerful and enduring influence on literacy throughout a child's life span. In fact, most experts in reading consider the early childhood years, when language typically is developing at a pace more rapid than at any other time, to be critical for literacy learning (Neuman & Dickinson 2001). The following findings underscore the importance of the early childhood teacher's role in promoting literacy:

• Early literacy intervention programs have demonstrated that with appropriate instructional support, children who are experiencing reading and writing difficulties can make significant progress (Hiebert & Taylor 2000).

• The reading level attained by a child by third grade is a powerful predictor not only of later attainment in reading but also of high school graduation (Slavin et al. 1994).

• Teachers daily have the opportunity to provide (or not) literacy experiences to an estimated five million American children who attend child care centers (Helburn 1994).

Early childhood practitioners are in a unique position to exert a powerful influence, positive or negative, on the future reading and writing abilities of all the children in their care. Sadly, only one in seven child care centers has been assessed as providing effective language and learning experiences (Helburn 1994).

Understanding emergent literacy

In the research literature, talk about *reading readiness*, which connoted that children's development was in a holding pattern until "real" reading commenced, shifted several decades ago to what is now termed *emergent literacy* (Holdaway 1979). Emergent literacy "refers to the reading and writing knowl-

---

Some Principles of Literacy Learning in Early Childhood

Gradual. The process of learning to read and write begins well before school and formal learning experiences. Literacy learning is a long and gradual process that commences in infancy.

Incremental. All children arrive at school with funds of knowledge about language. The responsibility of teachers is to respect and build on what children know so children will use literacy to accomplish personally significant tasks and to participate more fully in work and in life.

Multidimensional. Literacy is no longer limited to paper-and-pencil practice with words. Simply enabling today's children to attain literacy with print is not sufficient, because they live in a society that requires them to be literate in more expansive ways. All of the traditional areas of the language arts (listening, speaking, reading, and writing), as well as the fine arts, media literacy, and computer literacy are interrelated, developed together, and demanded by society.

Meaningful. Opportunities to participate in literacy events in meaningful contexts—situations where language is used to accomplish goals of importance for the individual child—stimulate the child's growth in literacy.

Interactional. The child's understanding of literacy concepts (e.g., book, story, word, read, write, sentence, punctuation) emerges from social interaction and from joint participation in a task that is focused on language, both oral and written.

Helpful. Young children's language learning is accelerated when language learning is supported by quality materials, scaffolded for the learner, and responsive to the learner's agenda.

Motivational. Children's growth in literacy is activated by the learner's motivation and interest and is extended through independent practice and opportunities to apply new skills.

Adapted from McGee & Richgels (2003).

How to Support Literacy through Picture Books

Provide a print-rich literacy environment. Create an inviting book center or corner, display some picture books with the covers out, display posters and mobiles of story characters, provide props for retelling (e.g., flannel board, toys, masks of story characters, puppets), demonstrate the use of the center, visit it yourself.

Read aloud to children and discuss books. Read aloud regularly. All children can profit from individual reading, particularly if they have had few experiences with books. Use volunteers to provide additional individual book experiences. As a rule of thumb, double the child's age as a rough estimate of how many children should be in a group (e.g., reading with small groups of six to eight for 3- and 4-year-olds). Try having older preschoolers and children in the primary grades discuss books using the RQL2 method developed by Dugan (1997):

• **R**espond—Say what you liked or disliked. Tell about your favorite part. Tell how the story makes you feel.

• **Q**uestion—Ask questions about the story. Ask other group members questions. Ask questions the whole group can answer.

• **L**isten—Be attentive to what your classmates say. Listen and respond to questions. Listen and join in the discussion.

• **L**ink—Relate events in the story. Link your experiences with the story. Link your ideas with the ideas of your classmates.

Help children to develop the concept of a symbol. Incorporate materials and experiences into the learning environment that help children understand the idea that a symbol is something that stands for something else. Materials can include familiar signs (e.g., stop, school crossing), alphabet blocks, flash cards with pictures and words, rebus stories.

Show support for emergent writing and drawing. Provide children with a wide array of writing and drawing implements and an ample supply of (scrap or recycled) paper for drawing and writing. Encourage them by saying, "Tell me about your picture" (rather than ask "What is it?"). Ask them to talk about their attempts to write, even if it is a scribble.

Point out features of print and build knowledge of the alphabet. Children need to understand the role of symbols as communication devices. Use predictable books that repeat words or phrases so children can note similarities in the text. Incorporate writing materials in play activities and in learning centers. Use alphabet books of various types.

Make children aware of the sound system of language. Use picture books to give children opportunities to explore the sound structure of oral and written language (Goswami 2001). Infants and toddlers can experiment with sounds, respond to familiar rhymes, participate in action rhymes, show interest in books that include pictures of familiar objects, and attempt to name objects or make sounds. Preschoolers can recognize their names, recognize rhymes and "sound alikes," and identify some letter sounds. Many older children are ready to learn more about phonics and can match letters and sounds, blend phonemes, and split syllables; change the first letter to create a new word (e.g., *man, fan, pan*); apply rules such as the e at the end of the word often signals a long vowel sound (e.g., *cake, mine*).

Teach children a vocabulary of literacy. Children need to use and understand terminology associated with literacy (e.g., *listen, read, picture, story, letter, word, spell, write, author, rhyme*). Use these terms in context while sharing picture books with children.

Statements in boldface adapted from Justice & Kaderavek (2002); McGee & Richgels (2003); and Stratton (1996).

Mary Renck Jalongo

edge and behavior of children who are not yet conventionally literate" (Justice & Kaderavek 2002, 8). In other words, emergent literacy describes all the manifestations that indicate children are learning to represent their ideas and feelings through oral language and drawing as well as through interaction with other types of symbols in their environments (such as signs, posters, billboards, shopping lists, logos and other advertising, notes, greeting cards, letters, newspapers and magazines, television and computer images, and that fusion of symbols designed specifically for them—the picture book). Stratton (1996) provides a useful perspective on emergent literacy:

> The process of emergent literacy begins at birth, involves all aspects of a child's development, and continues throughout life. It begins with the child's early nonverbal and verbal interactions with others, awareness of the environment, and explorations. It continues as the child gains intentional language, broadens explorations, and builds concepts. It progresses as the child gains an understanding of the function of symbols and language, has experiences with books, and experiments with writing. The focus of emergent literacy is on learning, rather than on teaching, and on the child as an active learner. The role of the adult is to facilitate and extend child-initiated learning. (177–8)

How do picture books lend support to these perspectives and principles? The box **How to Support Literacy through Picture Books** identifies the teacher's roles and the literacy concepts that young children need to develop to become literate.

The sequence of emergent literacy begins when lullabies are shared with infants, when lap babies learn some bounce-on-the-knee rhymes, and when toddlers point at the pictures in board books. (For more, see the box **Practical Suggestions for Sharing Picture Books with Toddlers in a Group**.) All of these activities share some commonalities: they are pleasurable, they invite the child to function as an active partner, and they are focused on language.

Acquiring basic understandings about books

What big ideas about literacy do young children acquire during adult-child interactions with picture books of various types? Snow and Ninio (1986) identify four messages that children get, which these researchers refer to as "the contracts of literacy."

Message 1: Books are unique objects. Through experience, children recognize that a book differs from a toy. They learn that picture books are "not for eating, throwing, chewing, or building towers" (Snow & Ninio 1986, 122). Children also learn to hold the book right side up, to begin at the beginning, and to turn the pages one at a time.

Message 2: Pictures have meaning. Children learn that pictures can be labeled and that pictures, "even though static, can represent dynamic actions, events, sequences, relations, motives, and consequences" (Snow & Ninio 1986, 132). Pictures are so powerful, at least initially, that children believe the pictures (rather than the words) are being read (Sulzby 1985).

This focus on the illustrations generates what Sulzby refers to as "picture-governed attempts" by young children at interpreting what they see. For

Practical Suggestions for Sharing Picture Books with Toddlers in a Group

Choose appropriate picture books. A key to success in conducting a read-aloud with toddlers is choosing developmentally appropriate books. Toddler books should be large and appealing, with simple text about subjects to which a very young child can relate; for example, *Time for Bed* (Fox) or *Flower Garden* (Bunting). Ideally, the story will also give a chance for the listeners to join in; for example, *I Love Animals* (McDonnell), which prompts the listeners to make animal sounds. Do not choose a book with much longer text and then try to pare it down yourself; save those books for the older children.

Adjust expectations for toddlers' behavior. Reading to a group of toddlers is much different than is reading in a one-on-one lap session at home. Although the children may neither sit perfectly still nor seem to concentrate on the story, they will settle down as they become familiar with the storytime routine. Therefore, persist at establishing storytime routines, just as you would persist at teaching a toddler other skills. Patiently coach and offer support as needed; promoting literacy is sufficiently important to merit a long-term commitment.

Plan your program with the youngest child in mind. Start with a song or rhyme that will be the same each time to establish an important signal for the children to focus on storytime. Remember, the opportunities you are providing are often the toddler's first group experiences with books, and it will take time to orient them to sharing books. If you have parent volunteers or aides available, invite them to sit with the children, not only to model attentive listening and participation but also to simulate lap reading by holding different children at various times on their laps.

Consider the pacing of the storytime. Today's children, even at the toddler stage, are accustomed to seeing many different images on the television or computer, from the car as they ride past billboards, or from the shopping cart as they pass hundreds of items. As a result, they amass experience with visual images that far exceeds that of previous generations. Therefore, keep things moving so their attention does not wane.

Plan for variety and participation. Alternate active times and quiet times, rather than expect children to listen quietly throughout. Provide plenty of opportunities for children to act out parts of the story by means of songs or finger rhymes. Put the most challenging story first, then follow up with a finger rhyme that gets the children involved. When leading finger rhymes or songs, use visual aids, finger puppets, or a hand puppet to focus the children's attention. The addition of a three-dimensional character such as a puppet is a welcome change to children after concentrating on the two-dimensional pages of a picture book and listening to a story. Puppets can be used to extend the story and bring a certain reality to it. Make each new activity a surprise by having the puppets or visual aids hidden from the toddlers' view, perhaps in a special storytime basket or box you have decorated. Next, begin one more short story, preferably with audience participation of some sort, and then have the children stand for another song or rhyme. Finally, a simple puppet show that involves just two puppets or a short video can round out the program. Close with the same song or rhyme each time as a signal to the toddlers that storytime is over for the day. A cooperative group game such as "Ring around the Rosy" is a good way to cap the storytime session.

The following plan presents a sample toddler storytime with a puppy theme:

• Opening—Sing "The More We Get Together" (used as the signal for storytime to begin).

• Picture book—Children listen to the story *Bubba and Beau, Best Friends* (Appelt), about a toddler's special bond of friendship with his dog.

• Action song—Sing "Bingo" and lead children in clapping to the spelling of the dog's name.

• Picture book—Invite children to participate in the predictable book *Bark, George* (Feiffer).

• Finger play—Lead the children in the "Bend and Stretch" action song.

• Puppet show—Present a puppet performance of *Claude the Dog* (Gackenbach). The story has just two characters, a privileged dog (Claude) and a stray dog without a home. Claude decides to share what he has.

• Closing—Sing "If You're Happy and You Know It" (used as the customary closing to the storytime).

Consult professional resources specifically for working with toddlers. Early childhood teachers who work with toddlers cannot simply "adapt" long picture books and storytime practices that are successful with children in kindergarten and the primary grades. Toddlers' literacy needs are very different, and developmentally appropriate and effective storytimes must be carefully planned with a toddler in mind. See Appendix D for more suggestions on appropriate books for toddlers and resources for teachers.

Compiled with Melissa Ann Renck, children's services librarian, Toledo Lucas County Library.

example, the following is a sample of 30-month-old Hua's dialogue about the book *Babies* (Fujikawa). The things that Hua chooses to mention are a mixture of details observed in the pictures, words heard from the text, discussions from previous story-reading sessions, and experience in her own young life. Hua has learned that pictures can do more than represent objects; effective interactions with books also can communicate behavior, motivation, and outcomes.

Text of the book	Retelling by Hua
Babies are very little, soft, warm and cuddly.	Baby! (*She points to the picture of a toddler*) Tat his big sister.
They're always lying around, eating, sleeping, laughing or crying.	Baby lyin' down. Baby eatin'. He's laughin', she's cryin'. Oh, baby sleepin' with her dolly.
They like to be changed and bathed and hugged and loved.	Baby takin' a tubby. Look, a quack, quack. Mommy huggin' baby, baby wanna story.
Then they eat and go to sleep again.	One, two, three baby, four, five babies. Babies eatin' and sleepin'. He tumblin' on his head.
And how they grow and grow	Baby playin' with kitty. Tat baby playin' ball. This baby crawlin'.
And grow.	He pushin' a car, car.
Before you know it, they will be running and chasing all around,	Babies runnin'. See kitty? Babies chasin' kitty and buderflies.
Oh, so busily . . .	Run little kitty, run away home.
And do lots of things by themselves.	Baby eatin' by herself. Puttin' on her socks. Baby readin' to kitty. Dada proud of baby.
Sometimes they are naughty	Oh! Bad baby. Momma mad.
And sometimes they are little angels.	(*She points to halo*) Wassat, momma? Baby sittin' with dolly.
But good or bad, all babies like to be hugged and cuddled and loved.	Momma huggin' and kissin' baby. Baby love momma. Momma love baby.

Mary Renck Jalongo

Gradually, as children have many opportunities with picture books, they begin to realize that the text is what is read, and they focus on what Sulzby (1985) refers to as "text-governed attempts." Kayla, a 4-year-old, uses a more text-governed approach to tell *The Doorbell Rang* (Hutchins). Notice how her words are beginning to reflect the language of the story.

Text of the book	Retelling by Kayla
"I've made some cookies for tea," said Ma. "Good," said Victoria and Sam. "We're starving." "Share them between yourselves," said Ma. "I made plenty."	"I made cookies," said Mom. "Good," said Sam. Mom said, "Share dem."
"That's six each," said Sam and Victoria. "They look as good as Grandma's," said Victoria. "They smell as good as Grandma's," said Sam.	"We can have some. They wook like Grama's. They smell like Grama's."
"No one makes cookies like Grandma," said Ma as the doorbell rang.	"No one makes cookies like Grama."
It was Tom and Hannah from next door. "Come in," said Ma. "You can share the cookies."	Tom an Anna came over to have cookies.
"That's three each," said Sam and Victoria. "They smell as good as your Grandma's," said Tom. "And look as good," said Hannah.	"That's six each. They smell like Grama's."
"No one makes cookies like Grandma," said Ma as the door bell rang . . .	"No one makes cookies like Grama."
"Oh dear," said Ma as the children stared at the cookies on their plates.	The kids looked at their plates.
"Perhaps you'd better eat them before we open the door." "We'll wait," said Sam.	"Don't open the door," said Sam.
It was Grandma with an enormous tray of cookies.	It was Grama!
"How nice to have so many friends to share them with," said Grandma. "It's a good thing I made a lot!"	She has lots of cookies.
"And no one makes cookies like Grandma," said Ma as the doorbell rang.	"No one makes cookies like Grama."

Copyright © 1986 by Pat Hutchins. Used by permission of HarperCollins Publishers.

An ability such as Kayla's was once disregarded and labeled as simple memorization. Experts now corroborate what veteran teachers have known intuitively all along—that this reading-like behavior is as closely related to learning to read as walking with support is to walking unassisted (see Jalongo 2003a).

Message 3: The book leads the reader. Children learn that during story sharing the picture book is the focus of the conversation, and that drawing relationships between pictured events and real-life events is one of the ways that books are discussed. After accumulating many such experiences that link literature with life, children learn to compare/contrast their experiences with what they see on the pages of picture books.

Message 4: Events in books are part of a different time frame and world. The young child who experiences stories soon realizes that the discussion of a book takes place in the here and now, and that imaginary characters can take on lives of their own. A "child can share a character's attitudes, approve or disapprove of [the character's] behavior, and can even exhort [the character] to act differently" (Snow & Ninio 1986, 135). As children gain experience with literature, their comments reflect an awareness that stories and characters exist independently of the children themselves, even though relationships may exist between books and the children's personal experiences.

In her retelling of Disney's *Lady and the Tramp,* 4-year-old Kiersten stops to comment on an issue she is resolving at home and at child care—where and when she is supposed to sleep. She also begins to talk directly to the main character:

Text of the book	Retelling by Kiersten
One Christmas Eve Jim Dear gave his wife Darling a present. Darling opened the present carefully. Out popped a little *puppy.* . . .	Once there was a man Burt who was married to his wife Darling. He gave Darling a present. It was a *very* nice one. It was a baby pup. She opened the gift.
"Oh, what a lovely puppy!" said Darling. "Let's call her Lady." . . .	He said, "How do you like it Darling?" She said, "I like it very much. Thank you, honey. I really like it. I really do. Maybe when he grows up he'll know better too."
At bedtime, Jim tucked Lady into a cozy basket. "That's your very own bed," said Jim.	This is your bed, Lady. It's your bed, Lady. Stay in there, Lady, or else you'll get tireder, so you better sleep in your own bed or Mrs. S. or Mrs. R. will get mad at you.

Book text reprinted, with permission, from *Lady and the Tramp* (New York: Random House), a Little Golden Book. Copyright © 1954 by The Walt Disney Company.

Mary Renck Jalongo

Kiersten has learned to regard picture books as part of a fictional world where characters take on lives of their own. She is also learning to interpret the language that she hears, and to use "book-like" vocabulary. Later in *Lady and the Tramp,* the text reads, "But some mean dogs barked at her. Lady ran and ran"; Kiersten says, "There were two dogs that dangered her." This use of *dangered* is a good example of Kiersten applying what she knows about language. She has heard words such as *danger, dangerous,* or perhaps *endangered.* Now she invents a verb to describe the story's meaning.

Eventually, after repeated read-alouds of their favorite book, preschoolers begin to tell the story in a way that more closely approximates the text of the book. These retellings often include some verbatim phrases from the story, as in 4-year-old Jonise's rendition of the Beatrix Potter classic *The Tale of Peter Rabbit:*

Text of the book	Retelling by Jonise
Once upon a time there were four little Rabbits, and their names were— Flopsy, Mopsy, Cotton-tail, and Peter.	Once 'pon a time there were Flopsy, Mopsy, and Peter Cottontail.
"Now, my dears," said old Mrs. Rabbit one morning, "you may go into the fields or down the lane, but don't go into Mr. McGregor's garden. . . . Now run along, and don't get into mischief. I am going out."	Mrs. Rabbit said, "Go an' play but don't go to old Mr. Gregor's garden." An' she left.
Then old Mrs. Rabbit took a basket and her umbrella, and went through the wood to the baker's. . . .	Mrs. Rabbit left with her basket to go shoppin'.
Flopsy, Mopsy, and Cotton-tail, who were good little bunnies, went down the lane to gather blackberries.	The three good rabbits went to get blackberries for dinner.
But Peter, who was very naughty, ran straight away to Mr. McGregor's garden, and squeezed under the gate! . . .	But Peter went to Mr. Gregor's garden under the gate. . . .
Peter got down very quietly off the wheelbarrow, and started running as fast as he could go. . . . He slipped underneath the gate, and was safe at last in the wood outside the garden.	Peter squished under the gate and escaped. (*Jonise pronounces this word as "x-scaped"*)
Mr. McGregor hung up the little jacket and the shoes for a scare-crow to frighten the blackbirds.	The scarecrow wore the jacket an' shoes.
Peter never stopped running or looked behind him till he got home to the big fir-tree. He was so tired that he flopped down upon the nice soft sand on the floor of the	Peter got home and flopped down on the floor. Mrs. Rabbit was cookin' when Peter came home an' wondered where his clothes were.

rabbit-hole and shut his eyes. His mother was busy cooking; she wondered what he had done with his clothes. . . .	
I am sorry to say that Peter was not very well during the evening. His mother put him to bed, and made some camomile tea; and she gave a dose of it to Peter! . . .	Peter's mom made some cammy tea 'cause he didn't feel well.
But Flopsy, Mopsy, and Cotton-tail had bread and milk and blackberries for supper.	Flopsy, Mopsy, and Peter Cotton-tail had a good supper.

Book text from *The Tale of Peter Rabbit* by Beatrix Potter, copyright © 1902 Frederick Warne & Co., reproduced by permission of Frederick Warne & Co.

Neuroscience suggests that each learning experience prepares the mind for future learning and that repeated exposure to a thought, idea, or experience enhances memory and recall (Diamond & Hopson 1998). Returning to the identical text again and again enables children to glimpse the structure of language—and of the story itself—to build a foundation for subsequent experiences. Repeated readings of the same story give young children an opportunity not only to bring their experience to the book but also to regard the book itself as an experience. The drawings opposite are examples of picture books captivating children and prompting them to draw their favorite characters.

Deciphering print with predictable books

The next stage in learning to read is to focus on deciphering print. Here again, picture books play a valuable role. Predictable books make it easier for children to guess what the words will say next, thus enabling them to gain a sense of accomplishment as more independent readers. Predictable books usually provide support to new readers by capitalizing on their prior knowledge (e.g., days of the week, ordinal numbers, lyrics of a familiar song) and by using repetition, rhyming patterns, or both (e.g., a refrain, a predictable question-and-answer structure) to help children correctly guess the words. In addition, using predictable books with groups of preschoolers and children in the primary grades approximates the lap reading experiences that many children have had at home. Whether the child is relying mostly on memory, mostly on illustrations, or actively trying to decode text, a predictable book can accommodate the child's needs.

Julia, a librarian working with a family literacy program in her community, is reading the book *From Head to Toe* (Carle) to a group of young children ranging from toddlers to third-graders. As she holds the book up, a preschooler calls out, "We read this one before!" In this story, which has a format similar to *Brown Bear, Brown Bear, What Do You See?* (Martin), each page introduces a new

Two 5-year-olds' drawings of their favorite story characters from *Mr. Rabbit and the Lovely Present* (Zolotow) right, and *The Polar Express* (Van Allsburg) below.

animal that demonstrates some physical ability ("I am ___ and I ___"), then asks the children, "Can you do it?" to which they are to respond in unison, "I can do it!" as they imitate the action. As Julia introduces each page, she sets the children's expectations for performing the corresponding actions:

Julia: Now, be very careful with this one.

Book text: *I am a donkey and I kick my legs. Can you do it?*

Children: I can do it!

Julia: I know that you know how to do this one . . .

Book text: *I am an elephant and I stomp my foot. Can you do it?*

Children: I can do it!

Julia: You can do this one while you are still sitting down.

Book text: *I am I and I wiggle my toe. Can you do it?*

Children: I can do it! I can do it!

A kindergarten teacher who observed this read-aloud session decided to use this same predictable book to teach reading. She began by showing the cover of the book and asked the kindergartners why a book might be called "from head to toe." When the teacher said that Eric Carle was the author and illustrator, some of the children recognized his artistic style. The teacher wrote "Eric Carle" on the board and let the children know they were going to be making a bulletin board together about him, using color copies of the covers of his books and information about him from the Internet.

Next, the teacher walked the children through all of the illustrations so they would be better able to predict what the printed words might say. She put a sentence strip up on the wall that read:

I am a ____ and I ____. Can you do it?
I can do it!

After she and the children read it together, the teacher provided the children with a "wild and crazy pointer" that they could use to lead their classmates through the words. The teacher had taken a glove, stuffed it with polyester fiber, attached it to a dowel rod, and put a big, gaudy ring on the index finger (with the other fingers stitched down to the palm). The children loved having a turn to use the pointer and leading their classmates through reading the text in unison.

Then the teacher posted a clip-art picture of each animal from the book and the word that described the physical activity each one demonstrated (e.g., a picture of a donkey and the phrase "kick my legs"). She mixed up the cards and animal pictures on the floor in front of the semicircle of children and had them take turns matching the phrase to the animal. They sounded out the words on the card together if a child faltered, but everyone was getting needed practice. She explained to the children that these picture-and-phrase pairs would become a matching game for them to play later on, and that corresponding stickers on the back of the cards would enable them to check their work.

Because *From Head to Toe* is predictable and the teacher has drawn the children's attention to the pattern, it offers a special form of support for readers

Mary Renck Jalongo

who are just learning how to figure out words. The children have practiced each animal's name and action, and if they get confused, the pictures in the book offer clues. By the second reading of the book, virtually all of the children are able to join in and gain a sense of fluency with the text that simulates that of more accomplished readers. Even those children in the class who are just learning English have a positive experience, because they can hear and see a picture book read aloud.

As a follow-up to the book, the teacher suggested that they make their own Big Book version of *From Head to Toe,* and the children decided to make a book about the animals at their school—a guinea pig that could whistle, a goldfish that could swim, a rabbit that could hop, and a therapy dog that could roll over.

For additional predictable books, see www.monroe.lib.in.us/childrens/children_booklists.html or other websites listed in Appendix B.

An apprenticeship toward comprehension

In a classroom setting, teachers often rely on poster-size Big Books for initial reading instruction. Many Big Books are also predictable books, and they can be useful as part of the *shared book experience* technique to teach reading. A teacher using the technique follows this general sequence:

• Introduction
   — Selects a book with repetition, rhyme, simple plot, predictable text, or some combination of these elements.
   — Familiarizes children with the book, using the book itself, a story chart of the plot, or appropriate visual aids.
   — Discusses pictures; asks and answers questions.

• Practice
   — Reads the book twice at one sitting, asking children to join in wherever possible.
   — Reads the book in unison, encouraging children to participate at their own level.
   — Teaches skills as children inquire about them.

• Extension
   — Incorporates other activities such as dramatizing; listening to audio-tapes; having children read in pairs or small groups; and having children dictate, illustrate, and read their own stories.

• Independence
   — Encourages children to read the book to a partner or partners.
   — Gives children small paperback copies to read.
   — Allows children to select other predictable books to read.

Consider for a moment some of the advantages of the shared book experience. First, it involves books that grab children's attention with oversize pages that enable children to see the pictures and the print more easily. Its process encourages children to join in, and allows each child to participate at his or her own level. The shared book experience is an enjoyable activity that provides needed practice in emergent and early reading skills. In addition, it uses high-quality illustrations and text as reading material. And finally, the interactions it promotes give children the experience of feeling like they are becoming success-ful readers. For more details on the shared book experience, see Slaughter (1993).

Fisher (2002) summarizes the benefits of shared reading as follows:

> Shared reading gives children the chance to "read" texts that they would not normally be able to read independently. The teacher, as the expert, reads a text that is beyond most children's ability to read independently. Either by supplying the more difficult words, sustaining interest by use of intonation, or enhancing comprehension through careful questioning, the teacher leads the less experienced reader into the world of texts at a level in advance of what they could do on their own. (42)

Picture books also offer support as readers gain independence and begin to read "all by themselves." A common misconception is that if children can sound out words, then they have learned to read. Actually, reading entails much more than such "word calling." Reading is all about making sense out of print, not merely parroting sounds and words. As Gallas (1997) points out,

> To really read a text, read it with understanding and insight, we must move inside of the text, pulling our lives along with us and incorporating the text and our lives into a new understanding of the world. Anything less is not a complete and informed reading. (252)

Thus, learning to read is the process through which one brings meaning to a text in order to get meaning from it (Weaver 1994). The moment that this *compre-hension* is lost, reading has ceased to occur (Smith 1997). Reading comprehension is the last outgrowth of a child's long apprenticeship in working with words, not the instant result of decoding them. In fact, literacy has been defined as "the ability and the willingness to use reading and writing to construct meaning from printed text, in ways which meet the requirements of a particular social context" (Au 1993, 20).

How does a child's apprenticeship with picture books support independent reading and comprehension of text? First of all, as children gain experience with books, they begin to understand three timeless questions of literature, as identi-fied by Rebecca Lukens (2003):

• What are people like?

• What do they need?

• Why do they do what they do?

Portraying human motives and foibles is one of the things that picture books do best. We know from child development research that children initially focus predominantly on appearance when predicting characters' behavior in narratives (Peskin & Olson 1997). Gradually children begin to understand that the mind is all about interpretation and representation and that our perceptions are sometimes wrong (Pelletier 1997). Szarkowicz (2000) conducted research on this using the book *Harry the Dirty Dog* (Zion). In the story, the white dog with black spots becomes so dirty that his owners do not recognize Harry as their pet. Unless children understand the concept of "misunderstanding"—in other words, realize that the characters can hold a false belief—they miss the point of the story. To study children's comprehension of this concept, the researcher posed the following questions:

- What color was Harry?
- Who do the family think this dog is?
- Who is this dog really?
- Who do the family think this is?
- Who is it really?
- Who do the children think they are giving a bath to?
- Who are they really giving a bath to?

Szarkowicz concluded:

> Children gain greater meaning of mentality in a story if they are supported during sharing by more experienced individuals. These individuals are able to help children "unpack" the text by defining internal state language and providing additional information about the mentality in the story. . . . For those who share literature with young children, these results reinforce the need to be interactive with children when sharing stories. Young children's thinking needs to be scaffolded during sharing to ensure that the mental states of characters are made explicit and coherent. Without support from more experienced individuals, young children may find it difficult to associate the mentality of the characters with their actions and, hence, may not access the meaning from a story that is assumed by adults. (2000, 79–80)

Evidently, one way in which young children develop an understanding of the mind is through their apprenticeship relationship with more-literate adults (Lewis et al. 1996).

Because one route of access to reading comprehension involves constructing understandings of picture books, children barraged by phonics, skills, and drill in the absence of that apprenticeship often experience a precipitous drop in comprehension. In fact, the phenomenon in which children who seemed to be progressing adequately in reading suddenly begin to falter is so commonplace that it has a name—"fourth grade slump." Suddenly the children who could circle the right picture and sound out the words experience failure and frustration as they attempt to "unpack" the meaning in texts, no doubt because they have had very few experiences with doing so (Block, Gambrell, & Pressley 2002; Snow 2002; Snow, Burns, & Griffin 1998). Their comprehension crumbles under the weight of content-area reading in mathematics, science, health, social studies, and so forth, around the fourth grade, where the expectations for understanding escalate and texts become increasingly complex.

Clearly, picture books, both fiction and nonfiction, are an important way to prepare young children for what lies ahead. Children are building reading comprehension when they:

- Understand what is read aloud to them
- Ask questions about stories and information books

- Learn to make inferences and "read between the lines"
- Recall details about the story or information
- Make predictions about the story or information
- Connect book information with their lives
- Notice similarities and differences between this book and other books

We know that different patterns of brain activity are associated with differences in reading ability (Olson & Gayan 2001). Scarborough's (2001) visual model of skilled reading plaits five different strands of language comprehension abilities (background knowledge, vocabulary, language structures, verbal reasoning, literacy knowledge) with three types of word recognition strategies (phonological awareness, decoding, sight recognition). This model asserts that to attain skilled reading, defined as "fluent execution and coordination of word recognition and text comprehension" (98), a child needs to orchestrate all of these skills in increasingly automatic and strategic ways.

Controlled vocabulary books, called *easy readers,* are another form of support for the budding reader. Easy reader books rely on high-frequency words (i.e., words such as *the, in,* and *a* that appear often in print), sight words (i.e., words such as *stop* and *no* that children recognize on sight), and words that are easy to decode (i.e., words that follow the general rules of phonics, and families of words that can be formed by changing the initial consonants for *-an, -un, -ate).* This control can support children who are just learning how to orchestrate the different demands of fluent reading.

Not all easy readers are created equal, however. The best books for budding readers have some combination of the following elements (Mitchell 2003):

- Uncomplicated pictures
- Humorous or delightful touches
- Solid themes of interest to children
- Short sentences and repeated words
- Rhyme and rhythm
- Alliteration and plays on words
- Frequent use of dialogue
- Grouping of words in meaningful sets
- Informative illustrations
- Animals as characters

Conclusion: How picture books build readers

Suppose that we wanted to "build a reader." What abilities, identified through research on emergent and early reading, would we use as a foundation? Research suggests that a number of abilities are predictive of a child's later success in reading, and opportunities to interact with picture books can support them all:

- Identifies and/or writes own name and other familiar names (Bloodgood 1999)

— *Supported through picture books:* Children's personal copies of books are marked with their names to show ownership.

— *Example:* A 3-year-old says, "My aunt got me this book *Minerva Louise* [Stoeke] for my birthday and she writed my name on it. See, here's a B. She writed her name too, right here."

• Identifies and/or writes some letters (Snow, Burns, & Griffin 1998)

— *Supported through picture books:* Children notice letters of the alphabet that correspond to those they have learned.

— *Example:* A 5-year-old listening to *Arf! Beg! Catch!: Dogs from A to Z* (Horenstein) sings "The Alphabet Song" as each letter is named.

• Understands some concepts about print (Clay 1985; Yaden et al. 2000)

— *Supported through picture books:* Children understand that print means something and that it often corresponds to what is pictured in a book.

— *Example:* A 4-year-old hears the book *The Grouchy Ladybug* (Carle) and at a later time looks at the cover and says, "This says 'grouchy ladybug'."

• Retells stories with a well-formed narrative structure (Morrow 2001)

— *Supported through picture books:* Children are presented with well-crafted stories to retell or adapt, creating original, new versions.

— *Example:* A kindergartner recalls her experience with Sue Williams's book *I Went Walking* and says, "We wrote a story like that, only our book had stuff you see at school, not stuff you see at a farm."

• Possesses a large and varied vocabulary (Dickinson & Tabors 2001)

— *Supported through picture books:* Children experience language that is decidedly different from everyday conversation.

— *Example:* A child hears *The Maggie B* (Haas) and asks, "What does 'good company' mean?"

• Demonstrates phonological awareness (Goswami 2001; Pullen & Justice 2003)

— *Supported through picture books:* Children attend to and recognize sounds and sound patterns in language, the core of phonological awareness (McGee & Richgels 2003).

— *Example:* A child hears the book *Hairy Maclary from Donaldson's Dairy* (Dodd) and comments, "This book has words in it that when you say them they sound alike, only different."

• Produces extended decontextualized language

— *Supported through picture books:* Children are motivated to relate past experiences, talk about a dream they had, or invent a new story, all of which represent decontextualized language, or description that occurs without the support of the immediate situation or another speaker (Dickinson & Smith 1994).

— *Example:* A 4-year-old listens to *Babies on the Go* (Dyer) and responds, "When my baby brother came, I got a T-shirt that said 'Big Brother' on it to wear to the hospital."

Debating whether an emergent reading program's emphasis should be on phonics or on meaningful interactions with literature is less productive than is considering the two as interdependent and complementary aspects of a balanced reading program (Au 1997; McGee 2003).

Effective teachers know how to make reading aloud an experience that will entice the young listener to want to become a reader and writer. Becky Rager, a child care provider, describes how a 4-year-old boy in her class who is learning to recognize and write letters of the alphabet became fascinated by the format of the book *Bunny Cakes* by Rosemary Wells. In this story, bossy big sister Ruby is intent upon baking an angel surprise cake with raspberry-fluff icing for Grandma's birthday. Little brother Max has a very different idea: He is going to make an earthworm cake and top it with red-hot marshmallow squirters. As each of various kitchen disasters occurs, Ruby sends her sibling to the store with a list on which she has neatly printed the name of the needed item. Max adds his scribble to the list, hoping that the grocer will be able to read it, but only big sister's legible writing works. Finally, Max draws a picture and succeeds in getting his candy garnish. The story concludes with a presentation of both bunny cakes to Grandma, and she is equally delighted by her grandchildren's creations.

This picture book subtly, yet effectively, gets the message across that the purpose of writing is to communicate. As Rager explains in her journal, she adjusted her sharing of the book to the child's curiosity about letters and words:

> Today I read 4-year-old Tony *Bunny Cakes* by Rosemary Wells. On each page there is a word written as it would look on a shopping list. Tony was very interested in these words. I asked what it said and he pointed to each letter with me as I said the letter. Then he repeated the letter after me, and then we would say the whole word together. He seemed to understand that words are arranged from left to right as we pointed to the letter of each word. If I did not point to each word as I read it, he would try to turn the page too soon. Tony seemed to be relying on this word-by-word reading to cue him about the exact moment to move on to the next page. (provided by Rebecca A. Rager)

As this example illustrates and this chapter has argued, experiences with high-quality picture books make a significant contribution to emergent and early literacy as they motivate, build comprehension, teach language skills, and engage children in the literacy events that build confidence and competence (Owocki 2003). Experiences with children's literature also offer something more, in that they provide children with the cultural tools they need:

> If education is aiming for lifelong literacy, in which the passion to read and write flourishes and grows in complexity, children need to see how the language arts enable them not merely to make marks but to make *their* mark. Early childhood educators and families witness this drive in children from the earliest days of life. We see it in the infant's cries and smiles that urge others to respond appropriately, the toddler's attraction to words that invite ("Hi") or control ("No!") social interaction, the kindergartner's pride at producing a drawing of her family labeled with their names, and the excitement of children in the primary grades as they discuss their journal writing entries with peers.

Max wanted Red-Hot Marshmallow Squirters for his earthworm cake. So he wrote "Red-Hot Marshmallow Squirters" on the list.

From *Bunny Cakes* by Rosemary Wells, copyright © 1997 by Rosemary Wells. Used by permission of Dial Books for Young Readers, A Division of Penguin Young Readers Group, A Member of Penguin Group (USA) Inc., 345 Hudson Street, New York, NY 10014. All rights reserved.

Such observations remind us that literacy is about having a voice, engaging in dialogue, and forging an identity. In a society struggling to fulfill the promises of democracy, the literacy learning set in motion during early childhood and amassed throughout a lifetime is worthwhile only if it leads to power—the power to influence people and society in ways that render them more compassionate, effective, and just. (Jalongo, Fennimore, & Stamp 2004, 82)

Families and Picture Books

My biggest regret was that I waited so long to understand that I had it in my power to make school like a family, a place where you enjoy the casual intrusion of those who are learning to love each other. . . . We keep the families out (of schools), and there is no reason to. Our jobs as educators are better when everyone is involved. We are on the wrong track if we feel we can educate children without the families.
—Vivian Paley, quoted in Sheerer (1998, 5)

A professor specializing in early childhood education is invited to speak to families of preschoolers who have enrolled in the local family literacy program. Rather than give a speech, she arranges to have six preschoolers listen to and discuss a picture book while the parents observe. The picture book the professor chooses is *Whose Mouse Are You?* (Kraus), converted into a big, poster-size version suitable for group sharing. The story is about a mouse family that is separated, then happily reunited. At first, the families of the children seem a bit uneasy as the little mouse reports that he is "nobody's mouse" because his father is inside the cat, his mother is caught in a trap, his sister is far from home, and his little brother—well, he has none. But the mood brightens quickly when Jose Aruego's illustrations humorously depict the brave little mouse saying how he will shake his father out of the cat! Free his mother from the trap! Find his sister and bring her home! And, meet his baby brother—he's brand new.

Why had the presenter chosen to share this picture book with the children and families? First, to demonstrate how to read and talk about a book with young children. Second, to show that children's literature can be surprising and entertaining. Third, to exemplify that picture books can deal deftly with very serious topics, such as the young child's fear of separation and abandonment. And fourth, to spark family interest in attending a Saturday workshop called "Reading to Your Young Child: Why and How."

Research Findings on the Influence of Families

Here's a sample of key findings:

• Of all the influences on children's language growth, the type of language environment that parents and families provide in the home is the most powerful (Educational Research Service 1998).

• Parents' attitudes toward education, their aspirations for children, the language models they provide, the literacy materials they supply, and the activities they encourage all make a substantial contribution to children's language development (Auerbach 1995a/b; Berger 1998; Macleod 1996; Mavrogenes 1990).

• A family's influence on literacy is deeply embedded in family life. Families influence literacy development through interpersonal interactions related to literacy; the physical environment and literacy materials in the home; and attitudes toward literacy, which affect emotions and motivation (Braunger & Lewis 1998).

• Enriched environments actually exert a positive developmental effect on the neural pathways in the brain (Diamond & Hopson 1998).

• Print-rich environments that include picture books, paper, and writing tools—all readily accessible to children and in frequent use—provide the best contexts for literacy learning (Matthias & Gulley 1995; Morrow 1995; Mulhern 1997; Neuman & Roskos 1998). "Print-rich" does not mean expensive or elaborate, however. It can include books borrowed from the library, recycled paper, and simple writing implements such as pencils and crayons.

• In typical homes that support young children's literacy, family members often practically trip over literacy materials because these items are in continuous use by children and adults (Taylor 1983).

• Types of family activities at home consistently associated with increases in school performance are: organizing and monitoring the child's time, helping with homework, discussing school matters with the child, and reading with young children (Finn 1998).

• A study involving several hundred parents who documented their 2-year-olds' vocabularies found that the range was enormous. Some parents reported their toddlers knowing as few as 50 and others as many as 550 words (Fenson et al. 1994). Reading aloud is a major influence on vocabulary development (Becher 1985).

• Preschool children from homes where literacy is supported have 1,000 to 1,700 hours of informal reading and writing encounters before coming to school, whereas children without similar family support have only 25 hours of these experiences during the preschool years (Adams 1990). Most children who have difficulties learning to read have been read to one-tenth as much as have those who are the most successful (Adams 1990).

• Activities that support literacy learning at home are: children observing family members who are reading and writing to accomplish important tasks; children interacting with parents, extended family, or community members in activities that include emergent reading and writing; and children engaging in literacy activities of their own choosing (Purcell-Gates 1996).

• Older students who improve the fastest in reading have read almost 50 times as much each year as those who progress slowly (Anderson, Wilson, & Fielding 1988).

The range of support services that a family literacy program provides is essential when one or more factors are making family support of children's growth in literacy a struggle. Perhaps the parents are English-language learners themselves. Or the family may be living in poverty. They may have completely different ideas about how children acquire literacy. Or key family members may think it is the teacher's job—not theirs—to motivate their child to read.

The Family Literacy Commission of the International Reading Association (www.reading.org) defines *family literacy program*, first of all, as a constellation of services involving more than one generation. The focus is on how parents, children, and extended family members use literacy at home and in the community. The National Center for Family Literacy (www.famlit.org) distinguishes family literacy services from typical *parent involvement activities*, in that family literacy services are more comprehensive. They are of sufficient duration to make sustainable changes in families. And family literacy programs not only enhance the child's opportunities to become literate but also educate families about assuming a more active role in the education of their children, support families' growth in literacy, and provide adults with training that leads to greater economic self-sufficiency. Family literacy projects that include developing the literacy skills of the adults in a family provide evidence that such a more holistic, total family approach to literacy is effective (Swick et al. 1998).

Whether the family needs additional support or whether they appear to be very skilled at fostering high levels of literacy in their children, one thing is certain: Families and communities exert a powerful influence on the course of children's lives as learners of language. The box **Research Findings on the Influence of Families** documents just how powerfully.

Young children learn more from the example that adults model than from verbal directions. One illustration of how books set the stage for reading is how young children attempt to imitate the adult readers they see. From 3½-year-old Scott's attempts to read *Marvin K. Mooney, Will You Please Go Now!*, a Dr. Seuss book he loves, we can infer that he has a sense of how the story goes; has heard this book read aloud many times; is trying to make sense of what he sees in the pictures and recalls of the words; is acquiring the abilities that will lead to reading; and is working hard, yet having fun, as he strives to offer an animated and fluent rendition of the story:

Text of the book	Retelling by Scott
"The time has come. The time is now."	It is time now!
"Just go. Go. GO! I don't care how."	GO! GO! GO! GO! I don't care. GO! GO!
"You can go by foot. You can go by cow. Marvin K. Mooney, will you please go now!"	Go by foot. Go by cow. Marbin K., GO!
"You can go on skates. You can go on skis."	GO by skateys or go . . . go . . . use skis.

"You can go in a hat. But please go. Please!" . . .	Go in a hat. A HAT that's silly!! GO! PLEASE GO!!!
"You can go in a Crunk-Car if you wish." . . .	Go in a clunk car.
"Or stamp yourself and go by mail. Marvin K. Mooney! Don't you know the time has come to go, Go, GO!"	Go in the mailman, Marbin K. K. . . . Time to go, GO! GO!!
"Get on your way! Please, Marvin K.! You might like going in a Zumble-Zay."	Go, Marbin K.! Go in a Bumbley Way!
"You can go by balloon or broomstick. OR you can go by camel in a bureau drawer." . . .	You can go by bullon or boomstick like witches!
"Get yourself a Ga-Zoom. You can go with a BOOM! Marvin, Marvin, Marvin! Will you leave this room!" . . .	Go with a BOOM BOOM! Marbin, Marbin, get outa da room!
"Marvin K. Mooney! Will you please GO NOW!"	Marbin K., GO NOW, GO NOW! GO! GO! GO!
"I said GO and GO I meant."	I said GO, GO, GO!!
The time had come. So Marvin WENT.	Time came so Marbin left! THE END!

From *Marvin K. Mooney, Will You Please Go Now!* by Dr. Seuss. Copyright © 1972 by Dr. Seuss and A.S. Geisel. Reprinted by permission of the publisher, Random House. All rights reserved.

As Scott's apparent interest in books, his motivation to "break the code," and his efforts to emulate adult reading behavior illustrate, early experiences with picture books pave the way for independent reading to occur.

> Studies have shown that those who have been read to from an early age have a far greater chance of becoming proficient readers themselves. Once children learn to read, they become better readers primarily by doing a vast amount of reading at an appropriate level of difficulty. These two statements summarize much of the research on literacy learning over the past century. However, discovering these "literacy truths" has not yet led to literacy for all. (Jennings 2001, 474)

Barriers to literacy for all

What are the major obstacles to literacy for all? At least three are apparent: access to high-quality materials, differences in home and school ideologies, and the effect of adult expectations on children.

Access to high-quality picture books

One of the motivations to read arises from having materials that are worth reading. Numerous studies have documented that all American children do not have equal access to high-quality literature, either at home or at school (Neuman & Celano 2001a). In a study of low-income families, for example, only 40 percent of the children younger than 5 years of age owned 10 or more books, and just 39 percent of the families mentioned reading as a favorite activity or reported sharing books at bedtime (High et al. 2000). Of course, the public library also is an important source of high-quality picture books. However, teachers and librarians need to be aware of the deterrents to library use that may exist for some families.

Evidently, even fairly simple interventions can encourage many families to support their children's acquisition of literacy. One study of Hispanic parents found that when pediatricians, during well-child medical check-ups, provided families with picture books, suggestions for sharing books with toddlers, and encouragement to read aloud at home, the parents were 10 times more likely than a control group was to read books with their children at least three days a week. Other studies of brief interventions have arrived at a similar conclusion. Whatever it takes, getting good books in children's hands and homes can reap remarkable benefits (Gregory & Morrison 1998; Sharif et al. 2003).

What Can Deter Families from Using the Library?

Worry over the expense of late fines or the child damaging or losing a book and having to replace it—which may be a hardship for families with financial difficulties.

Lack of familiarity with the policies of the library—which may be particularly true for families who come from countries without public library systems and who do not understand that services here typically are free of charge.

Requirement to show identification for a library card—which may be particularly threatening for families with immigration status issues.

Misconceptions about library services—assuming, for instance, that the library's collection is limited to books only and is intended for independent readers only. Such misunderstandings may cause families to overlook materials and services that would be ideal for their child, for example, books on tape for vision-impaired children, storytime sessions for toddlers and preschoolers, books written in English and in Spanish, captioned videos of favorite picture books, and activities to promote reading during the summer months.

Lack of transportation or limited hours of operation—which may be a major issue for working families in rural areas that have small community libraries with inadequate staffing or in areas that have only bookmobile services.

Service fees for patrons outside a library's community—which may be prohibitive for low-income families without a library in their own community.

Adapted from Jalongo, Fennimore, & Stamp (2004) and Margolis (2001).

Differences in home and school ideologies

As society changes, the definition of "family" changes too. As families change, so do the roles and responsibilities that parents and other family members perform (Kagan & Weissbourd 1994). The family is a remarkably adaptable human institution,

> able to modify its characteristics to meet those of the society in which it lives. . . . Rather than suggest that the family is under siege, it is more accurate to suggest . . . that our image of family may need to be broadened to accept diversity. It may be more important to concentrate on what families do, rather than what they look like. Family may be more about content than about form. (Gestwicki 2000, 3, 5)

Of course, the content of families also is shaped by *culture*, "the customs, practices, and traditions that characterize, distinguish, and give stability to a group . . . knowledge of shared norms and rules" (Bullough & Gitlin 2001, 112).

Sometimes we teachers are surprised by the diversity among families, that all parents or other family members may not be eager to have their child cared for outside the home or are not entirely convinced of the value of early childhood education (Schwartz 1996). We also sometimes forget how variously defined "family" and the roles of its members in raising a child can be (Copple 2002). Clearly, "there are differences in values and beliefs about the role of teachers, literacy, education, and schools held by parents" (Ernst-Slavit, Han, & Wenger 2001, 200). These differences are reflected in at least three dimensions of the family literacy environment (Britto 2001):

• Language and verbal interactions—the language children are exposed to in the home (Garcia 2003)

• Learning climate—access to printed material and support for learning in the home

• Social and emotional climate—interaction, play, and support between adults and children

Rather than criticize or judge families for failing to read aloud to young children at home, we need instead to systematically address the factors that influence whether or not they do so: the family's educational beliefs, its views of the purposes for reading, its approaches to sharing literature (e.g., didactic versus interactive), and its individual members' personal experiences with literacy, both as adults and during childhood (Bus 2001). In one project to promote reading at home, for example, one set of newly immigrated parents required their child to painstakingly copy the entire text of a picture book that was sent home because, in keeping with their own experience of rote learning, copying was the way to support a child's literacy development. Families in the project also thought the teacher was failing to perform her duties when they were asked to work at home with their children on reading.

Conflicting viewpoints on the importance of literacy and on the best ways to develop it in young children often interfere with effective home-school collaboration that is intended to support literacy. To best serve families of various ethnic backgrounds, schools must gain insights into those families' particular cultures (Hidalgo et al. 1995).

Promoting Reading Aloud in Diverse Families

Below are key issues to consider, and some suggested strategies.

Show respect for language differences. Accept that children are members of diverse family and community systems and that they bring multiple gifts of language, culture, and wisdom (McCarthey 1999). Set aside negative myths and common misconceptions you may hold. Assure the child and family that their native language and culture are valued (Garcia 2003). Realize that bilingualism is more about culture than about language. Hundreds of different patterns of language use exist (e.g., a language spoken either by virtually no one else in the community or by practically everyone; one language used during worship, another for school, and yet another for family interaction). Become better informed about children's and families' language use. Suggestions:

• If at all possible, communicate in the family's first language. Investigate websites and e-mail services available in the family's first language or that will translate for you.

• Check out the ¡Colorín colorado! website (www.colorincolorado.org), produced by Reading Rockets, a service of the public broadcasting station WETA in Washington, DC, with funding from a U.S. Department of Education grant. It provides a wealth of information in English and in Spanish about supporting young children's reading at home. The artwork on the website is by Caldecott Award–winning illustrator David Diaz.

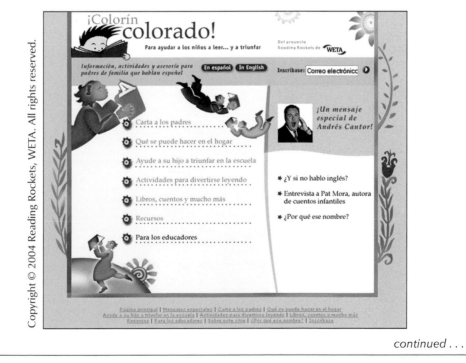

continued . . .

Promoting Reading Aloud, continued

• Work with community volunteers and older students to create listening and reading materials in the child's home language. Wordless picture books often can be used as the basis for stories in the child's first language. Families who are not accustomed to reading aloud may also respond favorably to the suggestion of using drawings or photographs as the basis for a story about their child and her or his activities.

• Consider a bookworm program staffed by senior citizens, secondary students, family members, and community members who can read aloud, share a talent related to a book theme, help assemble and keep track of book packs, staff a toy book lending library, or talk with children about the books they have read.

• For more "family friendly" ideas on working with families, see the U.S. government publications by Benjamin & Lord (1996), Fuller (1998), Funkhouser & Gonzales (1997), and Moles (1996).

Offer comprehensive services. Take a family literacy approach and provide English classes for families so they can participate more directly in literacy learning and see its positive effects. Endorse policies that address the needs of young, diverse language learners. Whenever possible, make services and information available at convenient times and places. Take the information to where the families are: workplaces, banks, malls, laundromats, stores. Realize that just because parents are polite and deferential toward school personnel does not mean that trust has been built (Hidalgo et al. 1995). Suggestions:

• Explore all of the resources that are available to get picture books into children's hands and homes. Be an advocate and use authoritative information to persuade those organizations and leaders who are capable of addressing young children's needs to become involved in supporting early literacy initiatives. Motivate local businesses to "adopt" a school or center, to disseminate reminders or tips on how adults can promote literacy (e.g., print a new tip on each week's pay stub), to donate funds or materials to the school, and to volunteer time at literacy events.

• Even if you cannot replicate a program such as Project EASE's Reading Circles project (Brooker 1997), you can study its key components (opportunities for storytelling and sharing books, parents teaching parents, a parent library, bookmaking activities, prepackaged literacy programs, training for parents about assisting their children with projects—including computer training for parents) and adapt those components for use in your setting.

Mary Renck Jalongo

Conduct an online search of professional journals and magazines to locate descriptions of how successful projects with families such as the National Network of Partnership Schools (Sanders 1999) were planned, carried out, and evaluated.

• Family journals that contain entries from both teachers and families are one way to foster family communication; children are able to borrow books to read at home with their families, and the family journals are used to communicate and write about what was read (Harding 1996).

• For additional recommended activities, see Bouchard (2001) and Eihorn (2001).

Create literacy environments that reflect diversity. Give children authentic, integrated opportunities to participate in a vital learning community (Soto, Smrekar, & Nekcovei 2001). Develop a sound philosophy of working with English-language learners (Cary 2000; Obiakor & Algozzine 2001). Accept errors as a normal part of language development and help families to accept them too (Soto, Smrekar, & Nekcovei 2001). Suggestions:

• Collect evidence of the child's language use both in the native language and in English. Report these findings in ways that can be shared with families during conferences. Invite parents and families to write encouraging comments about the children's early reading and writing efforts.

• Consider sponsoring a book fair that includes storytelling, author talks, puppet shows, games with a children's literature theme, and musical performances. During the event, invite children to dress as their favorite storybook characters. Adults who work at the booths also can dress in character.

• Hold a Breakfast with Books where children and families attend early in the morning before school begins. The children and caregivers eat breakfast together as well as read and discuss books. Have an "author's tea" to celebrate the publication of the children's own works—books to which each child contributed one page, Big Books designed by kindergartners or first-graders, or hardcover books created by children in the primary grades.

• Organize a book exchange. By pooling resources in the community, families can exchange books that are no longer at the child's reading or interest level for books that are. Some sources for books include the following: discards from the public library that are still usable, books that would otherwise be sold at a garage sale, books that just did not appeal to a particular child, and free books that teachers get from book clubs as dividends.

Compiled with Natalie K. Conrad, doctoral candidate, Indiana University of Pennsylvania.

Adult expectations about outcomes

Families' and teachers' expectations affect children's achievement. Family members with low expectations may be assuming that because they experienced difficulty with learning to read, their children will too. Or families may look around them and be demoralized to see that for many, literacy's promise has not been fulfilled; that for many, successfully learning to read and write did not bring the promised jobs or opportunities for advancement or fair treatment in society. Furthermore, some of what passes for literacy teaching in school appears to be—and is—irrelevant to the lives of children and their families.

The history of formal literacy instruction in the United States is replete with examples of literacy teaching that failed to live up to the nation's democratic ideals. First, there were the McGuffey Readers of the 1800s, filled with heavy-handed preaching and reserved for those children who were permitted to attend school and whose families could afford to lose them as workers. In the 1950s, generations of children were taught to read using the fair-haired, blue-eyed, neatly attired trio of Sally, Dick, and Jane whose strange way of talking ("Look, Sally. Look. See Spot run.") and their perfect home and family made nearly everyone else's seem sorely lacking. Such examples illustrate that language learning is about who has power and who does not—the power to influence what goes into the books, the power to decide who is warmly welcomed into the world of reading, and the power to decide what "counts" as having attained literacy.

It is beyond obvious that learning to read and write effectively remains a desirable outcome of schooling. But a larger question has become, to what end? From a *critical literacy* perspective, attaining literacy is a worthwhile task only if it enables the person to participate more fully in life and work. Literacy advocate Paulo Freire (1987) sees literacy as a cultural tool; therefore, literacy is political, it is all about power. He argues persuasively that literacy is about reading the *world*, not merely reading the *words*. From a critical literacy perspective, a sterile curriculum that emphasizes decoding skills, for example, is powerless to promote social justice.

While there is compelling evidence that skills such as decoding strategies and phonological awareness are essential to learning to read (e.g., see Snow, Burns, & Griffin 1998), they are not sufficient to turn children into enthusiastic and able readers. Families play a critical role in promoting reading. Until families see literacy as leading to power and economic stability, they will not fully buy into the message being sold in schools—that literacy is a key to a better life.

For literacy to have value, children must use reading and writing to accomplish tasks that have personal significance for them and their families. This is one reason that early childhood educators need on-the-job training in connecting with families of varying races, languages, and cultures and in taking into account what matters to those families. Teachers also need to learn strategies for furthering cross-cultural communication (e.g., effective use of translators) and assessment strategies suited to diverse children and families (Schwartz 1996).

For our part, when we teachers have low expectations for children, it can lead us to designate particular children or groups for repetitive, boring tasks instead of lively and challenging discussions about books, because we anticipate the latter would be too intellectually challenging (McGee & Richgels 2003). If a sense of hopelessness prevails among teachers, parents, and families, it holds young children back from reaching their full potential as listeners, readers, and writers.

Why read picture books?

The early childhood educator's recommendation to families to read aloud to their children is more than good, old-fashioned advice. We need to make sure that families understand that research shows that reading aloud to children

• increases their reading achievement scores, listening and speaking abilities, letter and symbol recognition, ability to use more complex sentences, reading comprehension, vocabulary and concept development, positive attitudes toward reading, and tendency to view reading as a valued activity (Becher 1985; van Kleeck, Stahl, & Bauer 2003); and

• is strongly and positively connected to their eventual success as independent readers (Educational Research Service 1998).

The box **How Reading Aloud Fosters Emergent Reading Skills** describes the basic skill areas fundamental to success in reading and explains how these skills are developed through reading aloud. The comments that children make during story sessions are one of the most useful indicators of the child's growth in literacy.

Knowing how to read is not sufficient, of course. Children must also want to practice this skill once they have acquired it. What motivates children to read? Martin and Brogran (1972) say that the emerging reader needs many favorite books to zoom through with joyous familiarity. Knowledge and enjoyment of numerous picture books come from children sharing literature with caring adults—especially family members (Taylor 1983).

When to begin reading picture books

The media often publicize cases in which a 2- or 3-year-old shows precocious mastery of reading skills. These reports may make some parents want to accelerate their own children's learning of letters or recognition of the alphabet. Some children do actually learn to read remarkably early, and most of them began with literature (rhymes, songs, finger plays, picture books) rather than with isolated memory tasks (Stainthorp & Hughes 1999). When children's experiences with the printed word begin with books, they approach the task of learning to read as appreciative listeners. They sense the value of being able to read. In contrast, children who are first taught to recognize words and letters may approach the task of learning to read as an abstract exercise that somehow pleases adults.

Inappropriate acceleration, in any domain of learning and development, creates problems. Young children who are pushed often show signs of stress and

Families and Picture Books

How Reading Aloud Fosters Emergent Reading Skills

Target Behaviors	How Reading Aloud Helps	Typical Comments from Child
Skill: Attends to visual cues		
The child turns pages of the book correctly; knows that books are read from left to right; has a concept of units of language (words, letters) and of matching spoken words to printed ones; and recognizes some words in the book.	Children have ample experience with book handling. Opportunities to hear the same story again and again enable them to get a sense of how a book "works."	"Let me hold it. I know how to turn the pages." "Is this where it says his name?" "Here comes the picture where he's wearing his hat." "Where does it say 'and that was that'?"
Skill: Uses intuitive knowledge of language; expects meaning from print		
The child can tell or invent a story based on illustrations; can relate the basic story from memory (including some exact book passages); and learns to expect a story from print.	Children acquire a "sense of story" and understand that stories have a beginning, a middle, and a conclusion.	"Watch me read this book." "And it was just right." "I can read the newspaper, too. Here, I'll read it to you."
Skill: Begins integration of visual and language cues		
The child begins to read single sentences word by word; uses knowledge of word order, some beginning sounds, the context, and the predictability of the story to read and to tell whether an error has been made.	Children often use repetitive books or books based on rhymes and songs they know to emulate reading adults.	"No! You're not reading it right. You forgot the part about the little old man." "This says 'The Little Red Hen,' right?" "This starts with s but it isn't her name. Her name has a big S."

Based on Clay (1979) and McDonnell & Osborn (1978).

self-doubt (McDevitt & Ormond 2001). Children have no way of knowing when adult expectations for them are inappropriate, and a child's sense of having failed him- or herself and disappointed important adults can adversely affect that child's learning for a lifetime.

What, then, is the recommended alternative? The preschool years are a crucial time for the development of language and literacy. Extensive observational research with young children and their families supports a more "natural" approach to early literacy. Parents and other family members who *invited* their children into the world of literacy (rather than dragged them into it, as harsh taskmasters) frequently say things later such as:

> I never really *taught* Leon how to read; we just kept lots of books around and read together and talked about them. Then we started to make books with family snapshots, and he dictated the captions. Pretty soon he was asking things like "Where does it say my name?" If I wrote a grocery list or a thank you note, he wanted to write, too. And gradually, he just started reading and writing.

So, the way to begin literacy learning is gently, gradually, with all of the care, concern, and supports in place that families demonstrate when children are taking their first hesitant steps across the living room floor. Under most circumstances, sharing opportunities for the young child to listen to stories is an ideal way to welcome him or her into the world of literature and create more opportunities for the emergent literacy described in Chapter 5 to flourish.

Building readers from infancy to independence

Toddlers who form secure attachments with family members and live in an intellectually stimulating environment are more likely to acquire competence in language (Murray & Yingling 2000). The sharing of picture books is one way to create closer emotional ties between children and adults and to provide that kind of environment. Caregivers who share books effectively with infants and toddlers display some common practices, such as selecting sturdy books suited to the very young, using the pictures as the basis for interaction with a child, and relating the story to the child's experiences (Bus 2001; Honig & Shin 2001).

One reason why many adults are skeptical of the value of reading aloud is because it seems that they are doing most of the work. But listening, especially for young language learners, involves much more than merely hearing the words. "Far from being passive, the listener is extremely busy participating in the re-creation of that story: for a successful listener needs to be a storyteller too" (Barton 1986, 9).

Many theorists and researchers have emphasized how important it is for a child to develop a "sense of story" (Applebee 1978; Favat 1977; Jacobs 1965; Snow 1983). Three-year-old Melanie illustrates how a sense of story is acquired as she retells Maurice Sendak's classic *Where the Wild Things Are*:

> That night he wears his wolf suit and made mischief of one kind. He be sent to his room with no food. That night the forest grew in his room and grew and grew and GREW! And there went an ocean tumbled down. And there was a private boat for Max. And in and out of weeks to where the wild things are.

When Children Seem Uninterested in Books

Some children appear not to enjoy book-reading activities (Kaderavek & Sulzby 1998). Research suggests a number of possible causes (see Justice & Kaderavek 2002; Marvin & Mirenda 1993). Perhaps such children have impaired language skills and are overwhelmed by the task demands. They may have attentional difficulties and need greater active engagement to focus and maintain their interest. Or maybe they have limited prior experience with literacy events, including being read to. Although teachers may not know precisely what mix of factors are behind a child's seemingly low interest in books, they can still try these practical strategies:

Present the book to the child individually. Young children who seem uninterested in books may have had few prior experiences with books or may not have had books presented effectively. In addition, they may not have been matched with books suited for their age or developmental level. Children who lack positive book experiences will sometimes respond more favorably when a book is shared on an individual basis rather than in a group setting.

Make the shared storybook reading more interactive. Think of the reading process as involving adult and child as equal partners, rather than as involving the adult as one who directs the child (Rabidoux & MacDonald 2000). Let the child choose the place to read and the book to be read from among a few appropriate selections. Allow the child to operate the book—hold it, turn the pages, announce "The End." After the child is thoroughly familiar with a book, invite him or her to pretend to read it, and offer encouragement for his or her attempts to tell the story or "read" the book.

Follow the child's lead. Choose books with the child's interests and abilities in mind. Make the interaction pleasurable and positive rather than competitive or coercive. Beware of books with too much text, because young children may lose interest. Avoid turning the story sharing into a harsh drill ("What's that?" "What's her name?" "How many animals are there?"). Constant questioning is not necessary; a thoughtful comment such as, "Hmm. I wonder what he will do now?" may be sufficient. Or, try simply pausing to let the child study the pictures or make a comment. Do not feel obligated to read the book word by word or to insist that the child remain quiet and still. Adapt the discussion of the story to suit the child.

Select books with more "toy-like" characteristics. Children who appear to be uninterested can often be enticed to interact and participate when presented books with moving parts. The reluctant child may be attracted to books with different textures to touch, such as the classic *Pat the Bunny* (Kunhardt); books with flaps to lift and pictures underneath to surprise, such as *Spot Bakes a Cake* (Hill); books with surprising moving parts and pop-ups, such as *How Many Bugs in a Box? A Pop-Up Counting Book* (Carter); or books with slots through which to thread yarn, such as *Ted and Dolly's Magic Carpet Ride* (Fowler). Alphabet books, predictable books, and books to build phonological awareness all play an important role in supporting reluctant readers, too.

When children with low interest in books are first being introduced to reading aloud, choose books that have no more than about five words per page, that display large print, and that contain illustrations that grab attention.

Some specific recommendations of books to support early literacy follow. For more, see Zeece (2002, 2003a/c).

Books with moving parts

Faulkner, K. *Do you have my quack?*

Faulkner, K. *Ten little monkeys.*

Ratnett, M. *Dracula steps out.*

Sharratt, N. *Ketchup on your cornflakes? A wacky mix and match book.*

Walsh, M. *Martha counts her kittens.*

Wilson-Max, K. *Little green tow truck.*

Alphabet books

Buckley, J. *Baseball ABC.*

Dorling Kindersley Publishing. *NFL ABC book.*

Edwards W. *Alphabeasts.*

Fleming, D. *Alphabet under construction.*

Hoban, T. *26 letters and 99 cents.*

Isadora, R. *ABC pop.*

Iwai, M. *B is for bulldozer: A construction ABC.*

Joyce, S. *ABC animal riddles.*

Kalman, M. *What Pete ate from A to Z.*

Kirk, D. *Miss Spider's ABC.*

Polacco, P. *G is for goat.*

Sierra, J. *There's a zoo in room 22.*

Slate, J. *Miss Bindergarten stays home from kindergarten.*

Wood, A. *Alphabet adventure.*

Predictable books

Appelt, K. *Bats around the clock.*

Ashman, L. *Can you make a piggy giggle?*

Beaton, C. *How big is a pig?*

Coxon, M. *Kitten's adventure.*

Fleming, D. *Where once there was a wood.*

Gray, L.M. *Is there room on the feather bed?*

Hutchins, P. *Rosie's walk.*

Kovalski, M. *The wheels on the bus.*

Mayer, M. *Snow day.*

Mole, J. *Copycat.*

Murphy, M. *Caterpillar's wish.*

Books to enhance phonological awareness

Andreae, G. *Giraffes can't dance.*

Edwards, P.D. *Warthogs in the kitchen: A sloppy counting book.*

Hoberman, M.A. *Miss Mary Mack.*

Martin, B., Jr., & S. Kellogg. *A beasty story.*

Mitton, R. *Down by the cool of the pool.*

Numeroff, L. *Monster munchies.*

Salisbury, K. *A bear ate my pear.*

Seeber, D. *A pup just for me/A boy just for me.*

Shaw, N. *Sheep in a jeep.*

Stickland, P., & H. Stickland. *Dinosaur roar!*

Weeks, S. *Oh my gosh, Mrs. McNosh.*

They roared their terrible teeth. And gnashed their terrible teeth. "Be still." He did a magic trick without blinking into his eyes. *(Melanie comments, "I heard this before, that's why I know all of this.")* He was the King of all and said, "Let the wild rumpus start!" He sent them to bed without any supper. *(Melanie notes, "They don't have anything to eat because giraffes just eat leaves.")*

He smelled food. He went home in a boat. Into his own bedroom alone where his supper was still hot.

Melanie already knows how a book "works." She understands elements of stories such as characters, action, sequence, and storybook language. She realizes that print is the spoken word written down and that practice with a book will make a person a more proficient reader. Most important, she is motivated to read and enjoys trying. Her abilities are the precursor to fluent reading. Reading is a complex process involving many subskills. These subskills are learned best when they are learned gradually through years of accumulated experience; they are exceedingly difficult when rushed or forced.

How to share picture books at home

If books are so important, why not just give them to families and schools? Research on book giveaways shows that whether the recipients are teachers or families, they need training and support in making literature and all of its benefits accessible to young children (McGill-Franzen & Allington 1999). The following sections emphasize two key steps in sharing picture books effectively and offer some general guidelines for parents and other family members. (For more on sharing books effectively, see Chapter 3.)

Choosing the book. For family members who lack much experience with children's books, consulting resources aimed at them, such as *For Reading Out Loud!* (Kimmel & Segel 1984), *The Read-Aloud Handbook* (Trelease 2001), or *Children's Reading Begins at Home* (Larrick 1980), can be especially helpful. Libraries also often have recommended reading lists free for the asking. When picking several picture books to read aloud, adults need to choose ones they think they might enjoy too, because, as Zeece points out, "Young listeners are not easily fooled by those who do not enjoy the book they are sharing" (2003b, 133).

Reading the book aloud. The quickest way to learn how to read a book to a child is to watch (or hear) someone else do it well. Family members could accompany the child to a story session sponsored by the library, or visit the school or center to observe a skilled early childhood teacher read aloud. Certain children's programs on television are another option. The public television show *Reading Rainbow* is a good example; each episode includes one complete book, such as *Aunt Flossie's Hats (and Crab Cakes Later)* (Howard), skillfully read aloud.

Choosing Picture Books for Infants, Toddlers, and 3-Year-Olds

For very young children, look for books that—

Contain appropriate themes or subject matter. Examples of themes that have appeal for very young children include learning to do something all by them-selves or being reassured that they are loved and protected. Subject matter includes the topics that have importance for very young children; for example, relationships with family members, playing with toys, and bonding with family pets.

Use language effectively and imaginatively. The words in picture books should be precise, eloquent, creative, and evocative. The text of the story should deftly set the scene and move the action along (Butler 1975). Very young children prefer books with little text and few words per page.

Include straightforward plots. Not all books for the very young are storybooks, but when a story is written for the very young, it should be direct and avoid tangents. *Who Is the Beast?* (Baker) is a good example of a clear, simple plot with the rhythm and rhyme that appeal to the very young child.

Build to a satisfying conclusion. A quality picture storybook comes to a swift resolution and ends on a positive note. The fact that the story has ended should be apparent, even to a child who is just learning how a book works. The book should have "form, unity, color, climax" (Butler 1975, 51).

Based on Butler (1975).

With practice, family members will become more attuned to children's needs and responses, and tailor their reading style accordingly.

The interaction of 18-month-old Claire and her mom illustrates the sort of accommodations by parents and other family members that can make book sharing more successful. With story sharing experiences like this, is it any wonder that Claire loves books?

> Claire is at an annual family reunion and, at first, she is a little overwhelmed by the unfamiliar people, pets, and new toys. Her mother wisely waits until afternoon when Claire has settled into her new surroundings to share some books together. Claire's mom sits on the floor and shows her the board book *Five Little Monkeys Jumping on the Bed* (Christelow), which is based on the familiar chant that goes, "Five little monkeys, jumping on the bed. One fell off and bumped his head. . . . "

> Claire is captivated. She studies the illustrations intently; the tips of two fingers are poised on her bottom lip as an outward sign of her concentration. As she turns a page, Mom asks teasingly, "Did *Claire* ever jump on the bed?"

Why Read Aloud to Children Who Can Read Independently?

Even after a child is reading independently, it makes sense for adults to continue sharing books with them.

To foster appreciation—Material that is too difficult for children to read independently can be enjoyed and shared when it is read aloud by adults.

To extend background and generate interest—Books read aloud can build children's knowledge and generate interest in a topic of study or upcoming activity.

To expand reading preferences—Read-aloud choices can include authors and types of books that children might otherwise overlook.

To develop listening comprehension—Books read aloud can build children's understanding of oral language; research has documented that a definite link exists between listening comprehension and reading comprehension (Neuman & Dickinson 2001).

To model what effective readers do—When adults read aloud to children, they demonstrate enthusiasm for books and invite children to mature into readers.

To share responses to literature with others—Stories can evoke a wide range of emotions, and the opportunity to share and discuss literary responses is a way to build motivation and interest.

To entertain and encourage children's development in the language arts—Reading aloud is an antidote to what is dull and routine. Reading aloud shows children that literacy has a value beyond schoolwork and that literacy can enrich life.

Compiled by Melissa Ann Renck, children's services librarian, Toledo Lucas County Library.

and the toddler shakes her head in an emphatic no. This causes Mom to reply in mock horror, "Yes, you have too jumped on the bed, I've seen you!" while tickling Claire's ribs a bit to let her know her mother enjoyed the joke. When they arrive at the book's end and it shows *mama* monkey jumping on the bed, it is evident that Claire is delighted and surprised. Her eyes grow wide, she smiles, and she cranes her neck around to look at her mother's face, as if to confirm her interpretation. Mom remarks, "Oh, look at that! Mama monkey is jumping on the bed after she told her monkey kids not to do it!"

Associating reading with pleasurable feelings and with the undivided attention of a caring adult is one of the ways that children learn to like reading. Children who become readers tend to come from environments in which adults model reading themselves and read aloud to their children (Trelease 2001). As Bernice Cullinan (1977) points out, children are dependent on adults to make literature a significant part of their lives. That responsibility begins with the

"Now I can go to bed!"

32

Illustration from *Five Little Monkeys Jumping on the Bed* by Eileen Christelow. Text and illustrations copyright © 1989 by Eileen Christelow. Reprinted with permission of Clarion Books/Houghton Mifflin Company. All rights reserved.

family and eventually grows to include early childhood teachers and all of us whose work reaches young children. Without adults to lead them to literature, the benefits of picture books can remain unrealized.

Conclusion: Making the commitment to reading aloud

An English teacher announces to her group of high school seniors that she is about to teach them the most important thing they will learn about literature all year. And this critical skill is?—How to read a book to a child. Reading to children truly is that important.

When parents and other family members recognize and act on that understanding, they become powerful forces in their children's lives, as this participant in a workshop on children's literature recalls, "My father was illiterate, and he wanted so much for his children to be readers. Every weekend, he would take us to the library. We would choose lots of different books, and he would admire our choices. I still have fond memories of those special Saturdays."

In her single-parent family, being able to read was valued even though the father had never learned how. What a strong person he must have been to admit his illiteracy in order to provide something better for his children. Until there was a reader in the house, he found relatives, friends, neighbors, and professionals who could fill in. But once his eldest, a 5-year-old girl, learned to read, she became the "resident reader" for the family, sharing with her siblings the books they admired and wondered about. She grew up to attend college and become a Head Start aide and a teacher. Even though their father could not read and the family income was very low, these children grew up in a print-rich environment. They all learned to read and, perhaps more important, to value reading. This father lived to see the promise of those well-spent Saturdays, his literacy dream for his children fulfilled: All of them became avid readers, excelled in school, and matured into successful professionals.

Young children seem to know that listening to stories read aloud is exactly what they need to master the reading process. Long before they are reading independently, children reach out with the words "Read me a story!" and "Read it again!" to have their literary needs met. And, in fact, they are correct. The classic case studies of young children (Bissex 1980; Butler 1975; Calkins 1983), as well as the more recent research on emergent reading abilities (e.g., Neuman & Dickinson 2001), send the consistent message that literature is the perfect place to start. All that remains is for families to commit to reading aloud as an important investment in their child's future reading, writing, and educational success.

Mary Renck Jalongo

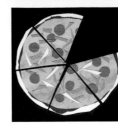

CHAPTER 7

Linking Picture Books with Curriculum

We can, through employment of picture books, bring a second and third teacher into the classroom. Authors and illustrators have done half our planning for us—and high-quality planning it is too—and we can piggy back on their talent and industry and use their books to jumpstart our own imaginations. Not to use these glorious and plentiful objects, designed absolutely for children, but a delight to all, is truly to look a gift horse in the mouth.

—Judith Graham, *Creativity and Picture Books* (2000, 67)

Today is the first day of nursery school and it's "Three Bears' Day." Four-year-old Nicholas felt confident when the teacher read Tomie de Paola's illustrated version of the familiar folktale. He participated in a dramatization of the story using simple props—three different-size bowls, chairs, and rugs (to represent the beds). At the cooking center, Nicholas followed a rebus recipe to make porridge (instant oatmeal with raisins) and ate some as a snack. In the family life corner, he found teddy bears of three different sizes. During quiet time, the preschoolers rested on their mats while watching a film version of *Corduroy* (Freeman), about a small bear in search of a button for his overalls. Other books about bears such as *The Three Bears Rhyme Book* (Yolen), *Emma's Vacation* (McPhail), *Mooncake* (Asch), *Deep in the Forest* (Turkle), *Alphabears* (Hague), and *Peace at Last* (Murphy) were displayed in the reading center. One of the manipulatives used with the flannel board was a classification game in which children arranged objects from smallest to largest. Two records, *Jamberry* (Degen) and *Unbearable Bears* (Roth), were in the listening center. The day concluded with a rhythm band march to the record from the song picture book *The Teddy Bears' Picnic* (Kennedy), after which each child received a small, pocket-size version of "The Three Bears" story printed on paper and folded into a book to color, keep, and share at home. As the children left the room, the teacher said good-bye and gave each one a sticker that read: "Ask me about Three Bears' Day!"

This stimulating day was one preschool teacher's way of making picture books come alive for her students and of making literature an integral part of the curriculum. Later that afternoon, when members of Nicholas's family asked about his day at school, he used the little book to offer his rendition of the story:

> Once upon a time there were three bears. Mommy Bear was cooking. Baby Bear was playing. Daddy Bear was reading. The three bears sat down to eat breakfast. The cereal is too hot, so Baby Bear said, "Let's go for a walk." Then a little girl walked in. She was a bad little girl. She saw three bowls of hot cereal on the table. "I'm hungry," she said. She tasted Daddy Bear's, it's too hot. Then she tried Mommy Bear's, it's too cold. Baby Bear's was ju … uu … st right. She ate it all up shirp! She sat on Baby Bear's chair and went up and down on it, and the chair broke—pu … sh and she fell. Laid down in Daddy Bear's bed, too hard. Laid down in Mommy Bear's bed, too soft. "My food are all gone" and then Baby Bear starts to cry. "Somebody broke my chair! Wee! Wee! Wee! Wee! Wee! Get out of my bed," said Baby Bear. "You can't sleep all the time."

Clearly, Nicholas's teacher has made picture books a focal point of her program. As a result, the 4-year-olds in her class are getting a warm invitation to join what Frank Smith (1988) refers to as "The Literacy Club"—consisting of all of the literate individuals in the community and society at large. Nicholas and his classmates are fortunate to be dramatizing books, retelling stories, listening to picture books read aloud, learning vocabulary in meaningful contexts, developing emergent literacy skills, reasoning mathematically, and participating in a community of language learners. Just think how different this 4-year-old's initial impressions of school would have been if, on his first day, the teacher instead had quizzed the children on their knowledge of the alphabet, or insisted that they sit quietly much of the day, or given them mindless activities intended to "keep little hands busy." As Judith Graham suggests, literature is a tremendous resource in the lifelong journey to becoming a better teacher.

Goals for picture books in the curriculum

The specific goals of an early childhood literature program should be consistent with the general objectives of the National Council of Teachers of English (1996), which include helping children to do the following:

• Identify with characters, understand interpersonal relationships, and gain insights from literature

• Appreciate the rhythms and beauty of language

• Understand the importance of literature as a mirror of human experience

• Develop effective ways of talking about literature

• Develop positive attitudes toward literature that carry over into adult life

• Become aware of quality books and their authors

What can early childhood teachers do to achieve these goals in their individual settings? In an observational study of teachers of young children in the United Kingdom, Fisher (2002) evaluated the academic achievement of students on standardized tests and then observed their teachers at work. Interestingly, virtually all of the classroom behaviors Fisher identified in the highly effective preschool teachers can be developed through interactions with picture books. These behaviors include the following (adapted from Fisher 2002):

• Selecting excellent books that are motivating to both teacher and children

• Displaying a genuine enthusiasm for books that seems to rub off on the children

• Showing sensitivity to children's developing abilities by devoting time to observing children's responses and listening to their comments about books

• Modeling what effective readers do, and making it visible to children by wondering aloud while reading

• Approaching interactions with books with a sense of purpose and focus, without being overly controlling or rushing through the experience

• Relating literature to children's previous experiences in and out of school to help them make sense of language

• Encouraging and valuing children's own interpretations and attempts rather than expecting them to guess what is on the teacher's mind

• Balancing opportunities for children to work with the support of peers, with teacher support, and independently

• Engaging in careful planning and preparation that results in an appropriate level of structure

• Adjusting the style of interaction to the purpose and making suitable adaptations for one-to-one, small group, and whole class learning experiences

• Avoiding "busywork" that reflects low expectations for children's intellects, and instead using more open-ended, exploratory literacy activities

• Developing the children's self-esteem during their early encounters with literacy and convincing them that learning to read and write is within their power

The role of the teacher

Early childhood teachers sometimes lose heart when a child arrives in their school or center having had very limited literacy experiences. But children who lack book experiences are the very ones who are counting most on us to turn that situation around and introduce them to the world of children's literature. In my view, a teacher who takes credit for the successes of children whose literacy backgrounds were extensively developed at home, yet absolves herself or himself of responsibility for children who lacked such privileges, is guilty of educational malpractice. Over and over again, the research on this issue has yielded the consistent message that ambitious teaching—defined as teachers having high expectations both for their ability to effect positive change and for their students' achievement—is a highly influential factor in successful teaching (Borich 1986; DEE 1998).

Effective teachers are a powerful force for good in shaping young children's literacy knowledge, skills, attitudes, and habits. Raphael and Au (1998) characterize that role in five different dimensions: (1) being knowledgeable about children's literature, (2) selecting books carefully, (3) presenting books effectively, (4) building a literature-based curriculum, and (5) assessing children's responses to literature. Ideally, teachers need to "bathe, immerse, soak, [and] drench" their students in good literature (Harwayne 1992, 1).

A common teacher misconception is that sharing picture books is a separate activity to be reserved for a storytime of a few minutes a day. Actually, teachers who are successful in promoting literacy infuse picture books into their entire program, by making their classrooms and centers places where books are shared, recommended, connected with all curricular areas, and supportive of the goals of diversity. The National Council of Teachers of English's standards concerning pedagogical principles of diversity include the following roles for teachers of the language arts:

1. Create learning environments that promote respect for and understanding of individual, academic, ethnic, racial, language, cultural, and gender differences.
2. Structure the classroom in a manner that encourages students to work independently and collaboratively.
3. Use a variety of materials and media.
4. Promote classroom discourse in which children's thinking is respected and challenged by the teacher and other students.
5. Enrich and expand the learner's language resources for different social and cultural settings. (NCTE 1996, 29)

For additional guidelines, see the NAEYC position statement "Responding to Linguistic and Cultural Diversity: Recommendations for Effective Early Childhood Education" (1995).

To accomplish these goals, teachers must accept at least three important responsibilities (Hickman 1984; Stewig 1980): (1) conveying an understanding and appreciation of literature, (2) using literature effectively to meet children's needs, and (3) creating a literature-rich environment.

Conveying an understanding and appreciation of literature

Observational studies both in homes and in schools have shown that children tend to emulate adults' responses to literature (Taylor 1983). One essential role of the teacher as a literate adult is to help children see that listening to stories, participating in discussions, learning to read, and mastering the writing process to become an author are worth all the effort. Reading aloud to children is one way to communicate these ideas. Children need to interact with adults who know and enjoy literature. In the role of appreciative reader, a teacher can enthusiastically recommend a book with a comment such as: "Sasha, I know you love to draw. Here is a book about a girl like you who loves to use her crayons. It's called *My Crayons Talk*" (Hubbard).

As a member of a community of readers and listeners, the teacher also can point out unique aspects of books that challenge the young child, for example, the detailed borders containing nursery rhyme characters in *Tomie de Paola's Favorite Nursery Tales* or the dedication page in *When I Was Young in the Mountains* (Rylant). A teacher of older children can let them in on inside information about illustrators and authors. For example, did you know that—

• Mercer Mayer includes his little white dog somewhere in every book?

• *On the Day You Were Born* was written by Debra Frasier as she waited for her infant daughter to be delivered?

• Dav Pilkey's *Dogzilla* and *Kat Kong* are spoofs of the movies *Godzilla* and *King Kong*?

• Lois Ehlert's book *Nuts to You!* was based on her interactions with a pesky squirrel outside the window of her city apartment?

• The harlequin Great Dane in the Pinkerton books by Steven Kellogg was inspired by his family pets?

• Donald Crews's stories *Bigmama's* and *Shortcut* are autobiographical?

For many other examples of interesting facts about picture book authors and illustrators, see Cummings (1992, 1993).

Picture books are central to the early childhood teacher's role as an enthusiastic and appreciative reader of literature. Reading aloud to children helps them become successful readers as they learn to enjoy books, develop a sense of how stories work, build a richer vocabulary, learn to make predictions, internalize grammatical structures, develop an understanding of literary language, and notice how different writers and illustrators create high-quality books (Routman 2002).

Using literature effectively to meet children's needs

Teachers exert a major influence on a child's perceptions of literature when they select books, structure the story session, determine the focus, and identify appropriate questions. Simply reading books is not enough. Teachers need to know how to present them effectively and discuss them with children, as described in Chapter 3. The box **Tips for Reading Aloud to Groups of Children** offers additional guidelines.

When teachers do not allow time to discuss a book, or conversely, they discuss the story in a very regimented way, children can miss the richness of literature. As Petrosky (1980) observes,

> Books are worlds. Books are experiences. Children need to talk with each other and with teachers about their encounters with those worlds, those experiences. We would do well to minimize our expectations of quick answers and fast responses. Meaning comes slowly. . . . We need to encourage children to talk to us and to each other about what they see, feel, think, and how they associate with what they read. (155)

Another way of conceptualizing the teacher's role in promoting literacy is to consider the Vygotskian (1962/1986) notion of the adult *scaffolding* the children's learning (Bruner 1983; Wood, Bruner, & Ross 1976). A helpful

Tips for Reading Aloud to Groups of Children

Familiarize yourself with the material in advance. This preparation enables you to establish eye contact with the listeners and glance at the page only occasionally. Make sure you know the correct pronunciation of new vocabulary and characters' names, particularly for books from other cultures.

Practice holding the book and turning the pages so the audience can always see the pictures. Consider the size of the book. For typical picture books, try holding the book with your index finger and thumb in front of the book's spine and your remaining fingers behind the book for support; turn the pages with the opposite hand. For big, poster-size books, try using an easel or have small groups of children kneel down in front of the book as it rests on the floor. If the book and pictures are very small, save it for reading with individual or pairs of children.

Plan the seating arrangement. Organize a manageable-size group, and arrange them in a semicircle. Put yourself at the children's eye level to get a sense of what they will see as you show the pictures. Position yourself so the children at the ends of the semicircle can see the book.

Use your voice effectively. Relax and speak clearly. Breathe deeply to project your voice. Vary the volume, pitch, and tone of your voice to suit the mood and style of the book. Read with feeling and alter your voice to match key characters' personalities, but do not be overly dramatic or get too complicated (e.g., using unfamiliar accents or dialects), which can detract from the book.

Draw children's attention to features of print as appropriate. For toddlers, perhaps point out the title only; for preschoolers, the title and illustrator; for older children, draw attention to such things as the dedication or historical notes. If the purpose of reading aloud is also to teach children how to read (as is often the case when using Big Books), try using a pointer to help them follow along. If the goal is to have the children choral speak/read the parts that are repeated, you may want to use removable highlighting tape, which comes on a roll and does not damage the book, to put a sheer, bright color over those particular words or phrases.

Consider the pace of the story. Adjust your reading to the action in the story. Pay attention to the pauses indicated by punctuation. Use the turn of the pages effectively—to pause when you want to build suspense, to smoothly transition to the rest of the sentence, and so forth.

Interject a few carefully selected comments as appropriate. Think out loud a bit to point out things that children must not miss if they are to understand the story. For example, "Uh oh, it looks like. . . . " "Hmm. I wonder if that is going to work?" "Did you notice that . . . ?" Often, these comments can be made during the second it takes you to turn the page and, if used judiciously, can help to maintain children's attention rather than become a distraction.

Pause at the end. Give listeners a chance to think the book over and savor the ending. If the group is small, consider giving each child a chance to comment. Invite children to relate this book to other books that have been shared and to connect the book with their personal experiences.

Compiled by Melissa Ann Renck, children's services librarian, Toledo Lucas County Library.

approach is to think of the teacher's support for children as having three levels (Bickler 1999), moving from most to least supportive:

• In *shared work,* the teacher assumes a major leadership role—for example, when sharing a Big Book with kindergarten children for the purpose of teaching them to read.

• In *guided work,* the children are encouraged to be independent, and the teacher offers support and instruction on an as-needed basis—for example, when kindergartners are drawing and writing in their journals in response to the picture books they have heard read aloud.

• In *independent work,* the children are doing something that they have already learned or are applying and practicing a familiar skill with very minimal support from the teacher—for example, when children are retelling a familiar story using flannel-board figures.

Creating a literature-rich environment

Teachers also are responsible for structuring children's physical environment for literacy development. Is evidence of a commitment to literacy apparent to anyone who might visit the classroom or center? Does the setting clearly indicate that picture books are valued and important? The items from **How Well Am I Doing as an Advocate for Picture Books?** can help teachers to self-assess.

Making books and related materials available to children is an important first step to becoming an effective advocate. Some classrooms and centers are stocked with a few battered copies of the books typical of discount stores. Although ordinary books are probably better than none, those kinds of materials are not representative of the best that picture books have to offer. The box **Choosing Books for the Classroom or Center** offers guidance in identifying high-quality literature.

When teachers set aside time for literature, present books in an engaging way, set children's expectations for books, and extend literature into other curricular areas, they let children know that books are important. Children see the physical evidence of taking time for books—for example, a library and a classroom display of their responses to literature. Children see evidence of special places for sharing literature, too—for example, a comfortable rocking chair or a semicircular seating arrangement marked on the floor with carpet squares. They also see extensions of literature—for example, a stack of hats to be used in enacting *Caps for Sale* (Slobodkina) to encourage dramatization of the story, or masks to wear when dramatizing *Who's in Rabbit's House?* (Aardema), or a mini trampoline to act out *Five Little Monkeys Jumping on the Bed* (Christelow), or a furry scarf for a tail to represent the squirrel in *Sody Salyratus* (Sloat). In addition, various materials are in the classroom that extend thinking about picture books—a collection of simple puppets, a set of simple costumes, computer software with a picture book theme, story baskets that contain the book and toys to inspire retelling, and learning games based on picture books. All of these elements set the stage for a literature-based curriculum.

How Well Am I Doing as an Advocate for Picture Books?

Instructions: Indicate how often each of these items occurs in your classroom by assigning yourself a score, using the scale below; then add up your scores.

<u>5=almost always 4=frequently 3=occasionally 2=seldom 1=almost never</u>

1. I set aside time for reading aloud to children each day.
2. I prepare for the use of picture books by reading them myself in advance.
3. I introduce stories with a motivational technique.
4. I relate children's books to other curricular areas.
5. I supplement the center's or school's collection with books borrowed from the library and other sources.
6. I use community resources such as librarians, parents, and other volunteers to enhance the children's literature program.
7. I keep current in children's literature through participation in professional conferences, inservice training, and college coursework and by reading book reviews.
8. I support/participate in programs such as Reading Is Fundamental (RIF) that provide children with books of their own.
9. When requested, I offer assistance to parents in choosing appropriate books for their children.
10. I make a special effort to locate books that are relevant to classroom activities or to the interests of individual children.
11. I prepare supplemental materials to accompany children's books, for example, puppets, dioramas, book displays, and activity boards.
12. I draw children's attention to aspects of books such as cover, title, author, illustrator; and I encourage them to identify their favorite books, authors, and illustrators.
13. I choose stories or books that offer rich vocabulary, and I take time before sharing the book to prepare the children for some of the new words they will encounter.
14. In selecting and reading books aloud, I consider and highlight language sounds such as rhyme and alliteration that are pleasing to the ear and promote children's phonological awareness.
15. I read aloud to groups using oversize books (Big Books) to enable children to notice print as well as pictures.
16. I not only read but also *tell* familiar stories to children.
17. I encourage children to discuss the books we read during storytime.
18. I respect children's preferences and permit them to choose some of the books we will read.
19. I encourage children's artistic responses (in art, drama, dance) to literature.
20. I acknowledge children's efforts to properly care for books.
21. I have an area in my classroom that is designated for reading and listening to books and records.
22. I select books that represent diversity in style, format, illustration, and literary genre.
23. The picture books I share depict ethnic groups, minorities, religious groups, females, and disabled people in positive, active roles.
24. I enjoy sharing picture books with young children.
25. I can identify from memory several outstanding children's book authors and illustrators.

Scoring: 125–100=Excellent, 100–85=Good, Below 85=Needs Improvement

Choosing Books for the Classroom or Center

The International Reading Association's special interest group on Children's Literature and Reading (IRA CL/R SIG) arrived at the following criteria to apply when selecting picture books as part of its Notable Books for a Global Society award program (Editors 2000). (For detailed criteria, see www.csulb.edu/org/childrens-lit/proj/nbgs/intro-nbgs.html.) In general, books should—

- Correlate with curriculum guides and national standards
- Reflect outstanding qualities such as high literary merit, rich factual content, and aesthetic design
- Meet the informational and recreational reading needs of students
- Reflect cultural, racial, and ethnic diversity
- Represent originality of concept, approach, or point of view
- Demonstrate strong reader appeal

In addition to these criteria, consider these points and questions:
- Impact—Can you imagine your students responding enthusiastically?
- Readability—Can you picture the listener(s)/reader(s) staying interested as you read through the book? Is it too wordy?
- Cohesiveness—Do the words, pictures, and other details (e.g., backgrounds, borders, end notes) of the book complement one another?
- Style—Do the words and illustrations match the message of the book?
- Format—Is the size, look, and feel of the book suited for the child or children?
- Endorsements—Is there evidence that the book is recommended by professional organizations and experts in the field?

Building a picture book collection

How can teachers with limited budgets get quality books into children's hands?

Use the public library. Librarians want picture books to be circulated to the public. Some communities even have a librarian who specializes in literature for children. Even if the local library is small, it may have cooperative arrangements with larger branches and be able to borrow from their collections. Establishing a good working relationship with a professional who keeps up to date with picture books can improve any teacher's literature curriculum.

Use family resources. For example, a customary practice in many schools is for a child to bring birthday treats to share with peers. One school set a policy that, instead of a sugary snack, the birthday child was to donate a picture book to the classroom library. The inside cover of each donated book got a card that recognized the donor by name. Because the teacher had shared with parents lists of recommended picture books and best picture books in paperback, most of the donations to the classroom library not only were appropriate but also cost families about the same as candy or cupcakes for the class would have. Within five years, this teacher's classroom library had acquired almost one hundred favorite picture books this way.

Another strategy is to participate in book clubs offered by distributors or publishers such as Scholastic (http://teacher.scholastic.com). In this system, club purchases by families earn the class bonus points that the teacher can exchange for additional books.

Use community resources. Early childhood teachers need to publicize that they are building a classroom library. The school's or center's newsletter, an ad in the local newspaper, or a public service message on the radio or television can announce the project. One Head Start teacher made this publicity task a project for several parent volunteers; they advertised for, obtained, and screened the contributed books. An administrator of a private child care center recruited two parents who enjoyed frequenting garage sales; they were coached on the types of books to select and purchased their finds with the proceeds from a bake sale. A teacher in a cooperative nursery school found a grandparent to build a bookcase for the book collection and visit the children several times to demonstrate the basics of woodworking.

Create books with the children. Another way to expand the book collection is by having children dictate their own stories for the teacher to record. Their dictation can be printed or typed by an adult on paper, then illustrated and signed by the child. If creating an entire story seems overwhelming to beginning writers, each child can contribute one page to the book. If children are not yet drawing representationally, they can select pictures cut out from magazines or computer clip art. Snapshots or digital camera photos also can be used as illustrations for an experience or event and arranged in sequence by the child. Children are interested in what other children have to say and in the pictures they draw, so they are motivated to read these homemade books.

Designing their own, original picture books also gives children an appreciation for the task facing authors and illustrators. Older children may even take on a challenge such as inventing their own versions of books with unusual formats. Some second-graders created a lift-the-flap format similar to Eric Hill's *Where's Spot?* and presented one of their creations each day to a group of kindergartners in their elementary school. Chelsea, a second-grader, inspired by picture books such as *Swimmy* (Lionni) and *The Rainbow Fish* (Pfister) that are about being different, decided to invent and illustrate a story of her own called "The Pink Tailed Mouse." Chelsea dictated the text for her story to Jessica, an early childhood student studying to become a teacher, and this text became the picture book shown opposite.

Picture books for curriculum planning

Following an exhaustive review of the literature, the National Commission on Reading issued a report on the status of literacy in America titled *Becoming a Nation of Readers* (Anderson et al. 1985). The Commission concluded:

> The single most important activity for building the knowledge required for eventual success in reading is reading aloud to children. . . . The benefits are greatest when the child is an active participant, discussing stories, identifying letters and words, and talking about the meaning of words. (23)

"The Pink Tailed Mouse," Dictated to Her Teacher Then Illustrated by Chelsea Dawne Feudale, Age 7

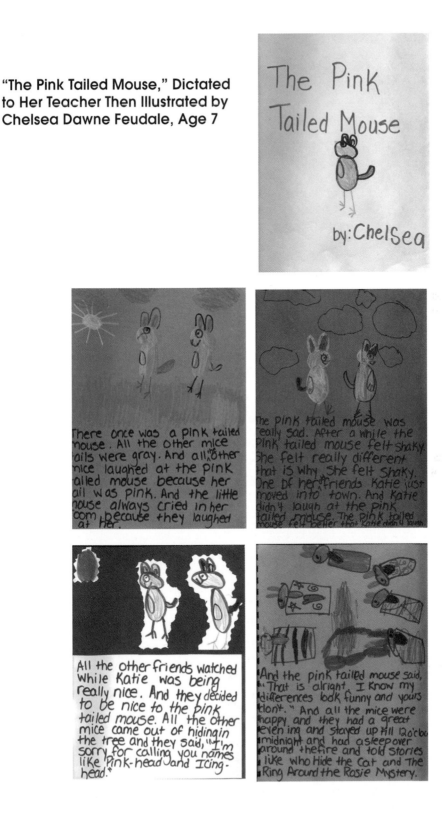

The Pink Tailed Mouse

by: Chelsea

There once was a pink tailed mouse. All the other mice tails were gray. And all other mice laughed at the pink tailed mouse because her tail was pink. And the little mouse always cried in her room because they laughed at her.

The pink tailed mouse was really sad. After a while the pink tailed mouse felt shaky. She felt really different that is why she felt shaky. One of her friends Katie just moved into town. And Katie didn't laugh at the pink tailed mouse. The pink tailed mouse felt better that Katie didn't laugh.

All the other friends watched while Katie was being really nice. And they decided to be nice to the pink tailed mouse. All the other mice came out of hiding in the tree and they said, "I'm sorry for calling you names like Pink-head and Icing-head."

And the pink tailed mouse said, "That is alright. I know my differences look funny and yours don't." And all the mice were happy and they had a great evening and stayed up till 12 o'clock midnight and had a sleepover around the fire and told stories like who Hide the Cat and The Ring Around the Rosie Mystery.

The importance of reading to children, with their active involvement, has long been appreciated as a route to literacy. More recently, there has been a proliferation of research that supports this view (see IRA/NAEYC 1998; Snow, Burns, & Griffin 1998). In other words, we know that most children learn to read from pleasurable experiences with favorite picture books.

Teachers can generate ideas, design related learning experiences, and enrich project work by beginning with a picture book. Three approaches to using picture books for curriculum building follow. Clearly, they can all be used in the same classroom; they are not mutually exclusive.

Organized by key concepts around a theme or project. Many early childhood teachers use the same themes year after year, often based on the calendar. But it can be preferable to select themes that have special significance for the children, rather than the same, tired old topics, and that might contribute to conceptual understandings that would support academic achievement. For example, a theme with great significance for emergent and early readers is literacy itself—its pleasures and uses, the challenges, and so on—yet few teachers select it. The box **Key Concepts in a "Literacy" Theme with Kindergarten and Primary Grade Children** suggests seven concepts about literacy and examples of picture books that would help to develop those concepts.

Likewise, teachers can use picture books centered around a project, in which children study something in depth that they can experience directly and then represent their understandings in a variety of ways—the school bus, for example (see Katz and Chard 2000). Once again, children's literature can be a resource for curriculum building. Preschoolers can pore over the details of a school bus in *School Bus* (Crews 1993*)* and emergent readers can learn to read using the predictable book *The Bus for Us* (Bloom) or the cumulative rhyme *The Little School Bus* (Roth). Children in the primary grades can use picture books to explore subject areas: math story problems in *The Smushy Bus* (Helakoski), science through the dozens of Magic School Bus series books by Joanna Cole (several are in Spanish, as well), or social studies in *A Bus of Our Own* (Evans) about racial discrimination in Mississippi.

Based in the learning domains. A second strategy for designing a literature-based curriculum is to designate the various learning domains, and list related activities under science, math, social studies, arts, and so on. The box **The Harvest** shows an example of a curriculum designed in this way for preschoolers.

Connected to developmental issues. By focusing on developmental issues that most members of an age group are facing, teachers can plan well-coordinated sequences of story choices. For example, the box **Sleeping and Waking** presents a web showing sequenced options for picture books related to that issue for infants and toddlers.

Mary Renck Jalongo

Key Concepts in a "Literacy" Theme with Kindergarten and Primary Grade Children

What are the different ways that people communicate?
- *I Hate English!* (Levine)
- *Moses Goes to School* (Millman)
- *My Grandma, My Pen Pal* (Koutsky)
- *Sitti's Secrets* (Nye)

What are the benefits of reading and writing?
- *Bunny Cakes* (Wells)
- *Mr. Pine's Mixed-Up Signs* (Kessler)
- *The Day of Ahmed's Secret* (Heide & Gilliland)
- *The Old Woman Who Loved to Read* (Winch)

Where can we go to read?
- *Check It Out! The Book about Libraries* (Gibbons)
- *Stella Louella's Runaway Book* (Ernst)
- *The Best Place to Read* (Bertram & Bloom)

What gets in the way of learning to read and write?
- *Aunt Chip and the Great Triple Creek Dam Affair* (Polacco)
- *Fix-It* (McPhail)
- *More Than Anything Else* (Bradby)
- *The Wretched Stone* (Van Allsburg)
- *Why I Will Never Ever Ever Ever Have Enough Time to Read This Book* (Charlip)

Who helps others to learn to read and write?
- *Read for Me, Mama* (Rahaman)
- *Thank You, Mr. Falker* (Polacco)
- *The Wednesday Surprise* (Bunting)
- *Tomás and the Library Lady* (Mora)

What might happen if animals could read and write?
- *A Story for Bear* (Haseley)
- *"Book! Book! Book!"* (Bruss)
- *Giggle, Giggle, Quack* (Cronin)
- *If You Take a Mouse to School* (Numeroff)

Why do people read?
- *I Love Going through This Book* (Burleigh)

Conclusion: Accepting responsibility for a literature-based curriculum

Rather than think of picture books as merely a pleasant diversion, a time filler, a way to calm children down after lunch or recess, we early childhood teachers need to view picture books as a key resource in our lifelong journey of becoming more competent and caring educators. Even when tight budgets prevent us from acquiring all the up-to-date resources and teaching materials we might like to have, we can visit the library and come out with a book bag full of fresh provisions—and fresh ideas, too—for engaging young children.

When we are at a loss for ideas to motivate and interest a particular child, settling down with a stack of picture books can be exactly what we need to think more creatively. . . . When the inevitable classroom conflicts arise, picture books

The Harvest: Activities Based in the Learning Domains for 4-, 5-, and 6-Year-Olds, Featuring *The Biggest Pumpkin Ever*

Language arts
- Listen to a recording of Hal Linden reading the story (Kroll).
- Read the poem "Mice" by Rose Fyleman.
- Share other stories about mice: *The Mother's Day Mice* (Bunting), *Come Out and Play, Little Mouse* (Kraus), *Sheila Rae, the Brave* (Henkes), *Mousekin's Golden House* (Miller), *Frederick* (Lionni).
- Read other books about gigantic food, such as *Cloudy with a Chance of Meatballs* (Barrett).

Science/cooking
- Visit a pumpkin patch.
- Experiment with sugar water as a way of stimulating a pumpkin's growth.
- Observe a real mouse and its proportion in relationship to a large pumpkin.
- Look for the first frost in the fall.
- Read a story about the seasons of the year, such as *A Year of Beasts* (Wolff).
- Roast and salt pumpkin seeds.
- Make pumpkin pie or pumpkin bread by following a rebus recipe.
- Cook pumpkin soup using a recipe from the colonial American era.
- Read *The Pumpkin Book* (Gibbons) and *It's Pumpkin Time* (Hall).

Mathematics
- Use magnetic geometric shapes and a pizza pan painted with lead-free orange paint to create different jack-o'-lantern faces.
- Have the children create a bulletin board to show the 100 mice on motorcycles; read books such as *Anno's Counting Book* (Anno) and *How Much Is a Million?* (Schwartz).
- Use children's drawings of pumpkins to categorize as small, medium, or large.
- Play a seriation game in which pumpkins drawn by the children are arranged from the smallest and greenest to largest and most orange.

Creative arts
- Create mouse finger puppets using peanut shells, finger tips from old gloves, or felt.
- Study the pictures in Lois Ehlert's *Red Leaf, Yellow Leaf,* and mix paints to replicate some of the colors seen on a fall walk.
- Use modeling dough to create something from the story.
- Sing and dramatize "In My Garden" and "Down on Grandpa's Farm" by Raffi.
- Sing the song picture book *The Fox Went Out on a Chilly Night* (Spier).

Social studies
- Coach children in role playing the scene where the two mice decide to share the pumpkin.
- Discuss *Best Friends* (Kellogg) and the girls' decision to share the puppy.

More books with a harvest or feast theme
- *My First Kwanzaa Book* (Chocolate)
- *Market Day: A Story Told with Folk Art* (Ehlert)
- *Mean Soup* (Everitt)
- *Latkes and Applesauce: A Hanukkah Story* (Manushkin)
- *Feast for Ten* (Falwell)
- *Celie and the Harvest Fiddler* (Flournoy)
- *Fall Leaves Fall!* (Hall)
- *One Tough Turkey* (Kroll)
- *This Is the Turkey* (Levine)

The two of them bumped heads and fell down.
"You've been feeding the pumpkin," said Clayton.
"You've been feeding the pumpkin," said Desmond.
"That's why it got so big," said Clayton.
"That's why it got so big," said Desmond.
They burst out laughing.

From *The Biggest Pumpkin Ever.* Text copyright © 1984 by Steven Kroll. Illustrations copyright © 1984 by Jeni Bassett. Reprinted by permission of Holiday House.

Sleeping and Waking: A Sequence of Picture Books Connected to Developmental Issues for 1-, 2-, and 3-Year-Olds

Getting Ready for Bed

Bathing and Changing Clothes

All by Myself (Hines)
Bathwater's Hot (Hughes)
Good Night, Monkey Boy (Krosoczka)
I Dance in My Red Pajamas (Hurd)
I Hate to Go to Bed (Davis)
The Practically Perfect Pajamas (Brooks)
The Tub People (Conrad)

Toys and Blankets

Everything to Spend the Night: From
 A to Z (Whitford Paul)
Ira Sleeps Over (Waber)
Max's Bedtime (Wells)
Ten Minutes Till Bedtime
 (Rathmann)
The Quilt Story (Johnston)
When I'm Sleepy (Howard)

Poetry

A Pocketful of Stars: Poems about the
 Night (Siegen-Smith)
Jump All the Morning: A Child's Day in
 Verse (Roche)
Night in the Country (Rylant)
When the Dark Comes Dancing
 (Larrick)
Wynken, Blynken, and Nod
 (Field)

Sleep

I Am Not Sleepy and I
 Will Not Go to Bed (Child)
Little Bunny's Sleepless Night
 (Roth)
Moonlight (Ormerod)
Roll Over! (Gerstein)
Sleep Tight, Ginger Kitten
 (Geras)
Slumber Party! (Caseley)
When Sheep Cannot Sleep
 (Kitamura)

Pleasant Dreams

Close Your Eyes (Marzollo)
If There Were Dreams to Sell
 (Lalicki)
The Donkey's Dream (Berger)
Fox's Dream (Tejima)

Bedtime Stories and Songs

Stories

Calf, Goodnight (Jewell)
Midnight Farm (Lindbergh)
The Baby's Lap Book (Chorao)

Lullabies

All the Pretty Horses (Jeffers)
Jumbo's Lullaby (Melmed)
Once: A Lullaby (Nichol)
One Grain of Sand: A Lullaby
  (Seeger)
The Lullaby Songbook (Yolen)

Waking Up

Early Morning in the Barn (Tafuri)
How Do I Put It On? (Watanabe)
Jesse Bear, What Will You Wear?
  (Carlstrom)
Junglewalk (Tafuri)
The Napping House (Wood)
What! Cried Granny: An Almost
  Bedtime Story (Lum)

Nightmares

No Elephants Allowed (Robison)
There's an Alligator under My
  Bed (Mayer)
What's under My Bed?
  (Stevenson)

can effectively demonstrate to young children ways of coping and teach them lessons about diversity and acceptance that will make centers and classrooms better places for everyone to spend their days. . . . And when tragedies and crises strike in children's lives, leaving us struggling to respond, a carefully chosen picture book often can help. At the end of this chapter is a resource list that will assist in locating just the right book for any occasion.

For all of these reasons, high-quality picture books are less like icing on a cake and more like a thick filling at its center, a filling that not only offers surprise but also holds the individual layers in place. Perhaps most important of all, that filling can transform a good cake into an excellent one. Picture books are (or should be) central to our practice. Good books lend cohesiveness to the components of curriculum; and quality books can elevate a good program into a better one.

Consider, for example, one of my favorite books, *Wilfrid Gordon McDonald Partridge,* by Mem Fox. In this story we meet a young boy with a long name who lives next door to a residential facility for the elderly. Although he knows them all and admires their special talents such as sharing stories and playing the organ, his favorite senior—Miss Nancy Alison Delacourt Cooper—has four names, just like Wilfrid does. When Wilfrid overhears his parents talking about Miss Nancy losing her memory, he asks each resident "What's a memory?" and gets different answers: something warm, something from long ago, something that makes you cry, something that makes you laugh, something as precious as gold. Wilfrid decides to look for things that might fit these definitions and present them to Miss Nancy. In his basket, he collects a warm hen's egg, a seashell, a medal, a puppet, and a football. Each of the items does prompt Miss Nancy's memory.

I have seen teachers develop curriculum by beginning with Fox's book. The gentle story led one third grade teacher to develop a theme she titled "What We Treasure: People, Places, and Things" and to get her students involved in activities such as interviewing family members, creating a classroom museum of family treasures and writing each item's story, and sharing the traditions of their cultural and ethnic heritages. A first grade teacher used the book to introduce an intergenerational project in which her students would write to senior pen pals for several weeks before visiting them and sharing stories together.

Experienced and proficient early childhood teachers would never try to teach children without using literature. They turn to picture books for inspiration and treat them as a resource. They use picture books to improve curriculum, teaching, and above all, the learning of every child.

Help in finding the right book for any curriculum

Beaty, J.J. 1996. *Building bridges with multicultural picture books: For children 3–5.* Upper Saddle River, NJ: Merrill/Prentice Hall.

Brown, J.C., & L.A. Oates, eds. 2002. *Books to grow on: African American literature for young children.* Brochure. Washington, DC: NAEYC.

Mary Renck Jalongo

Then Wilfrid Gordon called on Miss Nancy
and gave her each thing one by one.

Reproduced, with permission, from Kane/Miller Book Publishers, *Wilfrid Gordon McDonald Partridge*
(La Jolla: Kane/Miller). Text copyright © 1984 by Mem Fox. Illustrations copyright © 1984 by Julie Vivas.

Freeman, J. 1990. *Books kids will sit still for: The complete read-aloud guide.* New York: Bowker.

Freeman, J. 2000. The best picture books of the twentieth century. *Instructor* 1101: 12–16.

Gillespie, J.T., & C.J. Naden. 1990. *Best books for children: Preschool through middle grades.* 4th ed. New York: Bowker.

Glantz, S. 2000. Picture books. *Library Talk* 133: 34–41.

Horning, K., G. Moore-Kruse, & M. Schliesman. 1999. *Cooperative children's book center choices 1998.* Madison, WI: Friends of the Cooperative Children's Book Center.

Hurst, C.O. 1990. *Once upon a time: An encyclopedia for successfully using literature with young children.* Allen, TX: DLM.

Kimmel, M.M., & E. Segal. 1990. *For reading out loud!* New York: Delacorte.

Lima, C.W., & J.A. Lima. 1989. *A to Zoo: Subject access to children's picture books.* 3d ed. New York: Bowker.

Schon, I. 2002. *Books to grow on: Latino literature for young children.* Brochure. Washington, DC: NAEYC.

Sierra, J., & R. Kaminski. 1991. *Twice upon a time: Stories to tell, retell, act out, and write about.* Bronx, NY: Wilson.

Trelease, J. 2001. *The new read-aloud handbook.* New York: Penguin.

Yokota, J., ed. 2001. *Kaleidoscope: A multicultural booklist of grades K–8.* 3d ed. Urbana, IL: National Council of Teachers of English.

Yopp, R.H., & H.K. Yopp. 1992. *Literature-based reading activities.* Boston, MA: Allyn & Bacon.

Zarnowsky, M., R.M. Kerper, & J.M. Jensen. 2001. *The best in children's nonfiction: Reading, writing, and teaching Orbis Pictus Award books.* Urbana, IL: National Council of Teachers of English.

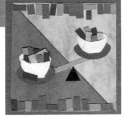

The Future of Picture Books

Picture books build an aesthetic sense in very young children, an appreciation of language and art that can be the beginning of a lifetime of cultural experience. They also build community between adults and children as they are so often a shared pleasure. I believe that all our children have the right to be introduced to these books.
—Robin Morrow, "The Picture Book" (1999, 41)

Part of the challenge confronting every generation of early childhood educators is preparing children for a future that we can barely imagine. What will stories and reading be like 10 or 20 years from now, when today's young children have become tomorrow's adults? One thing seems certain: The literacy with print that makes it possible for us to function today in society will prove inadequate in the future . . . in fact, it already is inadequate in many ways. The paper-and-pencil–driven literacy taught in most schools now, though necessary, is not sufficient to operate at the highest levels of our society, where the ability to move seamlessly from one type of symbol system to another and to expertly blend ideas with images and words is prized. And we need only to look around us to see that *media literacy*—defined as the ability to understand, interpret, and make responsible decisions about a variety of mass media and media messages including advertising, television, the Internet, newspapers, magazines, and videos (McBrien 1999)—is a survival skill. For children to acquire these proficiencies, teachers will need to embrace a "pedagogy of multiliteracies" (New London Group 1996).

Yet, as the world becomes increasingly wired, networked, high tech, and instantaneous, faster is not always better. This new communications environment, for example, does not encourage—even discourages—sustained interest and concentrated focus. Instead, the new media are more suited to "surfing" and "scanning" than to study and reflection. As Derrick de Kerckhove (1997) notes, this characteristic may be one explanation for the persistence of the printed page. He notes

> [A book is] a resting place for words. It sounds trite, but in fact the printed page is the only place where words do have a rest. Everywhere else, they are moving: when you speak, when you see them on a screen, when you see them on the Net, words are moving. But a book is a restful place. The printed word is, and always was, still. (107)

In spite of the technology's many contributions, the Internet "still has not found the equivalent of a novel" (Hunt 2000, 111).

Some experts argue that the picture book will endure because, in many ways, it is already adapted to an image-driven society. Children's books represent a synthesis of graphics and text that renders them "powerful allies for learning some very complicated reading strategies. . . . Picture books offer the stability of print but at the same time they open the doors for readers to make connections with many different kinds of texts in their own lives" (Mackey & McClay 2000, 192). Others wonder whether publishing for children and for adults will go their separate ways, with children remaining with picture books while adults go to electronic (e-book) formats. The entire children's book publishing industry is still trying to anticipate which way or even whether to move on e-books for children.

Still others foresee fundamental changes in the way we define "story" and in readers' roles as interpreters of or participants in the construction of narratives.

 "Electronic media are not simply changing the way we tell stories; they are changing the very nature of story, of what we understand (or do not understand) to be narratives" (Hunt 2000, 111). Innovations such as *hypermedia* (which links sounds and words electronically) and MUDs (*multiuser domains* that create multi-layered texts, both old and new, that readers can help to write, annotate, or respond to) set different expectations for what a story is and what the act of reading means (Hunt 2000). Under these circumstances, as Janet Murray (1997) contends, books, films, and plays begin to push "against the boundaries of linear storytelling . . . like a two-dimensional picture trying to burst out of its frame" (28–29).

In the future, picture books may become far less linear and far more interactive than we now envision—more virtual reality than ink on paper. Tomorrow's child, immersed from birth in a flow of rapidly fleeting images, may find those new formats more soothing and pleasurable than what we, as yesterday's children, find appealing about books today—the feel of the paper; the opportunity to pause, reflect, and relook or reread; the ability to stop completely and return later, knowing that nothing will have changed.

Despite what new paths literature may take, one thing is reasonably certain: Young children will still need caring adults to introduce and guide them. Whatever the future holds for adult readers and writers, the world of the very young must always move a bit slower as young children experience the world afresh and uninitiated.

For the time being though, the picture books that we know and love are safe. For some fortunate adults, their love affair with picture books begins when they are young children. Pauline Davey Zeece (2003b) gives us a touching example in her story about a kindergartner whose affection for Ezra Jack Keats's work lasted a lifetime. Keats produced a variety of groundbreaking children's books during the 1970s and 1980s; in 2002, a collection of his classic stories was re-released. Zeece begins her story this way:

> The small child slowly entered the classroom with the other kindergarten children. The dust from a glorious playground digging adventure covered her with a fine coating of grit. Tiny strands of perspiration trickled down the side of her cheeks, leaving her face almost striped in appearance. . . . She was, however, undaunted as she negotiated her way through a group of adults who had encircled a very special visitor. Reaching the front of the room, she looked up and in an almost inaudible whisper asked: "Are you *really* Ezra Jack Keats?"
>
> With an immediate sensitivity to her question, Mr. Keats turned to the 5-year-old fan and said, "Why yes I am!" Quickly the child reached from behind her back and produced a small bouquet of beleaguered dandelions. Whispering again, she offered the flowers and said, "I love you, Ezra Jack Keats." The meticulously appointed Caldecott author-illustrator gently took the small yellow flowers and slipped one into the lapel of his suit as he replied, "Thank you, I love you too!" (2003b, 133)

The tale ends 20 years later, with Zeece encountering that same child in a bookstore, grown into an adult but again lovingly turning the pages of a Keats story, a smile on her lips as she studies the familiar illustrations in the reissued version. That kindergartner's love of picture books remained undiminished.

Other adults come to an appreciation of picture books much later, perhaps while raising their own children or, like me, while studying children's literature in their teacher preparation program. They are awed by the beauty of the illustrations, captivated by the crafting of the words, delighted by the humor, and amazed to discover that a whole world of children's literature is out there for them to discover. They realize they have some catching up to do, and waste no time. They dive into picture books at the library while helping their child to choose, browse the children's book section at the bookstore, collect lists of recommended picture books, borrow from a college faculty member's shelf, and begin building their own collections at home or at school. These adults may not have connected with picture books early in life, but they manage to make up for it. Often, a strong connection with one particular picture book creates the occasion to forge this kind of commitment.

The issue of when an appreciation for picture books occurs matters less than whether it occurs at all. What is important is that adults who care about children must, at some point, learn to care about this particular form of literature best suited to the young child—*the picture book.* Any early childhood educator who fails to mine the riches of picture books is missing out on a tremendous source of inspiration for effective teaching. Any child whose teacher fails to make picture books part of the program is deprived of a natural resource for learning.

Like a children's story, this book now comes full circle and revisits the dual thesis of engagement and enjoyment. One can attain literacy in many ways. Literature is the most compelling and wondrous way. Young children need to listen, retell, enact, and read picture book stories; relish rhymes and songs; and illustrate and write their own picture books. Those satisfying interactions with adults and peers that are focused on the pages of picture books are the ones through which children glimpse the value of literacy in their lives and learn to pursue adult literacy with passion and purpose.

 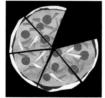 

Mary Renck Jalongo

References

A note to grownups. 1985. Brochure. Natick, MA: Picture Book Studio.

Adams, M.J. 1990. *Beginning to read: Thinking and learning about print.* Cambridge, MA: MIT Press.

Aiken, J. 1982. *The way to write for children.* New York: St. Martin's.

Allor, J.H., & R.B. McCathren. 2003. Developing emergent literacy skills through storybook reading. *Intervention in School and Clinic* 39 (2): 72–9.

American Booksellers Association. 2003, September 17. Children's book market suffers decline. *Bookselling This Week.* Available online: http://news.bookweb.org/news/1803.html

Anderson, R.C., E.H. Hiebert, J.A. Scott, & I.A.G. Wilkinson. 1985. *Becoming a nation of readers: The report of the Commission on Reading.* Washington, DC: U.S. Department of Education, National Institute of Education.

Anderson, R.C., P.Y. Wilson, & L. Fielding. 1988. Growth in reading and how children spend their time outside of school. *Reading Research Quarterly* 23: 285–303.

Applebee, A.N. 1978. *A child's concept of story: Ages two to five.* Chicago: University of Chicago Press.

Armington, D. 1997. *The living classroom: Reading, writing, and beyond.* Washington, DC: NAEYC.

Astbury, R. 1998. Editorial. *School Librarian* 46 (2): 57.

Au, K 1993. *Literacy instruction in multicultural settings.* Orlando, FL: Harcourt Brace.

Au, K. 1997. Literacy for all students: Ten steps toward making a difference. *The Reading Teacher* 51 (3): 186–94.

Auerbach, E.R. 1995a. From deficit to strength: Changing perspectives on family literacy. In *Immigrant learners and their families: Literature to connect the generations,* eds. G. Weinstein-Shr & E. Quintero, 59–62. McHenry, IL: Center for Applied Linguistics.

Auerbach, E.R. 1995b. Which way for family literacy: Intervention or empowerment? In *Family literacy: Connections in schools and communities,* ed. L.M. Morrow, 11–27. Newark, DE: International Reading Association.

Ayers, W., ed. 1995. *To become a teacher: Making a difference in children's lives.* New York: Teachers College Press.

Bader, B. 1998. American picture books from Max's metaphorical monsters to Lilly's purple plastic purse [Special Issue on Picture Books]. *The Horn Book Magazine* 74 (March/April): 141–56.

Bainbridge, J.M., S. Pantaleo, & M. Ellis. 1999. Multicultural picture books: Perspectives from Canada. *The Social Studies* 90 (July/August): 183–88.

Baker, A., & E. Greene. 1987. *Storytelling: Art and technique.* 2d ed. New York: Bowker.

Baker, S., D. Simmons, & E.J. Kameenui. 1998. Vocabulary acquisition: Instructional and curricular basics and implications. In *What reading research tells us about children with diverse learning needs,* eds. D.C. Simmons & E. Kameenui, 219–38. Hillsdale, NJ: Erlbaum.

Bamford, R., & J.V. Kristo, eds. 1998. *Making facts come alive: Choosing quality nonfiction literature K–8.* Norwood, MA: Christopher-Gordon.

Barbour, A. 1998–99. Home literacy bags promote family involvement. *Childhood Education* 75 (2): 71–75.

Barchers, S.I. 2000. *Multicultural folktales: Readers' theatre for elementary students.* Englewood, CO: Libraries Unlimited.

Barton, B. 1986. *Tell me another.* Exeter, NH: Heinemann.

Bauer, C.F. 1987. *Presenting reader's theater.* New York: H.W. Wilson.

Bauer, C.F. 1993. *New handbook for storytellers.* Chicago: American Library Association.

Becher, R.M. 1985. Parent involvement and reading achievement: A review of research and implications for practice. *Childhood Education* 62 (1): 44–50.

Benjamin, L.A., & J. Lord. 1996. *Family literacy.* Washington, DC: Office of Educational Research and Improvement.

Benton, M. 1979. Children's responses to stories. *Children's Literature in Education* 10: 68–85.

Berger, E. H. 1998. Reaching parents through literacy. *Early Childhood Education Journal* 25 (3): 211–15.

Berman, R.A. 2001. Setting the narrative scene: How children begin to tell a story. In *Children's language: Developing narrative and discourse competence,* eds. K.E. Nelson, A. Aksu-Koc, & C.E. Johnson, 1–30. Mahwah, NJ: Lawrence Erlbaum Associates.

Bettelheim, B. 1976. *The uses of enchantment: The meaning and importance of fairy tales.* New York: Knopf.

Bickler, S. 1999. Creating a mental set for learning. In *Understanding the literacy hour,* eds. R. Fisher & H. Arnold. Royston, England: United Kingdom Reading Association.

Billings, J.A. 1998. Toward equity: Bringing the community into the school. *Our Children: The National PTA Magazine* 23 (8): 34–35.

Bishop, R.S. 1992. Multicultural literature for children: Making informed choices. In *Teaching multicultural literature in grades K–8,* ed. V.J. Harris, 37–53. Norwood, MA: Christopher-Gordon.

Bissex, G.L. 1980. *GYNS AT WRK: A child learns to write and read.* Cambridge, MA: Harvard University Press.

Block, C.C., L.B. Gambrell, & M. Pressley, eds. 2002. *Improving comprehension instruction: Rethinking research, theory, and classroom practice.* San Francisco, CA: Jossey-Bass.

Bloodgood, J.W. 1999. What's in a name? Children's name writing and literacy acquisition. *Reading Research Quarterly* 34: 342–67.

Bodart, J. 1988. *Booktalk!* Chicago: American Library Association.

Bohn, A.H., & C.E. Sleeter. 2001. Will multicultural education survive the standards movement? *Education Digest* 66 (5): 17–24.

Borich, G. 1986. *Effective teaching methods.* 3d ed. New York: Macmillan.

Bouchard, M. 2001. *ESL Smart! Ready-to-use life skills and academic activities for grades K-8.* Bloomington, IN: Center for Applied Research in Education.

Braunger, J., & J.P. Lewis. 1998. *Building a knowledge base in reading.* 2d ed. Portland, OR: Northwest Regional Laboratory.

Braus, N., & M. Geidel. 2000. *Everyone's kids' books: A guide to multicultural, socially conscious books for children.* St. Brattleboro, VT: Everyone's Books.

Bredekamp, S., & C. Copple, eds. 1997. *Developmentally appropriate practice in early childhood programs.* Rev. ed. Washington, DC: NAEYC.

British Broadcasting Corporation (BBC). 1999, March 31. Year of Reading puts 23 million books in schools. *BBC News.* Available online: http://news.bbc.co.uk/1/hi/education/308506.stm

Britto, P.R. 2001. Family literacy environments and young children's emerging literacy skills. *Reading Research Quarterly* 36 (4): 346–48.

Bromley, K.D. 1996. *Webbing with literature: Creating story maps with children's books.* 2d ed. Boston: Allyn & Bacon.

Brooker, M. 1997. Bringing parents into the schools. *Reading Today* 15 (1): 13.

Brown, J.C., & L.A. Oates. 2001. *Books to grow on: African American literature for young children.* Brochure. Washington, DC: NAEYC.

Brown, M., R. Althouse, & C. Anfin. 1993. Guided dramatization: Fostering social development in children with disabilities. *Young Children* 48 (2): 68–71.

Bruner, J. 1983. *Child's talk: Learning to use language.* Oxford: Oxford University Press.

Bruner, J. 1990. *Acts of meaning.* Cambridge, MA: Harvard University Press.

Buckleitner, W. 1996. Literacy on-screen. *Scholastic Early Childhood Today* 11 (2): 8.

Bullough, R.V., & A.D. Gitlin. 2001. *Becoming a student of teaching: Linking knowledge production and practice.* 2d ed. New York: Routledge Falmer.

Burns, M.M., & A.A. Flowers. 1999. What ever happened to…? A list of recovered favorites and what makes a book memorable after all. *The Horn Book Magazine* 75 (September/October): 574–86.

Bus, A.G. 2001. Joint caregiver-child storybook reading: A route to literacy development. In *Handbook of early literacy research,* eds. S.B. Neuman & D.K. Dickinson, 179–91. New York: Guilford.

Butler, D. 1975. *Cushla and her books.* Boston: The Horn Book.

Caine, G., & R.N. Caine. 1997. *Education on the edge of possibility.* Alexandria, VA: Association for Supervision and Curriculum Development.

Calkins, L. 1983. *Lessons from a child.* Portsmouth, NH: Heinemann.

Cambourne, B. 2001. Conditions for literacy learning: Why do some students fail to learn to read? Ockham's razor and the conditions of learning. *The Reading Teacher* 54 (8): 784–86.

Campbell, P.B., & J. Wirtenberg. 1980. How books influence children: What the research shows. *Interracial Books for Children Bulletin* 11 (6): 3.

Cardenas, J., M. Robledo, & D. Waggoner. 1988. The undereducation of American youth. ERIC, ED309201.

Cartledge, G., & M.W. Kiarie. 2001. Learning social skills through literature for children and adolescents. *Teaching Exceptional Children* 34 (2): 40–47.

Cary, S. 2000. *Working with second language learners: Answers to teachers' top ten questions.* Portsmouth, NH: Heinemann.

Chambers, B. 1983. Counteracting racism and sexism in children's books. In *Understanding the multicultural experience in early childhood education,* eds. O. Saracho & B. Spodek, 91–105. Washington, DC: NAEYC.

Chandler, K. 2000. Functional illiteracy. *The Advisor* 26: 3.

Cianciolo, P.J. 1984. Illustrations in children's books. In *The Scott, Foresman anthology of children's literature,* eds. Z. Sutherland & M.C. Livingston, 846–78. Glenview, IL: Scott, Foresman.

Cianciolo, P.J. 2000. *Informational picture books for children.* Chicago: American Library Association.

Clay, M.M. 1979. *Reading: The patterning of complex behaviour.* 2d ed. Auckland, New Zealand: Heinemann Education NZ.

Clay, M.M. 1985. *Early detection of reading difficulties.* 3d ed. Auckland, NZ: Heinemann.

Cliatt, M.J.P., & J.M. Shaw. 1988. The storytime exchange: Ways to enhance it. *Childhood Education* 64 (5): 293–98.

Clifton, L. 1981. Writing for black children. *The Advocate* 1: 32–4

Coats, K. 2001. Fish stories: Teaching children's literature in a postmodern world. *Pedagogy* 1 (2): 405–409.

Cohen, L.E. 1997. How I developed my kindergarten book backpack program. *Young Children* 52 (2): 69–71.

Collins, N.L.D., & M.B. Shaeffer. 1997. Look, listen, and learn to read. *Young Children* 52 (5): 65–67.

Conrad, N.K., Y. Gong, L. Sipp, & L.D. Wright. 2003. Using text talk as a gateway to culturally responsive teaching. *Early Childhood Education Journal* 31 (3): 187–94.

Copple, C., ed. 2002. *A world of difference: Readings on teaching young children in a diverse society.* Washington, DC: NAEYC.

Council on Interracial Books for Children. 1978. *Identifying racism and sexism in children's books.* Filmstrip. New York: Racism and Sexism Resource Center for Educators.

Creany, A.D. 1999. Censorship: Evaluating quality without imposing agendas. In *Resisting the pendulum swing: Informed perspectives on education controversy,* ed. M. Jalongo, 17–27. Olney, MD: Association for Childhood Education International.

Cress, S.W., & D.T. Holm. 2000. Developing empathy through children's literature. *Education* 120 (3): 593–97.

Cullinan, B.E. 1977. Books in the life of the young child. In *Literature and young children,* eds. B.E. Cullinan & C.W. Carmichael, 1–16. Urbana, IL: National Council of Teachers of English.

Cullinan, B.E., & L. Galda. 1994. *Literature and the child.* 3d ed. New York: Harcourt Brace.

Cummings, P. 1992. *Talking with artists.* New York: Bradbury.

Cummings, P. 1993. *Talking with artists II.* New York: Bradbury.

Daniels, H. 1994. *Literature circles: Voice and choice in the student-centered classroom.* York, ME: Stenhouse.

de Kerckhove, D. 1997. *Connected intelligence: The arrival of the Web society.* Toronto, Canada: Somerville House.

de la Mare, W. 1942. *Bells and grass.* Reissue ed. New York: Viking.

DEE (Department for Education and Employment). 1998. *The national literacy strategy: Framework for teaching.* London: Author.

DeGeorge, K.L. 1998. Friendship and stories: Using children's literature to teach friendship skills to children with learning disabilities. *Intervention in School and Clinic* 3 (3): 157–62.

Diamond, B., & M. Moore. 1995. *Multicultural literacy: Mirroring the reality of the classroom.* White Plains, NY: Longman.

Diamond, M., & J. Hopson. 1998. *Magic trees of the mind: How to nurture your child's intelligence, creativity, and healthy emotions from birth through adolescence.* New York: Penguin/Putnam.

Dickinson, D., & P.O. Tabors, eds. 2001. *Beginning literacy with language: Young children learning at home and school.* Baltimore: Paul H. Brookes.

Dickinson, D.K., & M.W. Smith. 1994. Long-term effects of preschool teachers' book readings on the language and literacy development of low-income children's vocabulary and story comprehension. *Reading Research Quarterly* 29: 104–22.

Dickman, F.C. 1998. Textile art as illustration. *Book Links* 7 (6): 49–51.

Doake, D. 1985. Reading-like behavior: Its role in learning to read. In *Observing the language learner,* eds. A. Jaggar & M. Trika Smith-Burke, 82–98. Newark, DE: International Reading Association.

Dugan, J. 1997. Transactional literature discussions: Engaging students in the appreciation and understanding of literature. *The Reading Teacher* 51 (2): 86–96.

Duke, N., & J. Kays. 1998. Can I say 'once upon a time'?: Kindergarten children developing knowledge of information book language. *Early Childhood Research Quarterly* 13 (2): 295–318.

Editors of *Reading Today.* 2000. SIG booklist features best books for children. *Reading Today* 18 (1): 33.

Edmiston, B. 1993. Going up the beanstalk: Discovering giant possibilities for responding to literature through drama. In *Journeying: Children responding to literature,* eds. K. Holland, R. Hungerford, & S. Ernst, 250–66. Portsmouth, NH: Heinemann.

Educational Research Service. 1998. *Reading aloud to children.* ERS Info-File #F1-342. Arlington, VA: Author.

Eihorn, K. 2001. *Easy & engaging ESL activities and mini-books for every classroom.* New York: Scholastic.

Elleman, B. 1986. Picture book art: Evaluation. *Booklist* 8 (2): 1548.

Enge, N. 1998–99. "Do I belong here?" Understanding the adopted, language-minority child. *Childhood Education* 75 (2): 106–09.

Ernst-Slavit, G., J. Han, & K.J. Wenger. 2001. Reading at home, reading at school: Conflict, communication, and collaboration when school and home cultures are different. In *Collaboration for diverse learners: Viewpoints and practices,* eds. V.J. Risko & K. Bromley, 289–309. Newark, DE: International Reading Association.

Favat, F.A. 1977. *Child and tale.* Urbana, IL: National Council of Teachers of English.

Fenson, L., P.S. Dale, J.S. Reznick, E. Bates, D.J. Thal, & S.J. Pethick. 1994. Variability in early communicative development. *Monographs of the Society for Research in Child Development* 59 (5): v–173.

Finazzo, D. 1997. *All for the children: Multicultural essentials of literature.* Albany, NY: Delmar/ ITP.

Finn, J.D. 1998. Parental engagement that makes a difference. *Educational Leadership* 55 (8): 20–24.

Fisher, R. 1995. *Teaching children to learn.* Cheltenham, England: Stanley Thornes.

Fisher, R. 2002. *Inside the literacy hour.* New York: Routledge Falmer.

Fox, D.L., & K.G. Short. 2003. *Stories matter: The complexity of cultural authenticity in children's literature.* Urbana, IL: National Council of Teachers of English.

Fox, M. 2001. *Reading magic: Why reading aloud to our children will change their lives forever.* San Diego, CA: Harvest/Harcourt Brace.

Fox, S. 1997. The controversy over Ebonics. *Phi Delta Kappan* 79 (3): 237–41.

Freire, P. 1987. The importance of the act of reading. In *Literacy: Reading the word and the world,* eds. P. Freire & D. Macedo, 29–36. Westport, CT: Bergin & Garvey.

Fuller, M.L. 1998. *Effective home-school relations: Working successfully with parents and families.* Boston: Allyn & Bacon.

Funkhouser, J.E., & M.R. Gonzales. 1997. *Family involvement in children's education: Successful local approaches.* Washington, DC: U.S. Department of Education, Office of Educational Research and Improvement, Office of Research.

Galda, L. 1983. Research in response to literature. *Journal of Research and Development in Education* 16 (3): 1–7.

Gallas, K. 1994. *The languages of learning: How children talk, write, dance, and sing their understanding of the world.* New York: Teachers College Press.

Gallas, K. 1997. Story time as a magical act open only to the initiated: What some children don't know about power and may not find out. *Language Arts* 74 (4): 248–54.

Garcia, E. 2003. Respecting children's home languages and cultures. In *A world of difference: Readings on teaching young children in a diverse society,* ed. C. Copple, 16. Washington, DC: NAEYC.

Gestwicki, C. 2000. *Home, school, and community relations: A guide to working with families.* 4th ed. Albany, NY: Delmar.

Giblin, J. 1996. Trends in children's books today. In *Only connect: Readings on children's literature,* 3d ed., eds. S.E. Egoff, G. Stuffs, R. Ashley, & W. Sutton, 337–42. New York: Oxford University Press.

Gillespie, J.T. 2001. *Best books for children: Preschool through grade 6.* Westport, CT: Greenwood.

Giorgis, C., & N. Johnson. 1999. Children's books: Visual literacy. *The Reading Teacher* 53 (2): 146–52.

Glazer, S.M. 1998. *Assessment is instruction: Reading, writing, spelling, and phonics for all learners.* Norwood, MA: Christopher-Gordon.

Gorter-Reu, M.S., & J.M. Anderson. 1998. Home kits, home visits, and more! *Young Children* 53 (3): 1–74.

Goswami, U. 2001. Early phonological development and the acquisition of literacy. In *Handbook of early literacy research,* eds. S.B. Neuman & D.K. Dickinson, 111–25. New York: Guilford.

Graham, J. 2000. Creativity and picture books. *Reading* 34 (July): 61–67.

Greenlaw, M.J. 1983. Reading interest research and children's choices. In *Children's choices: Teaching with books children like,* eds. N. Reser & M. Frith, 90–119. Newark, DE: International Reading Association.

Gregory, L.P., & T.G. Morrison. 1998. Lap reading for young at-risk children: Introducing families to books. *Early Childhood Education Journal* 26 (3): 67–78.

Guthrie, J.T., & A. Wigfield, eds. 1997. *Reading engagement: Motivating readers through integrated instruction.* Newark, DE: International Reading Association.

Hade, D.D. 2001. Curious George gets branded: Reading as consuming. *Theory into Practice* 40 (3): 158–65.

Hall, C., & M. Coles. 1999. *Children's reading choices.* London: Routledge.

Harding, N. 1996. Family journals: The bridge from school to home and back again. *Young Children* 51 (2): 27–30.

Harms, J.M., & L. Lettow. 1996. *Picture books to enhance the curriculum.* Chicago: Wilson.

Harper, G. 2001. Enfranchising the child: Picture books, primacy, and discourse. *Style* 35 (3): 393–409.

Harris, V., ed. 1997. *Using multiethnic literature in the K–8 classroom.* Norwood, MA: Christopher-Gordon.

Harwayne, S. 1992. *Lasting impressions: Weaving literature into the writing workshop.* Portsmouth, NH: Heinemann.

Hearne, B. 2000. *Choosing books for children: A common sense guide.* 3d ed. Champaign, IL: University of Illinois Press.

Hefflin, B.R., & M.A. Barksdale-Ladd. 2001. African American children's literature that helps students find themselves: Selection guidelines for grades K–3. *The Reading Teacher* 54 (8): 810–19.

Helburn, S. 1994. *Cost, quality and child outcomes in child care centers.* Denver, CO: Department of Economics, Center for Research in Economics and Social Policy, University of Colorado at Denver.

Hepler, S.J., & J. Hickman. 1982. The book was okay. I love you. Social aspects of responses to literature. *Theory into Practice* 21: 278–83.

Hickman, J. 1984. Research currents: Researching children's response to literature. *Language Arts* 61: 278–84.

Hidalgo, N.M., S.-F. Siu, J.A. Bright, S.M. Swap, & J.L. Epstein. 1995. Research on families, schools, and communities: A multicultural perspective. In *Handbook of research on multicultural education,* eds. J.A. Banks & C.A.M. Banks, 498–524. New York: Macmillan.

Hiebert, E., & B. Taylor. 2000. Beginning reading instruction: Research on early interventions. In *Handbook of reading research, Vol. 3,* eds. M. Kamil, P. Mosenthal, P. Pearson, & R. Barr, 455–82. Mahwah, NJ: Erlbaum.

High, P.C., L. LaGasse, S. Becker, I. Ahlgren, & A. Gardner. 2000. Literacy promotion in primary care pediatrics: Can we make a difference? *Pediatrics* 105 (4): 927–34.

Hodges, J. 1995. Conflict resolution for the young child. ERIC Clearinghouse on Elementary and Early Childhood ERIC Document Reproduction Service No. ED 356 100.

Hoffman, S., & N. Knipping. 1988. Learning through literature. Paper presented at the Meeting of the Association for Childhood Education International, April, Salt Lake City, Utah.

Holdaway, D. 1979. *The foundations of literacy.* Sydney, Australia: Ashton/Scholastic.

Honig, A.S., & M. Shin. 2001. Reading aloud with infants and toddlers in child care settings: An observational study. *Early Childhood Education Journal* 28 (3): 193–97.

Horning, K., G. Moore-Kruse, & M. Schliesman. 1999. *Cooperative children's book center choices 1998.* Madison, WI: Friends of the Cooperative Children's Book Center.

Horning, K.T. 1997. *From cover to cover: Evaluating and reviewing children's books.* New York: HarperTrophy.

Huck, C., S. Hepler, J. Hickman, & B. Kiefer. 2000. *Children's literature in the elementary school.* 7th ed. New York: McGraw-Hill.

Hunt, P. 2000. Futures for children's literature: Evolution or radical break? *Cambridge Journal of Education* 30: 111–17.

IRA (International Reading Association) & NAEYC. 1998. Joint Position Statement. Learning to read and write: Developmentally appropriate practices for young children. *Young Children* 53 (4): 30–46.

Isenberg, J.P., & M.R. Jalongo. 2000. *Creative expression and play in early childhood.* 3d ed. Upper Saddle River, NJ: Merrill/Prentice Hall.

Jacobs, J.S., T.G. Morrison, & W.R. Swinyard. 2000. Reading aloud to students: A national probability study of classroom reading practices of elementary school teachers. *Reading Psychology* 21: 171–93.

Jacobs, L. 1965. *Using literature with young children.* New York: Teachers College Press.

Jalongo, M.R. 1986. Using crisis-oriented books with young children. In *Reducing stress in young children's lives,* ed. J.B. McCracken, 41–46. Washington, DC: NAEYC.

Jalongo, M.R. 2002. Constructing a childhood. Editorial. *Early Childhood Education Journal* 30 (1): 1–2.

Jalongo, M.R. 2003a. *Early childhood language arts.* 3d ed. Boston: Allyn & Bacon.

Jalongo, M.R. 2003b. The child's right to creative thought and expression. International Position Paper of the Association for Childhood Education International. *Childhood Education* 79 (4): 218–28.

Jalongo, M.R., N.K. Conrad, D. Dragich, & A. Zhang. 2002. Using wordless picture books to support young children's literacy growth. *Early Childhood Education Journal* 29 (3): 167–77.

Jalongo, M.R., B.S. Fennimore, & L.N. Stamp. 2004. The acquisition of literacy: Reframing definitions, paradigms, ideologies, and practices. In *Contemporary perspectives on language education and language policy in early childhood education,* eds. O. Saracho & B. Spodek, 65–86. Greenwich, CT: Information Age Publishing.

Jalongo, M.R., & M.A. Renck. 1984. Looking homeward: Nostalgia in children's literature. *School Library Journal* 31: 36–39.

Jalongo, M.R., & D. Ribblett. 1997. Using song picture books to support emergent literacy. *Childhood Education* 74 (1): 15–22.

Jennings, M. 2001. Two very special service-learning projects. *Phi Delta Kappan* 82 (6): 474–75.

Jensen, E. 1998. *Teaching with the brain in mind.* Alexandria, VA: Association for Supervision and Curriculum Development.

Jobson, E. 2001. Joining the children's cyber marketplace: A challenge for publishers. *Publishing Research Quarterly* 17 (1): 21–8.

Jones, E., & J. Nimmo. 1999. Collaboration, conflict, and change: Thoughts on education as provocation. *Young Children* 54 (1): 5–10.

Justice, L.M., & J. Kaderavek. 2002. Using shared storybook reading to promote emergent literacy. *Teaching Exceptional Children* 34 (4): 8–13.

Kaderavek, J.N., & E. Sulzby. 1998. Parent-child joint book reading: An observational protocol for young children. *American Journal of Speech-Language Pathology* 7: 33–47.

Kagan, S.L., & B. Weissbourd. 1994. *Putting families first: America's family support movement and the challenge of change.* San Francisco: Jossey-Bass.

Katz, L.G. 1988. What should young children be doing? *American Educator* 12: 28–33, 44.

Katz, L.G., & S.C. Chard. 2000. *Engaging children's minds: The project approach.* 2d ed. Norwood, NJ: Ablex.

Kiefer, B. 1985. Looking beyond picture book preferences. *The Horn Book Magazine* 61 (November/December): 705–13.

Kiefer, B. 1995. *The potential of picture books: From visual literacy to aesthetic understanding.* Englewood Cliffs, NJ: Merrill/Prentice Hall.

Kimmel, M.M., & E. Segel. 1984. *For reading out loud! A guide to sharing books with children.* New York: Dell.

Koeller, S., & P.M. Mitchell. 1996. From Ben's story to your story: Encouraging young writers, authentic voices, and learning engagement. *The Reading Teacher* 50 (4): 328–36.

Kohl, H. 1995. *Should we burn Babar? Essays on children's literature and the power of stories.* New York: New Press.

Kozol, J. 1998. Learning with our students: Growing as teachers. Opening speech at the Annual Convention of the National Council of Teachers of English, November 19–24, Nashville, Tennessee.

Krashen, S. 1993. *The power of reading: Insights from the research.* Englewood, CO: Libraries Unlimited.

Krashen, S. 1997. *Every person a reader: An alternative to the California Task Force Report on Reading.* Portsmouth, NH: Heinemann.

Lacy, L.E. 1986. *Art and design in children's picture books.* Chicago: American Library Association.

Lamme, L.L., V. Cox, J. Matanzo, & M. Olson. 1980. *Raising readers: A guide to sharing literature with young children.* New York: Walker.

Larrick, N. 1980. *Children's reading begins at home.* Winston-Salem, NC: Starstream Products.

Lechner, J.V. 1995. Images of African Americans in picture books for children. In *The all white world of children's books and African American children's literature,* ed. O. Sayimense, 75–89. Trenton, NJ: Africa World.

Levine, D.E. 2003. *Teaching young children in violent times: Building a peaceable classroom.* 2d ed. Cambridge, MA: Educators for Social Responsibility; and Washington, DC: NAEYC.

Levine, M. 1998. *See no evil: A guide to protecting our children from media violence.* San Francisco, CA: Jossey-Bass.

Lewis, C. 1981. *Writing for young children.* Garden City, NY: Anchor Press/Doubleday.

Lewis, C., N.H. Freeman, C. Kyriakidou, K. Maridaki-Kassotaki, & D.M. Berridge. 1996. Social influences on false belief access: Specific sibling influences or apprenticeship? *Child Development* 67: 2930–47.

Lima, C.W., & J.A. Lima. 2001. *A to zoo: Subject access to picture books.* 6th ed. New York: Greenwood.

Lonigan, C.J., & G.J. Whitehurst. 1998. Relative efficacy of parent and teacher involvement in shared-reading intervention for preschool children with low-income backgrounds. *Early Childhood Research Quarterly* 13 (2): 263–90.

Lukens, R. 2003. *A critical handbook of children's literature.* 7th ed. Boston: Allyn & Bacon.

Lynch-Brown, C., & C.M. Tomlinson. 1999. *Essentials of children's literature.* 3d ed. Boston: Allyn & Bacon.

MacCann, D. 1998. *White supremacy in children's literature: Characterizations of African Americans, 1830–1900.* New York: Garland.

Mackey, M., & J.K. McClay. 2000. Graphic routes to electronic literacy: Polysemy and picture books. *Changing English* 7: 191–201.

Macleod, F. 1996. Integrating home and school resources to raise literacy levels of parents and children. *Early Child Development and Care* 117 (7): 123–32.

Margolis, R. 2001. The best little library in Texas: The Terrazas Branch Library is the winner of the Giant Step Award. *School Library Journal* 47 (1): 54–58.

Marshall, C.S. 1998. Using children's storybooks to encourage discussions among diverse populations. *Childhood Education* 74 (4): 194–99.

Martin, B., & P. Brogran. 1972. *Teacher's guide, instant readers.* New York: Holt, Rinehart & Winston.

Marvin, C., & P. Mirenda. 1993. Home literacy experiences of preschoolers in Head Start and special education programs. *Journal of Early Intervention* 17: 351–67.

Matthias, M., & B. Gulley, eds. 1995. *Celebrating family literacy through intergenerational programming.* Olney, MD: Association for Childhood Education International.

Maughan, S. 1999, August 16. Children's books go Hollywood. *Publisher'sWeekly.com.* Available online: www.publishersweekly.com.

Mavrogenes, N.A. 1990. Helping parents help their children become literate. *Young Children* 45 (4): 4–9.

Mayr, D. 1999. Ten tips on writing picture books. *Writer* 112 (6): 14–16.

McBrien, J.L. 1999. New texts, new tools: An argument for media literacy. *Educational Leadership* 57 (2): 76–79.

McCarthey, S.J. 1999. Identifying teacher practices that connect home and school. *Education and Urban Society* 31 (1): 83–107.

McDevitt, T., & J.E. Ormond. 2001. *Child development and education.* Upper Saddle River, NJ: Prentice Hall.

McDonnell, G.M., & E.B. Osborn. 1978. New thoughts about reading readiness. *Language Arts* 55 (1): 26–29.

McGee, L.M. 2003. Shaking the very foundations of emergent literacy: Book reading versus phonemic awareness. In *Major trends and issues in early childhood education: Challenges, con-*

troversies, and insights, eds. J.P. Isenberg & M.R. Jalongo, 2d ed., 114–25. New York: Teachers College Press.

McGee, L.M., & D.J. Richgels. 2003. *Designing early literacy programs: Strategies for at-risk preschool and kindergarten children*. New York: Guilford.

McGill-Franzen, A., & R.L. Allington. 1999. Putting books in the classroom seems necessary but not sufficient. *The Journal of Educational Research* 93 (2): 67–74.

McGuire-Raskin, L. 1996. Multiculturalism in children's picture books: An analysis of insider vs. outsider texts. *Journal of Children's Literature* 22 (1): 22–27.

Meek, M. 1991. *On being literate*. London: The Bodley Head.

Mehren, E. 1999, December 23. Reading by 9: Toy tie-ins rate an "A" with children's book publishers. *Los Angeles Times*, A1.

Millard, E. 1997. *Differently literate: Boys, girls, and the schooling of literacy*. London: Falmer Press.

Minkel, W. 2000. Digital audiobooks can help kids learn. *School Library Journal* 46 (10): 24.

Mitchell, D. 2003. *Children's literature: An invitation to the world*. Boston: Allyn & Bacon.

Moles, O.C., ed. 1996. *Reaching all families: Creating family-friendly schools*. Washington, DC: U.S. Department of Education, Office of Educational Research and Improvement.

Monson, D.L. 1985. *Adventuring with books: A booklist for pre-K–grade 6*. Urbana, IL: National Council of Teachers of English.

Morrow, L.M., ed. 1995. *Family literacy: Connections in schools and communities*. Newark, DE: International Reading Association.

Morrow, L.M. 2001. *Literacy development in the early years: Helping children read and write*. 4th ed. Boston: Allyn & Bacon.

Morrow, R. 1999. The picture book: Unique art form or good vibes? *Orana* 35 (2): 37–42.

Mosenthal, P.B. 1999. Understanding engagement: Historical and political contexts. In *Engaged reading*, eds. J.T. Guthrie & D.E. Alverman, 1–16. New York: Teachers College Press.

Moss, M., & M. Puma, M. 1992. The congressionally mandated study of educational growth and opportunity. Cambridge, MA: ABT Associates. ERIC, ED394334

Mulhern, M.W. 1997. Doing his own thing: A Mexican-American kindergartner becomes literate at home and school. *Language Arts* 74 (6): 468–76.

Murray, A.D., & J.L. Yingling. 2000. Competence in language at 24 months: Relation with attachment security and home stimulation. *Journal of Genetic Psychology* 161 (2): 133–40.

Murray, J.H. 1997. *Hamlet on the holodeck: The future of narrative in cyberspace*. New York: The Free Press.

NAEYC. 1995. Responding to linguistic and cultural diversity: Recommendations for effective early childhood education. Position Statement. Available online: www.naeyc.org/resources/position_statements/psdiv98.htm

Nagy, W. & J. Scott. 2000. Vocabulary processes. In *Handbook of reading research, Vol. 3,* eds. M.L. Kamil, P.B. Mosenthal, P.D. Pearson, & R. Barr, 269-84. Hillsdale, NJ: Erlbaum.

National Assessment of Educational Progress. 2003. Statement on NAEP 2003 Mathematics and Reading Results. Available online: www.nagb.org/release/statement_11_03.html

National Council for Accreditation of Teacher Education (NCATE). 2002. *Professional standards for the accreditation of schools, colleges, and departments of education*. Washington, DC: Author. Available online: www.ncate.org/2000/unit_stnds_2002.pdf

National Council of Teachers of English (NCTE). 1996. *Guidelines for the preparation of teachers of English language arts*. Urbana, IL: Author.

Nelson, K.E., A. Aksu-Koc, & C.E. Johnson. 2001. *Children's language: Developing narrative and discourse competence*. Mahwah, NJ: Erlbaum.

Neuman, S.B. 1999. Books make a difference: A study of access to literacy. *Reading Research Quarterly* 34: 286–311.

Neuman, S.B., & D. Celano. 2001a. Access to print in low-income and middle-income communities: An ecological study of four neighborhoods. *Reading Research Quarterly* 36 (1): 8–26.

Neuman, S.B., & D. Celano. 2001b. Books aloud: A campaign to "put books in children's hands." *The Reading Teacher* 54 (6): 550–57.

Neuman, S.B., C. Copple, & S. Bredekamp. 2000. *Learning to read and write: Developmentally appropriate practices for young children.* Washington, DC: NAEYC.

Neuman, S.B., & D.K. Dickinson, eds. 2001. *Handbook of early literacy research.* New York: Guilford.

Neuman, S.B., & K.A. Roskos, eds. 1998. *Children achieving: Best practices in early literacy.* Newark, DE: International Reading Association.

New London Group, The. 1996. A pedagogy of multiliteracies: Designing social futures. *Harvard Educational Review* 66: 60–92.

Nilges, L.M., & A.F. Spencer. 2002. The pictorial representation of gender and physical activity level in Caldecott Medal winning children's literature 1940–1999: A relational analysis of physical culture. *Sport, Education & Society* 7 (2): 135–140.

Nilsen, A., R. Peterson, & L. Searfoss. 1980. The adult as critic vs. child as reader. *Language Arts* 57: 530–39.

Nodelman, P., & M. Reimer. 2003. *The pleasures of literature.* 3d ed. Boston: Allyn & Bacon.

Norton, D.E. 1999. *Through the eyes of a child: An introduction to children's literature.* 5th ed. Columbus, OH: Merrill.

Norvell, G.W. 1973. *The reading interests of young people.* East Lansing, MI: Michigan State University Press.

Nyberg, J. 1996. *Charts for children: Print awareness activities for young children.* Glenview, IL: GoodYear.

O'Malley, J. 1998. Quilting stories. *Book Links* 7 (6): 52–4.

Obiakor, F.E., & B. Algozzine. 2001. *It even happens in "good" schools: Responding to cultural diversity in today's classrooms.* Thousand Oaks, CA: Corwin Press.

Ogbu, J. 1988. Class stratification, racial stratification, and schooling. In *Class, race, and gender in American education,* ed. L. Weis, 106–25. Albany, NY: State University of New York Press.

Olson, R.K., & J. Gayan. 2001. Brain, genes, and reading development. In *Handbook of early literacy research,* eds. S.B. Neuman & D.K. Dickinson, 81–96. New York: Guilford.

Owens, W.T., & L.S. Nowell. 2001. More than just pictures: Using picture story books to broaden young learners' social consciousness. *Social Studies* 92 (1): 33–40.

Owocki, G. 2003. *Comprehension: Strategic instruction for K–3 students.* Portsmouth, NH: Heinemann.

Paley, V.G. 1981. *Wally's stories.* Cambridge, MA: Harvard University Press.

Papalia, D.E., & S.W. Olds. 1998. *A child's world: Infancy through adolescence.* 7th ed. New York: McGraw Hill.

Pelletier, J. 1997. Action, consciousness, and theory of mind in children's story retelling. Paper presented at the Biennial Meeting of the Society for Research in Child Development, April 3–6, Washington, DC.

Pellowski, A. 1984. *The story vine: A source book of unusual and easy-to-tell stories from around the world.* New York: Macmillan.

Pellowski, A. 1995. *The storytelling handbook: A young people's collection of unusual tales and helpful hints on how to tell them.* New York: Simon & Schuster.

Peskin, J., & D. Olson. 1997. Children's understanding of misleading appearance in characterization. Paper presented at the Biennial Meeting of the Society for Research in Child Development, April 3-6, Washington, DC.

Peterson, R., & M. Eeds. 1990. *Grand conversations: Literature groups in action.* New York: Scholastic.

Petrosky, A.R. 1980. The inferences we make: Children and literature. *Language Arts* 57: 149–56.

Piaget, J. 1962. *Play, dreams and imitation in childhood.* Translated by F.M. Hodgson. New York: W.W. Norton.

Prescott, O. 1965. *A father reads to his children.* New York: Dutton.

Prudhoe, C.M. 2003. Picture books and the art of collage. *Childhood Education* 80 (1): 6–11.

Pullen, P.C., & L.M. Justice. 2003. Enhancing phonological awareness, print awareness, and oral language skills in preschool children. *Intervention in School and Clinic* 39 (2): 87–98.

Purcell-Gates, V. 1996. Stories, coupons, and the *TV Guide:* Relationships between home literacy experiences and emergent literacy knowledge. *Reading Research Quarterly* 31: 406–28.

Purves, A.C., & D.L. Monson. 1984. *Experiencing children's literature.* Glenview, IL: Scott, Foresman.

Rabidoux, P.C., & J.D. MacDonald. 2000. An interactive taxonomy of mothers and children during storybook interactions. *American Journal of Speech-Language Pathology* 9 (4). 331–44.

Rand, D., T. Parker, & S. Foster. 1998. *Black books galore! Guide to great African American children's books.* New York: Wiley.

Rand, M.K. 1984. Story schema: Theory, research and practice. *Reading Teacher* 37: 377–82.

Raphael, T.E., & K. Au, eds. 1998. *Literature-based instruction: Reshaping the curriculum.* Norwood, MA: Christopher-Gordon.

Raugust, K.R. 1999, June 28. Licensing '99: Franchises at the forefront. *Publisher'sWeekly.com.* Available online: www.publishersweekly.com.

Raugust, K.R. 2000, May 1. Food for thought. *Publisher'sWeekly.com.* Available online: www.publishersweekly.com.

Reutzel, D.R., K. Camperell, & J. Smith. 2002. Hitting the wall: Helping struggling readers comprehend. In *Improving comprehension instruction: Rethinking research, theory, and classroom practice,* eds. C.C. Block, L.B. Gambrell, & M. Pressley, 321–53. San Francisco, CA: Jossey-Bass.

Risher, D., & N. MacDonald. 2001. The interaction between music and early literacy instruction: Listen to literacy! *Reading Improvement* 38 (3): 106–15.

Roberts, E. 1984. *The children's picture book.* Cincinnati, OH: Writer's Digest.

Roberts, P. 1997. *Multicultural friendship stories and activities for children, ages 5–15.* Lanham, MD: Scarecrow Press.

Rosenblatt, L.M. 1978. *The reader, the text, the poem: The transactional theory of the literary work.* Carbondale, IL: Southern Illinois University Press.

Rosenblatt, L.M. 1982. The literacy transaction: Evocation and response. *Theory Into Practice* 21: 268–77.

Roser, N., & M. Martinez. 1985. Roles adults play in preschoolers' response to literature. *Language Arts* 62: 485–90.

Routman, R. 1994. *Invitations: Changing as teachers and learners.* 2d ed. Portsmouth, NH: Heinemann.

Routman, R. 2002. *Reading essentials: The specifics you need to teach reading.* Portsmouth, NH: Heinemann.

Rubright, L. 1996. *Beyond the beanstalk: Interdisciplinary learning through storytelling.* Portsmouth, NH: Heinemann.

Rumelhart, D.E. 1980. Schemata: The building blocks of cognition. In *Theoretical issues in reading comprehension,* eds. R.J. Spiro, B.C. Borce, & W.F. Brewer, 33–57. Hillsdale, NJ: Erlbaum.

Rushton, S., & E. Larkin. 2001. Shaping the learning environment: Connecting developmentally appropriate practices to brain research. *Early Childhood Education Journal* 29 (1): 25–34.

Sanders, M.G. 1999. Schools' programs and progress in the national network of partnership schools. *Journal of Educational Research* 92 (4): 220–29.

Saracho, O.N. 2003. Supporting literacy-related play: Roles for teachers of young children. *Early Childhood Education Journal* 31 (3): 203–8.

Scarborough, H.S. 2001. Connecting early language and literacy to later reading (dis)abilities: Evidence, theory, and practice. In *Handbook of early literacy research,* eds. S.B. Neuman & D.K. Dickinson, 97–110. New York: Guilford.

Schon, I. 2002. Books to grow on: Latino literature for young children. Brochure. Washington, DC: NAEYC.

Schwartz, W. 1996. Hispanic preschool education: An important opportunity. New York: ERIC Clearinghouse on Urban Education. (ERIC/CUE Digest No. 113; Report No. EDO-UD-96-2)

Semali, L.M. 2003. Defining new literacies in curricular practice. Available online: http://readingonline.org/newliteracies/lit_index.asp?HREF=semali1/index.html

Sharif, I., P.O. Ozuah, E.I. Dinkevich, & M. Mulvihill. 2003. Impact of a brief literacy intervention on urban preschoolers. *Early Childhood Education Journal* 30 (3): 177–80.

Sheerer, M. 1998. Perspectives: Let the dialogue begin. *Educational Leadership* 55 (8): 5.

Shulevitz, U. 1989. What is a picture book? *The Five Owls* 2 (4): 49–53.

Silvey, A. 2002. *The essential guide to children's books and their creators.* New York: Mariner/Houghton Mifflin.

Sims, R. 1982. *Shadow and substance: Afro-American experience in contemporary children's fiction.* Urbana, IL: National Council of Teachers of English.

Sitarz, P.G. 1997. *Story time sampler: Read alouds, booktalks, and activities for children.* Englewood, CO: Libraries Unlimited.

Slaughter, J.P. 1993. *Beyond storybooks: Young children and the shared book experience.* Newark, DE: International Reading Association.

Slavin, R., B. Karweit, N. Wasik, N. Madden, & L. Dolan. 1994. *Preventing early school failure.* Boston: Allyn & Bacon.

Smith, F. 1988. *Joining the literacy club: Further essays into education.* Portsmouth, NH: Heinemann.

Smith, F. 1989. Overselling literacy. *Phi Delta Kappan* 70 (5): 352–59.

Smith, F. 1997. *Reading without nonsense.* 3d ed. New York: Teachers College Press.

Snow, C., & A. Ninio. 1986. The contracts of literacy: What children learn from learning to read books. In *Emergent literacy: Writing and reading,* eds. W. Teale & E. Sulzby, 116–38. Norwood, NJ: Ablex.

Snow, C.E. 1983. Literacy and language: Relationships during the preschool years. *Harvard Educational Review* 53: 165–89.

Snow, C.E. 2002. *Reading for understanding: Toward an R&D program in reading comprehension.* Santa Monica, CA: RAND.

Snow, C.E., M.S. Burns, & P. Griffin, eds. 1998. *Preventing reading difficulties in young children.* Washington, DC: National Research Council.

Solsken, J.W. 1985. Authors of their own learning. *Language Arts* 62: 491–99.

Sorgen, M. 1999. *Applying brain research to classroom practice.* Materials presented at the University of South Florida Brain/Mind Connections Conference, June, Sarasota, Florida.

Soriano-Nagurski, L. 1998. And the walls came tumbling down: Including children who are differently abled in typical early childhood educational settings. *Young Children* 53 (2): 40–41.

Soto, L.D., J.L. Smrekar, & D.L. Nekcovei. 2001, Spring. Preserving home languages and cultures in the classroom: Challenges and opportunities. *Directions in Language and Education,* no. 13. Washington, DC: National Clearinghouse for Bilingual Education. Available online: www.ncela.gwu.edu/ncbepubs/directions/13.htm

Spitz, E.H. 1999. *Inside picture books.* New Haven, CT: Yale University Press.

Stainthorp, R., & D. Hughes. 1999. *Learning from children who read at an early age.* London: Routledge.

Steiner, S.F. 2001. *Promoting a global community through multicultural children's literature.* Englewood, CO: Libraries Unlimited.

Stewig, J.W. 1980. *Children and literature.* Boston: Houghton Mifflin.

Stratton, J.M. 1996. Emergent literacy: A new perspective. *Journal of Visual Impairment and Blindness* 90 (3): 177–83.

Strube, P. 1996. *Getting the most from literature groups.* Jefferson City, MO: Scholastic Professional Books.

Sulzby, E. 1985. Children's emergent reading of favorite storybooks: A developmental study. *Reading Research Quarterly* 20: 458–81.

Sutherland, Z. 1997. *Children and books.* 9th ed. Boston, MA: Addison-Wesley.

Swick, K.J., R. Grafwallner, M. Cocky, & P. Barton. 1998. Parents as leaders in nurturing family-school involvement. *Contemporary Education* 70 (1): 47–50.

Sylwester, R. 1995. *A celebration of neurons: An educator's guide to the human brain.* Alexandria, VA: Association for Supervision and Curriculum Development.

Szarkowicz, D.L. 2000. When they wash him they'll know he'll be Harry: Young children's thinking about thinking within a story context. *International Journal of Early Years Education* 8 (1): 71–81.

Taylor, D. 1983. *Family literacy: Young children teaming to read and write*. Portsmouth, NH: Heinemann.

Temple, C., M. Martinez, J. Yokota, & A. Naylor. 1998. *Children's books in children's hands: An introduction to their literature*. Needham Heights, MA: Allyn & Bacon.

Thomas, R. 1993. *Primary plots 2: A book talk guide for use with readers ages 4–8*. New Providence, NJ: Bowker.

Thomas, W.P., & V.T. Collier. 1997. School effectiveness for language minority students. Washington, DC: National Clearinghouse for Bilingual Education.

Tomlinson, C.M., & C. Lynch-Brown. 2003. *Essentials of children's literature*. 5th ed. Boston: Allyn & Bacon.

Trelease, J. 2001. *The read-aloud handbook*. New York: Penguin.

Trumbo, J. 1999. Visual literacy and science communication. *Science Communication* 20 (4): 409–26.

Turner, J.C. 1997. Starting right: Strategies for engaging young literacy learners. In *Reading engagement: Motivating readers through integrated instruction*, eds. J.T. Guthrie & A. Wigfield, 183–204. Newark, DE: International Reading Association.

Tway, E. 1982. *Reading ladders for human relations*. Urbana, IL: National Council of Teachers of English.

van Kleeck, A., S.A. Stahl, & E.B. Bauer, eds. 2003. *On reading books to children: Parents and teachers*. Mahwah, NJ: Lawrence Erlbaum.

Van Schuyver, J.M. 1993. *Storytelling made easy with puppets*. Phoenix, AZ: Oryx Press.

Vardell, S.M., & K.A. Copeland. 1992. Reading aloud and responding to nonfiction: Let's talk about it. In *Using nonfiction tradebooks in the elementary classroom: From ants to zeppelins*, eds. E.B. Freeman & D.G. Pearson, 76–85. Urbana, IL: National Council of Teachers of English.

Vasquez, V. 2003. *Getting beyond "I like the book": Creating space for critical literacy in K–6 classrooms*. Newark: DE: International Reading Association.

Vygotsky, L.S. 1962/1986. *Thought and language*. Cambridge, MA: MIT Press.

Wade, R. C. 2000. Service-learning for multicultural teaching competency: Insights from the literature for teacher education. *Equity and Excellence in Education* 33 (3): 21–29.

Waggoner, D. 1994. Language minority school age population now totals 9.9 million. *NABE News* 18 (1): 24–26.

Walters, T.S. 2002. Images, voices, choices: Literature to nurture children's literacy development. In *Love to read: Essays in development and enhancing early literacy skills of African American children* ed. B. Bowman, 72–81. Washington, DC: National Black Child Development Institute.

Weaver, C. 1994. *Reading process and practice: From sociolinguistics to whole language*. 2d ed. Portsmouth, NH: Heinemann.

Wells, G. 1986. *The meaning makers: Children learning language and using language to learn*. Portsmouth, NH: Heinemann.

Wham, M.A., J. Barnhart, & G. Cook. 1996. Enhancing multicultural awareness through storybook reading experience. *Journal of Research and Development in Education* 30 (10): 1–9.

Wiles, J. 1999. *Curriculum essentials: A resource for educators*. Boston: Allyn & Bacon.

Wood, D.J., J.S. Bruner, & G. Ross. 1976. The role of tutoring in problem solving. *Journal of Child Psychology and Psychiatry* 17: 89–100.

Yaden, D. 1988. Understanding stories through repeated read-alouds: How many does it take? *The Reading Teacher* 41: 556–60.

Yaden, D.B., A. Tam, P. Madrigal, D. Brassell, J. Massa, L.S. Altamirano, & J. Armendariz. 2000. Center for the Improvement of Early Reading Achievement: Early literacy for inner-city children: The effects of reading and writing interventions in English and Spanish during the preschool years. *The Reading Teacher* 54 (2): 186–89.

Yolen, J. 1977. How basic is shazam? *Language Arts* 54: 645–51.

Zack, V. 1983. The parent—the preschool child 0–3—the book: Ring around the joyful telling. *The Advocate* 8 (6): 86–94.

Zeece, P.D. 1999. And the winner is: Children's literature awards and accolades. *Early Childhood Education Journal* 26 (4): 233–44.

Zeece, P.D. 2000. Books about feelings and feelings about books: Literature choices that support emotional development. *Early Childhood Education Journal* 28 (2): 111–15.

Zeece, P.D. 2001a. Meeting children's needs with quality literature: Part one. *Early Childhood Education Journal* 28 (3): 175–80.

Zeece, P.D. 2001b. Meeting children's needs with quality literature: Part two. *Early Childhood Education Journal* 28 (4): 237–41.

Zeece, P.D. 2002. Free reading and reading freely. *Early Childhood Education Journal* 29 (3): 185–90.

Zeece, P.D. 2003a. Growing readers: The role of early childhood professionals. *Early Childhood Education Journal* 30 (4): 259–65.

Zeece, P.D. 2003b. The personal value of literature: Finding books children love. *Early Childhood Education Journal* 31 (2): 133–38.

Zeece, P.D. 2003c. Using literature to support prereading strategies. *Early Childhood Education Journal* 30 (3): 181–86.

Zipes, J. 1995. *Creative storytelling: Building community, changing lives.* London: Routledge.

Outstanding Picture Book Authors and Illustrators

A
Aardema, Verna
Ackerman, Karen
Ahlberg, Allan
Ahlberg, Janet
Alexander, Martha
Aliki
Allard, Harry
Ancona, George
Anno, Mitsumaso
Aruego, Jose
Asch, Frank

B
Baker, Keith
Bang, Molly
Binch, Caroline
Bond, Felicia
Brett, Jan
Bridwell, Norman
Brown, Marc
Brown, Margaret Wise
Bruna, Dick
Bryan, Ashley
Bunting, Eve
Burningham, John

C
Caines, Jeannette
Carle, Eric
Carlstrom, Nancy
Cauley, Lorinda Bryan
Chorao, Kay
Cleary, Beverly
Cohen, Barbara
Cohen, Miriam
Cole, Joanna
Conover, Chris
Cooney, Barbara
Crews, Donald
Cronin, Doreen

D
Degen, Bruce
Demi
de Paola, Tomie
Dillon, Leo
Dillon, Diane
Dorros, Arthur
Dyer, Jane

E, F
Eastman, P.D.
Ehlert, Lois
Emberley, Ed
Flack, Marjorie
Fleming, Denise
Florian, Douglas
Fox, Mem

G
Gackenbach, Dick
Galdone, Paul
Giff, Patricia Reilly
Goble, Paul
Goode, Diane
Greenfield, Eloise
Grifalconi, Ann

H
Hafner, Marilyn
Hall, Donald
Hazen, Barbara
Henkes, Kevin
Hest, Amy
Hoban, Lillian
Hoban, Russell
Hoban, Tana
Hoberman, Mary Ann
Hoffman, Mary
Hughes, Shirley
Hutchins, Pat
Hyman, Trina Schart

I, J, K
Isadora, Rachel
Jeffers, Susan

Johnston, Tony
Jonas, Ann
Kasza, Keiko
Keats, Ezra Jack
Keller, Holly
Kellogg, Steven
Kimmel, Eric A.
Kroll, Steven

L
Lester, Julius
Lionni, Leo
Lobel, Arnold
Locker, Thomas

M
Marcellino, Fred
Marshall, James
Martin, Bill, Jr.
Mayer, Marianna
Mayer, Mercer
McCloskey, Robert
McDermott, Gerald
McDonnell, Flora
McKissack, Patricia
McMillan, Bruce
McPhail, David
Merriam, Eve
Milne, A.A.
Mora, Pat
Morris, Ann

O, P
Ormerod, Jan
Oxenbury, Helen
Peet, Bill
Pinkney, Brian
Polacco, Patricia
Prelutsky, Jack
Provensen, Alice
Provensen, Martin

R
Rathmann, Peggy
Rey, H.A.
Rice, Eve
Ringgold, Faith
Rockwell, Anne
Rockwell, Harlow
Rosen, Michael
Rylant, Cynthia

S, T
Say, Allen
Schulevitz, Uri
Scieszka, Jon
Selsam, Millicent E.
Sendak, Maurice
Seuss, Dr.
Sharmat, Marjorie
    Weinman
Simon, Seymour
Soentpiet, Chris K.
Soto, Gary
Spier, Peter

Steig, William
Steptoe, John
Stock, Catherine
Szilagyi, Mary
Tejima

U, V
Ungerer, Tomi
Van Allsburg, Chris
Viorst, Judith
Vivas, Julie

W
Waber, Bernard
Waddell, Martin
Wells, Rosemary
Wildsmith, Brian
Williams, Garth
Williams, Karen Lynn
Williams, Vera B.
Winter, Paula
Winthrop, Elizabeth
Wood, Audrey
Wood, Don

Y, Z
Yashima, Taro
Yolen, Jane
Young, Ed
Zemach, Harve
Zemach, Margot
Zion, Eugene (Gene)
Zolotow, Charlotte

Internet Resources on Children's Literature

Directories of Web links on children's literature

Children's Lit.com (subscription)—www.childrenslit.com
Children's Literature on the Web—http://frankrogers.home.mindspring.com/
The Children's Literature Web Guide—www.acs.ucalgary.ca/~dkbrown/
**Index to Internet Sites: Children's and Young Adults' Authors and
    Illustrators**—http://falcon.jmu.edu/~ramseyil/biochildhome.htm

Listserv

KIDLIT-L (to participate in online discussions about children's books)—
    listserv@bingvmb.cc.binghamton.edu

Organizations, professional publications, and projects committed to reading

American Library Association—www.ala.org
America Reads—www.ed.gov/inits/americareads
Center for Children's Books—www.lis.uiuc.edu/~ccb
Children's Book Council—www.cbcbooks.org
The Horn Book—www.hbook.com
International Reading Association—www.reading.org
National Council of Teachers of English—www.ncte.org
National Education Association—www.nea.org/readacross/parents.html
Reading Is Fundamental—www.rif.org

Literature awards and honors

American Library Association—www.ala.org
Awards in Children's Literature—www.literature-awards.com/
    childrens_literature.htm
International Reading Association Choices Book Lists—www.reading.org
    choices/

Author and illustrator information

Authors—general information

http://childrensbooks.about.com/cs/authorsillustrato/
http://dir.yahoo.com/Arts/Humanities/Literature/Authors/Children_s/
http://edcen.ehhs.cmich.edu/~tbushey/author.html
www.edupaperback.org/
www.ortakales.com
www.scils.rutgers.edu/~kvander/AuthorSite/

Poets—general information

www.poets.org/

Illustrators—general information

Every Picture Tells a Story—http://everypicture.com

Authors—individual websites

Frank Asch—www.frankasch.com
Jan Brett—www.janbrett.com
Eve Bunting—www.murrieta.k12.ca.us/alta/library/bunting
Lynne Cherry—www.friend.ly.net/scoop/biographies/cherrylynne/
Beverly Cleary—www.beverlycleary.com
Barbara Cooney—www.hbook.com/cooney.shtml
Tomie de Paola—www.tomie.com
Kevin Henkes—www.kevinhenkes.com/
Eric Hill—www.funwithspot.com
Lillian Hoban—www.lillianhoban.com
Patricia Polacco—www.patriciapolacco.com/
Dr. Seuss's Seussville—www.randomhouse.com/seussville
Jim Trelease—http://trelease-on-reading.com/
Chris Van Allsburg—www.eduplace.com/author/index_flash.html
Audrey Wood Clubhouse—www.audreywood.com

Lists of recommended books

Books to Grow On—www.kcls.org/webkids/btgo/index.cfm
Children's Literature Resources—http://falcon.jmu.edu/~ramseyil/
childlit.htm
Fairrosa Cyber Library—www.fairrosa.info
School Library Journal (subscription)—www.schoollibraryjournal.com

Selecting Culturally and Linguistically Appropriate Materials: Suggestions for Service Providers—http://ecap.crc.uiuc.edu/eecearchive/digests/1999/santos99.html

Sites for children

Kid's Storytelling Club—www.storycraft.com
Houghton Mifflin Kids' Clubhouse—www.eduplace.com/kids
Public Broadcasting Service—www.pbs.org

Teacher resources

Booklists of Children's Literature, Monroe County (Indiana) Public Library—www.monroe.lib.in.us/childrens/children_booklists.html
Children's Picture Book Database at Miami University—www.lib.muohio.edu/pictbks/
Early Childhood Language Arts: To Literacy through Literature—http://wps.ablongman.com/ab_jalongo_earlychild_3
Homework Spot/Storytelling—http://homeworkspot.com/reference/readingroom/storytelling.htm
Lesson Plans, Teaching Guides, and Themed Collections—www.childrenslit.com
Literature for Children and Young Adults—www.lesley.edu/library/guides/research/literature_children.htm
Multicultural Book Review Homepage—www.isomedia.com/homes/jmele/homepage.html
National Institute for Literacy—www.nifl.gov (click on "LINCS")
National Storytelling Network—www.storynet.org
StoryArts Online—www.storyarts.org
Story Palace—www.storypalace.ourfamily.com
Storyteller.net—www.storyteller.net
The Role of Storytelling in Early Literacy Development—www.home.aone.net.au/stories/doc/childhd.htm
Teaching Books.net—www.teachingbooks.net

Sources of songs and lyrics

Between the Lions, Songs—http://pbskids.org/lions/songs/index.html
Kididdles, MoJo's Musical Mouseum—www.kididdles.com/mouseum/
KidsRanch, Music—www.kidsranch.org/music/divtune/singalong.htm
Kinder Planet, Sing a Song—www.kinderplanet.com/music.htm
Mama Lisa's World, Children's Songs and Rhymes of All Nations—www.mamalisa.com/world/

National Institute of Environmental Health Sciences (NIEHS), Kids' Pages,
  Sing-Along Songs—www.niehs.nih.gov/kids/music.htm
The Teachers' Guide, Children's Songs—www.theteachersguide.com/
  ChildrensSongs.htm

Sources for lesson plans and activities

Busy Teachers' Website K–12—www.ceismc.gatech.edu/busyt
Classroom Connect—www.classroom.net/home.asp
Discovery Channel School—www.school.discovery.com/schoolhome.html
Early Childhood.com—www.earlychildhood.com
Early Childhood Educator—www.edpsych.com/
Early Childhood Special Education Thematic Units—www.sbcss.K12.ca.us/
  sbcss/specialeducation/ecthematic/index.html
Education Resources Created by Peggy Reihl—http://home.sprintmail.com/
  ~peggyriehl/
The Educator's Reference Desk—www.eduref.org
The Gateway to Educational Materials—www.thegateway.org
Instructor Magazine—http://teacher.scholastic.com/products/instructor.htm
Kathy Schrock's Guide for Educators—http://discoveryschool.com/
  schrockguide/
Language Arts Lesson Plans—www.col-ed.org/cur/lang.html
Scholastic Books—www.scholastic.com
Sites for Teachers—www.learningpage.com
TeachersFirst.com—www.teachersfirst.com/lesn-read.shtml

Resources for writing children's books

Become a Children's Book Author—www.fabjob.com/childauthor.asp
Highlights Foundation: Writers' Resources—www.highlightsfoundation.org/
  pages/current/resources_top.html?src=overture

Board Books

Board books have heavy cardboard pages rather than pages made of paper. This makes the pages easier to turn for the youngest children and makes the books able to withstand hard use in the classroom. Many old and familiar favorites have been reissued as board books. Reissue can sometimes give the original illustrations a face lift due to advances in color printing processes since the book was first released. Many new books—most often those intended for infants and toddlers—are issued from the very start as board book editions. Consider collecting several of the following titles for your classroom library.

Alborough, J. *Hug.*

Alexander, M. (illustrator). *A you're adorable.*

Aruego, J. *We hide, you seek board book.*

Barton, B. *Machines at work.*

Barton, B. *The Little Red Hen board book.*

Barton, B. *The three bears board book.*

Barton, B. *Trains board book.*

Bond, F. *Tumble bumble board book.*

Boynton, S. *Moo baa la la la.*

Brett, J. *The mitten: A Ukrainian folktale.*

Briggs, R. *The Snowman: A fun shaped play book.*

Brown, M.W. *Good night, Moon board book.*

Brown, M.W. *The runaway bunny.*

Burningham, J. *Mr. Gumpy's outing board book.*

Carle, E. *From head to toe.*

Carle, E. *The grouchy ladybug board book.*

Carlstrom, N.W. *Jesse bear, what will you wear?*

Cousins, L. *Maisy's favorite toys.*

Crews, D. *Freight train board book.*

Crews, D. *School bus board book.*

Degen, B. *Jamberry.*

Dorling Kindersley Publishing. *My first phonics book.*

Dorling Kindersley Publishing. *Touch and feel animals box set.*

Dyer, J. *Time for bed.*

Emberley, R. *My animals/Mis animales.*

Emberley, R. *My clothes/Mi ropa.*

Emberley, R. *My food/Mi comida.*

Emberley, R. *My toys/Mis juguetes.*

Fleming, D. *Barnyard banter board book.*

Hoberman, M.A. *I know an old lady who swallowed a fly.*

Hoberman, M.A. *Miss Mary Mack.*

Hutchins, P. *Rosie's walk.*

Kalan, R. *Jump, frog, jump!*

Katz, K. *Counting kisses.*

Keats, E.J. *The snowy day.*

Keats, E.J. *Whistle for Willie.*

Kirk, D. *Miss Spider's ABC.*

Krauss, R. *The carrot seed.*

Martin, Jr., B. *Brown Bear, Brown Bear, what do you see?*

Marzollo, J. *Mama Mama/Papa Papa flip board book.*

McBratney, S. *Guess how much I love you.*

Murphy, J. *Five minutes' peace.*

Perkins, A. *Hand, hand, fingers, thumb.*

Pinkney, A., & B. Pinkney. *Pretty brown face.*

Rathmann, P. *Good night, Gorilla.*

Root, P. *One duck stuck.*

Rosen, M. *We're going on a bear hunt.*

Saltzberg, B. *Animal kisses.*

Scott, A.H. *On Mother's lap.*

Seuss, Dr. *Mr. Brown can moo! Can you?*

Seuss, Dr. *There's a wocket in my pocket!*

Shaw, C.G. *It looked like spilt milk.*

Steig, W. *Pete's a pizza.*

Stickland, P., & H. Stickland. *Dinosaur roar!*

Walsh, E.S. *Mouse paint.*

Whatley, B. *The teddy bears' picnic board book and tape.*

Williams, V.B. *"More more more," said the baby.*

Winthrop, E. *Shoes.*

Wolff, A. *Oh, the colors/De colores.*

Wood, A. *Piggies.*

Wood, A. *The napping house.*

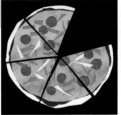

Selected Books for Toddlers, and Resources for Teachers

Compiled by Melissa Ann Renck, children's services librarian at Toledo Lucas County Library

Picture books

Appelt, K. *Bubba and Beau, best friends.*
Bornstein, R. *Little Gorilla.*
Brown, M.W. *Goodnight, Moon.*
Bunting, E. *Flower garden.*
Campbell, R. *Dear zoo.*
Carle, E. *The very hungry caterpillar.*
Cousins, L. *Maisy's pool.*
Dann, P. *Five in the bed.*
Ehlert, L. *Fish eyes: A book you can count on.*
Feiffer, J. *Bark, George.*
Fleming, D. *In the tall, tall grass.*
Fox, M. *Time for bed.*
Gackenbach, D. *Claude the dog.*
Galdone, P. *The Little Red Hen.*
Hill, E. *Where's Spot?*
Keats, E.J. *The snowy day.*
McBratney, S. *Guess how much I love you.*
McDonnell, F. *Splash!*
Pryor, A. *The baby blue cat and the whole batch of cookies.*
Rice, E. *Sam who never forgets.*
Walter, V. *"Hi, Pizza Man!"*
Williams, S. *I went walking.*
Williams, V.B. *"More more more," said the baby.*

Teacher resources

Briggs, D. 1997. *52 programs for preschoolers: The librarian's year-round planner.* Chicago: American Library Association.
Davis, R.W. 1998. *Toddle on over: Developing infant & toddler literature programs.* Fort Atkinson, WI: Alleyside Press.
Friedberg, J.B. 1995. *Super storytimes: Why, how and what to read to young children.* Urbana, IL: National Council of Teachers of English.
Jeffrey, D.A. 1995. *Literate beginnings: Programs for babies and toddlers.* Chicago: American Library Association.
Kupetz, B.N., & E.J. Green. 1997. Sharing books with infants and toddlers: Facing the challenges. *Young Children* 52 (2): 22–7.
Nichols, J. 1998. *Storytimes for two-year olds.* 2d ed. Chicago: American Library Association.
Zeece, P.D. 2001. First stories: Emergent literacy in infants and toddlers. *Early Childhood Education Journal* 29 (2): 101–4.

More Literacy Resources from NAEYC

Learning to Read and Write: Developmentally Appropriate Practices for Young Children
Susan B. Neuman, Carol Copple, & Sue Bredekamp

Developmentally appropriate, research-based strategies for promoting children's literacy learning in preschool, kindergarten, and elementary class-rooms and infant/toddler settings. This engaging book offers crystal-clear guidance and exciting ideas for teachers to help young children on the road to reading and writing competence. Includes NAEYC's joint position statement with the International Reading Association. **Item #161** (Spanish translation **#161S**)

A stand-alone version of the IRA/NAEYC position statement is also available (Item #759).

Much More than the ABCs: The Early Stages of Reading and Writing
Judith A. Schickedanz

A rich picture of children's early literacy that helps teachers, caregivers, and parents nurture both children's enjoyment of reading/writing and their skills. Gives concrete suggestions, based on topics such as reading aloud with children, setting up a book corner and writing center, and introducing the alphabet in meaningful ways. Book lists assist in choosing good books for kids at different ages. **Item #204**

Love to Read: Essays in Developing and Enhancing Early Literacy Skills of African American Children

Barbara Bowman, Ed.

Leading experts document African American children's current reading achievement, focus on how teachers and families can promote significant progress, and discuss policy considerations in boosting all children's mastery of literacy. From the National Black Child Development Institute. **Item #251**

Spotlight on Young Children and Language

Derry G. Koralek, Ed.

A rich language environment in the early years is key to children's success in many areas. This collection of engaging, research-based articles (from *Young Children*) describes powerful ways to promote language throughout the early childhood curriculum. Includes a resource list and carefully designed questions and activities to aid readers in reflecting on the articles. **Item #283**

For other valuable literacy resources, see NAEYC's online catalog at **www.naeyc.org.** Look for *Literacy through Play* **(#162),** *Make Way for Literacy: Teaching the Way Young Children Learn* **(#159),** the brochure *Raising a Reader, Raising a Writer: How Parents Can Help* **(#530, #530S),** and others.